T0348368

The Art of Shralpinism

The Art of Shralpinism

LESSONS FROM THE MOUNTAINS

Jeremy Jones

MOUNTAINEERS
BOOKS

MOUNTAINEERS BOOKS is dedicated to the exploration, preservation, and enjoyment of outdoor and wilderness areas.

1001 SW Klickitat Way, Suite 201, Seattle, WA 98134
800-553-4453, www.mountaineersbooks.org

Copyright © 2022 by Jeremy Jones
All rights reserved. No part of this book may be reproduced or utilized in any form, or by any electronic, mechanical, or other means, without the prior written permission of the publisher.

Mountaineers Books and its colophon are registered trademarks of The Mountaineers organization.

Printed in Canada
Distributed in the United Kingdom by Cordee, www.cordee.co.uk
26 25 24 23   2 3 4 5 6

Editor: Chris Crossen
Copyeditor: Amy Smith Bell
Design and layout: Jen Grable
Back cover photograph: Ming Poon
Technical illustrator: Mike Daniel
All other illustrations by Jeremy Jones

Library of Congress Control Number: 2022935918

Disclaimer: Please use common sense. This book is not intended as a substitute for professional instruction, physical training, careful planning, and/or your own good judgment. It is incumbent upon any users of this guide to assess their own skills, experience, fitness, and equipment. Readers will recognize the inherent dangers found in mountain settings and assume responsibility for their own actions and safety, including awareness of changing or unfavorable conditions and dangerous or unstable snow. Ultimately, this book contains only the personal opinions and experiences of the author, and the publisher and author are expressly not responsible for any adverse consequences resulting directly or indirectly from information contained in this book.

Mountaineers Books titles may be purchased for corporate, educational, or other promotional sales, and our authors are available for a wide range of events. For information on special discounts or booking an author, contact our customer service at 800-553-4453 or mbooks@mountaineersbooks.org.

Printed on recycled and FSC-certified materials with vegetable-based inks

ISBN (paperback): 978-1-68051-330-1
ISBN (ebook): 978-1-68051-331-8

ENVIRONMENTAL BENEFITS STATEMENT
Mountaineers Books saved the following resources by printing the pages of this book on chlorine free paper made with 30% post-consumer waste.

TREES	WATER	ENERGY	SOLID WASTE	GREENHOUSE GASES
81	6,000	35	300	35,000
FULLY GROWN	GALLONS	MILLION BTUs	POUNDS	POUNDS

Environmental impact estimates were made using the Environmental Paper Network Paper Calculator 4.0. For more information visit www.papercalculator.org

An independent nonprofit publisher since 1960

Contents

Mountains should be climbed with as little effort as possible and without desire. The reality of your own nature should determine the speed. If you become restless, speed up. If you become winded, slow down. You climb the mountain in an equilibrium between restlessness and exhaustion. Then, when you're no longer thinking ahead, each footstep isn't just a means to an end but a unique event in itself. This leaf has jagged edges. This rock looks loose. From this place the snow is less visible, even though closer. These are things you should notice anyway. To live only for some future goal is shallow. It's the sides of the mountain which sustain life, not the top. Here's where things grow.

—*Robert M. Pirsig,* Zen and the Art of Motorcycle Maintenance

Prologue

**My mind is burning a hole through the blind rollover below me.
What's behind it? How steep is the face? Am I in the right spot? I
stave off dry heaves with deep, controlled breaths. My snowboard
is strapped to my feet, below me a 3,200-foot spine wall in Alaska's Fairweather Range. The closest town is 50 miles away. The
bottom of the face is guarded by a horizontal cliffband ranging
from 20 to 200 feet tall. There's no feeling in my toes, and my
boots are loose because of frozen laces.**

Yesterday afternoon, my riding partner, local Alaskan Ryland Bell, and I left the
comforts of base camp with the hopes of being where I am right now, at exactly
this moment. So much perseverance despite a sea of doubt, the efforts to cross the
bergschrund and wallow and claw our way up the couloir. Topping out at twilight, we
celebrated with a hug and a cheer before digging into the side of the mountain and
getting some fitful sleep.

It is the moment of truth. I crank my bindings one last time, take a final deep
breath, swing my board, and let unchecked gravity take me toward the abyss. One
side of my brain screams, "Stop, stop, stop!" while the other fights back with "You
got this! Hold the line!" I am playing a zero-mistake game of chicken with gravity
and Russian roulette with the snowpack. The descent has played out in my head a
hundred times. I have planned every turn, anticipated every blind spot and every

type of snow texture, but now I let go. The world becomes quiet, my focus acute but not forced. The moment takes me.

An onlooker might call me crazy. An adrenaline junkie daredevil. But they don't know the whole story. They don't know that I've been sleeping under this peak for weeks building up to this moment. They don't see the person who is in the perfect spot to dig me out if I *do* get into an avalanche. They don't know that my life's focus since I was fourteen has built up to my being here at this very moment. They don't see the young kid who dominated amateur competition, got third in his first pro race at sixteen, and kept riding just fast enough to pay some bills, travel on the world tour, and *almost* make the Olympics. They don't know I have two older brothers who taught me the fine art of dirtbagging and ski bumming, who called me at nineteen with the message "Sell everything, bring CLIF Bars and a sleeping bag, and get up to Alaska—we have a spot in our tent on Thompson Pass."

That fateful afternoon in Alaska, when I followed my brother's track in the waning dusk over the first blind roll of my life, it didn't feel wrong, like I was willingly riding off the end of the earth to my death. I pushed through the fear and over the roll where the steepest, longest, most beautiful slope of snow lay below. In the pink light of the sunset my turns grew bigger and bigger, and I reached speeds I had only hit in a Super-G course. I was at ease and in total control.

Alaska's grasp on my life was immediate. Things that had never been done before in the mountains elsewhere could frequently be done in Alaska's stable, coastal snowpack that covered its steep, glacier-laden mountains. Within two years my brothers would start their movie company Teton Gravity Research, and my goal of being the fastest snowboarder on the World Cup circuit dissipated. My new compass heading was to push my snowboarding to new levels on the world's best mountains and document it on film. Too many close calls too early on led to avalanche classes and a hyperfocus on risk management. We built a protocol—a method of mountain travel that limits risk—with the help of more experienced teammates, which enabled us to consistently find the edge, tickle it at times, but never cross it.

To understand when the portal opens so we can dance with the dragons has been my life's focus, although my approach has slowly evolved and morphed over time as I've gained more knowledge. When I was thirty, my career was about as solid as a pro snowboard career could be. My paycheck was based on being in snowboard movies and magazines, and I was in both, more than anyone else in the world. Most riders work all year for a single movie part, while I had just finished my most successful year ever, racking up a total of five parts. I was a master with a helicopter, where I could film a video part in three or four sunny days. But my body was breaking down, as was my mind. I had come to the edge of where I could take my snowboarding, as well as where I could take a helicopter or a snowmobile. That stagnation is the death of the brain and the antithesis of progression is a concept to which I've always held firm: I felt that if I wasn't pushing the sport forward, then I should get out of the way so the next kid could.

The other major factor was what I was seeing happening to the mountains, specifically the effect climate change was having on them—shrinking glaciers, summit rainfall in January, low-elevation resorts struggling to open. These changes meshed with what the scientific world had been warning us about. It did not sit well with me that my personal carbon footprint was negatively affecting the very thing my life was centered around: snow. At this time I turned toward "foot-powered" snowboarding and riding the best line of my life in the backcountry. And getting there under my own power.

I wrote about this change of perspective in my journal in 2007: "We were like big game hunters equipped with spotlights and rifles. It was time to grab the bow and arrow and camping gear—time to give these mountains the respect they deserved. Time to sleep under these dream lines, to learn from them and live with them. Then when the time became right, to tiptoe up them and snowboard back down."

With a whole new crew of riders and filmers, I set out to make my first foot-powered snowboarding film, *Deeper*, which I thought might be my last film ever. A year into filming, with hardly a thought, I left my sponsor of nineteen years, Rossignol,

and started Jones Snowboards because the splitboards I needed to achieve my new goals didn't exist—I had to design my own.

Two years into backcountry filming, Ryland and I are poised to drop into the biggest spine wall of our lives. We had climbed and bivied at the top of the face, waiting for morning to come. Picking up speed, I find my flow. Even though I'm in total control, there is no way I can stop. The slope is too steep and each turn creates small sluffs that build into small avalanches. These are predictable slides, and depending on my appetite, I mix it up and play with them like a surfer plays with a wave. We call this "sluff management." But my internal Spidey sense knows that I have monster sluff building above me and to my left. Moving at the same speed as the sluff, I feel the weight starting to grab the tail of my snowboard. An essential rule in sluff management is to never sluff your exit—or at least get to your exit before your sluff does or find a safe spot to pull up on an "island of safety" while the sluff cascades through your line. This is poor sluff management, something I try to avoid at all costs.

My exit is to my right, off the smallest part of the cliff. I purposefully do not ride above it until the end of my line in order to leave it clean. This means that the majority of my line is over the biggest part of the cliff. Cut over too early and I sluff my exit, too late and I'm dragged off a huge cliff and get seriously hurt or worse. As much as I wrestled with this in the days leading up to my line, my mind is totally free of any such thought. I bounce down the spines and dabble with a rare "white moment." Everything is quiet, despite the rush of my sluff and the wind. Hundreds of micro-decisions and adjustments are being made, but I give them no thought. My mind and body are one. I perfectly position myself over my exit air just as my sluff reaches it. Together we fly through the air like I am jumping a snow waterfall. The landing is soft and steep, and although it is now partially hidden from the explosion of my sluff off the cliff, I stomp the landing. Coming out of the smoke, I wait a few seconds and then lean into a few celebratory powder turns before straight running toward the glacier valley below. My body shakes. Uncontrollable screams are followed by sobs and tears.

Ryland and I have just ridden one of the best lines of our lives, all under our own power. A huge achievement for the time. That line will stay with me forever, but all I can really think about is that I will see my infant daughter and wife again. That I will live to ride another day. The sad truth is that too many of my friends, heroes, and mentors have not lived to ride another day.

What follows in these pages are the people and experiences that define me. I'm not proud of every decision I've made in the mountains, but often we learn the most from our mistakes. The trick is not dying in the process. I'm not better than those who've fallen to the mountains. I've tried to be honest about the risks, stack the deck as much as possible, pick the right time to walk on the moon and with the right plan and the right people. I've tried to be present enough to know when the mountains lie down and welcome you, or when the danger scale tilts too far in the wrong direction and it is time to back off.

At the heart of this passion is the ability to push through significant mental and physical barriers when the struggle is grand but also to have the wherewithal and awareness to recognize nature's subtle signs that turn a green light to red in an instant, requiring you to abandon one of your life's greatest goals. This mix of gusto and humility, fearlessness and fear, grit and sensitivity, requires a deep understanding of who you are as a person at your innermost core, as well as an intimate connection with nature and your partners, plus a deep understanding of the behaviors, characteristics, and subtleties of all things snow. This is the Art of Shralpinism.

Intro: Why I Ride

A guide once told me: "Experience is something you get just after you need it." The trick is to become experienced without getting killed. My hope is that you learn from my "experiences," so you do not make all the same mistakes I've made along the way. This book should complement, not replace, traditional avalanche classes and on-the-slope experience. It's loosely organized into three parts: Wisdom, Science, and Art. This is from the perspective of a rider who has spent a lot of time out *in* it, pushing the envelope, gaining experience, and looking back over a long, fortunate career. I have been snowboarding for almost four decades—first as an amateur before racing on the international circuit, then as a freerider in front of (and now also behind) the camera in a range of snowboarding movies, and eventually developing my own snowboard designs. All of it aimed at helping to pioneer foot-powered backcountry riding.

Numerous winding paths have led to a life spent exploring mountains and wilderness. Along the way, I've slowly created a toolbox for navigating safely and having fun. Similarly, your approach should always be evolving. Ideally, as you get older, you'll understand better which tools you need and which you don't, and your strategy will become more refined, allowing you to enjoy the mountains even more.

Curiosity is the root of discovery, and it begins with the question "why?" Asking why something is is the basis of science. Intrigue, curiosity, and wonder are three words that are at the root of my snowboard discoveries, but certainly not what I felt as a kid sitting in science class studying periodic tables and struggling to get a passing grade. However, the scientific method stuck with me. Test, tweak, repeat.

My approach has developed over the years, and my passion for the sport and connection with nature are stronger than ever. The mountains are my power source, where I go to refuel my body and mind. They are the places that make the most sense to me, and where I'm most inspired and humbled. The more I immerse myself in the mountains, the more I get out of them. The mountains have always been my greatest teacher, and the lessons they've taught have led to the highest highs and, sadly, the lowest lows. I love riding anywhere, including the resort, where I still do about 40 percent of my riding. But exploring and traveling into the backcountry, riding lines with a few friends, away from the crowds, has the strongest pull for me.

Why the backcountry? It has a simplicity—fewer people, better snow, endless amounts of untouched terrain. Harder to explain is the feeling of smallness, the reward of traveling into new landscapes, discovering new lines, and figuring out how to safely ride them. The more remote and obscure, the greater the reward. It's in these

hard-to-reach, zero-mistake places that I learn the most. The lessons that come from exposing yourself to much larger forces, interwoven with experiencing wilderness, develop creativity, problem-solving, planning, and friendships. It's a unique feeling putting all of these pieces together to travel into and ride remote areas, away from humanity's presence. The backcountry offers many more dimensions than the resort, more challenges and more rewards.

Becoming an experienced backcountry traveler is a lifelong pursuit. To be in an uncontrolled world, coexisting with nature and learning to understand its subtle signs, is a never-ending quest that requires total presence and humility. Embrace the journey and every step along the way. If a ten-minute hike off a chairlift is new ground for you, celebrate it. Don't get caught up in what others are doing—we all have our own paths, our own losses and wins. For me, curiosity and wonder are the driving forces. Curiosity is a powerful thing; it can motivate us to do great things, but it can also get us in over our heads. Stepping into the mountains—whether resort, sidecountry, or backcountry—is always serious business.

There are no shortcuts or hacks when it comes to staying safe in the mountains. When you come close to dying in the mountains, or witness someone almost die or worse, that experience becomes part of your makeup. My mistakes have left mental scars that will never heal, nor should they. During my ongoing quest to send serious

lines in perfect conditions, the real lessons, the character-building ones, have come from the tough days in the mountains when things have not gone perfectly. It's for these days, the missed calls, that I write this book.

The reality is that gaining competency in backcountry travel cannot *all* come from a book, classroom, or course. Sure, formal education is an absolute must. However, an Avy Level 1, 2, or 3 class does not give you the green light to charge into the mountains and ride serious lines. Really bad accidents and problems can happen in the mountains. And the new norm of extreme weather only increases the incidence of unforeseeable events. Survival and success are a mix of experience, science, honest fear, and the ability to quiet the noise of real-world distractions, pressures, and expectations. No matter how fit you are, how big you go, or how many classes you've taken, if you've spent only a few years in the backcountry, you're still a beginner.

By age twenty, even though I was making a living as a competitive snowboarder, I knew my focus would eventually be riding the best lines in primo conditions and

in the best style. Much to my surprise, by twenty-four, I had done just that. But I was taking unsustainable risks, deep down knowing that eventually my bluff would get called. Many times I'd been closer to the edge of safety than I'd ever intended. A half-weighted foot with the abyss below me, the world cracking all around, sending me 70 miles per hour down the mountainside or cartwheeling out of control down narrow, walled chutes. In order to play the game for life, I needed more education, more discipline, and some protocols for handling serious backcountry terrain, so I could come home to my family every night. I realized that an understanding of snow science, routefinding, mountaineering skills, and wilderness first aid were essential.

Perhaps even more important than classes are mentors. Commit your life to the mountains, and you will find your teachers. They come in all shapes and sizes and ages. I'm the sum of everyone I've ever ridden and traveled with, as I always observe, listen, and ask questions. I seek out specialists, understand their different styles, take what works for me, and then progress. I'm extremely fortunate to have learned from some of the best. Throughout this book you'll also learn from my mentors and partners as I share critical lessons I still use today.

When dissecting my miscues, it's clear that individual psychology, group dynamics, and decision-making also play huge roles. In the aftermath of an unfortunate event, rather than really investigating what happened along the way and why potential warning signs were ignored, we tend to focus on the one missed call. Instead we need to try to expand our understanding of these events and all the dynamics at play. How did we forget about proper rider spacing on the uphill? Why did we ride into an obvious wind-loaded pocket halfway down? The mental game is just as important as the tactical game.

Big mountain riding is an art form and comes in many forms and styles. And as with art, various tools can be used to create your singular vision. I consider science to be part of the equation too, informing the tools you use to make the art. Embrace the science and include your art—the exact techniques, systems, gear, and protocols you use to make decisions are up to you—the possibilities are endless, the creativity limitless. There are plenty of crossover techniques among artists, but they rarely ever follow the exact same rules. Wisdom + science = art. My art is an extension of the knowledge and styles passed on from my mentors and partners. This sharing of knowledge has been going on for multiple generations. This book is a handoff of sorts—I'm merely one link in the chain. It's important for me to write while I'm still focused on charging, because too many times I see older teachers discrediting the younger generations as reckless daredevils. My hope is to turn the reckless into the calculated. Mountains are dynamic, living, raw beings, and there's no way to eliminate all risk. And this is the point—to be exposed, out in it, where we're very small. To understand this feeling is important.

Put simply, I'm a lover of shredding and alpinism—a Shralpinist.

PART ONE

Wisdom

Snowboarders ride for a lot of different reasons. I'm psyched most every-where in the mountains, but I'm happiest in the backcountry. It takes a lot of time to develop the skills to be capable and confident away from the resorts. To improve, you need to love what you're doing, push it every once in a while, and figure out the best way to train to reach your goals.

Begin by building a foundation, and get better every year. This is easy for the first ten, fifteen years; it's why I envy the beginner snowboarder. New riders have so much progression sitting right in front of them. It comes in many forms: learning new tricks and assessing risk, stepping up to expert terrain, making good turns in bad snow, figuring out deep days, firm days, and stomping your biggest cliff. As I've grown older, it's safe to say I've probably stomped the biggest cliff I'm ever going to hit, and I have a hard time bombing bumpy hardpack like I used to, but I'm still committed to progressing. Stagnation is not an option.

The simplest barometer for me is when I think, *I couldn't reach this moment any sooner than now, because I've needed all my knowledge and experience to be standing here.* The multiday, self-supported foot-powered trips take me deeper into the wilderness than I've ever gone before. It's slower speed but grander. I'm largely against the "first descent" claim, but I'm confident that in this ever more crowded world, I'm making turns where no one has before, and I'm doing so under my own power. This confirms to me that forty years into this magical sport, I'm still breaking new ground. At the same time, the resort and mellower terrain in my local mountains continue to play a huge part in getting to these new places.

CHAPTER 1

Building a Foundation

There are no shortcuts to success in the mountains or life. Ride with purpose and intent on every run day after day for years on end and see where it gets you.

I'm a huge sports fan. I grew up on Cape Cod, and it was a family affair with sports. Some of my few memories of hanging out with my grandfather are sitting on the floor next to his recliner, watching games on TV. As a kid, I played all the traditional sports: baseball, soccer, hockey, football, surfing, skateboarding, and lacrosse. I treated each sport like I was going to be a pro. Any free time was spent focused on whatever sport was in season. Because I hailed from the Cape, hockey was the most serious. We converted our basement into a mini street hockey rink. My grandfather, dad, and brothers were first and foremost hockey players. By second grade, I was playing eleven months a year. My first dawn patrols were for hockey practice before school. I slept in my gear sometimes to squeeze in extra sleep. My earliest memory is getting frostbite in kindergarten at a 5:30 a.m. hockey practice.

Finding the Mountains

My grandfather discovered Stowe, Vermont, before I was born. I say "discovered" because crossing the bridge that connected Cape Cod to the rest of the world was a big deal. Driving to Boston, an hour away, was something you did on a school field trip once or twice a year to see Paul Revere's house or Bunker Hill. Driving five hours to Vermont felt like an expedition to Antarctica, but my parents had fallen in love with skiing by the time I was four. We had a two-room condo at the base and made the pilgrimage every weekend.

The goal wasn't to turn us into ski racers or even expert skiers. There was never talk of being a part of the local ski club. My parents had their own friends on the mountain. The kids would meet them for lunch and take a run or two together. I learned the basics in a kids' program and, as soon as I could keep up, I was on my own. If I could hang with my brothers, they would let me ski with them. If I fell behind,

they ditched me. I skied a lot by myself at a young age. Thankfully, I had cousins. My mother is an identical twin and, not by chance, she and her sister had kids at the same time. My aunt's youngest, Adam Hostetter, was my wingman before I could walk.

I started snowboarding at age nine, and the progression couldn't have been any slower for the first few years. The first snowboard I ever saw was in the basement of Shaw's General Store. I'm not sure why I went down to the small clearance section, but I somehow found a Burton Backhill collecting dust. I grabbed the board without asking and stood on it, letting my imagination run free with new possibilities. On the floor were a couple six-page Burton catalogs. I brought one home and studied every word, every spec, every photo.

Because resorts didn't allow snowboards early on, I hiked and rode local hills with the wooden Burton Backhill—no metal edges and rubber foot straps. I learned every grab I'd ever tried on my skateboard in a matter of days, and I could make basic powder turns right away. However, as I lived on the East Coast, finding powder was extremely rare. When it came to making turns on hardpack, I failed miserably. Run after run, I would hike up the hill, stand on the board, pick up speed, lean over to make a turn, and then starfish, sliding away on my chest. There were no videos to watch, no how-tos, no one to teach me.

Snowboarding Leaps into the Modern Era

It'd be three years before I was actually allowed on a chairlift with my snowboard. During this time, I learned the hard lesson that dreams are cheap and reality doesn't care. The boards improved rapidly, though, and Shaw's had a great program that let you trade in your old board for credit on a new one.

Snowboarding leaped into the modern era around 1986, when the highback binding was invented. This innovation, along with the metal edges and p-tex (thank you, skiing!), is what took snowboarding from stand-up sledding to the sport we have today. Burton's new model became my sole focus. Unfortunately, my old Backhill didn't fetch enough trade-in dollars. However, three boards did. My brothers weren't as committed as I was, and I made the bold decision to trade in their boards without ever asking. It cost me some serious bruises, but progression requires risk and sacrifice. The new board was going to solve all my problems.

Except—it didn't. A few days in with my new board I was at peak frustration. With tears in my eyes, I hiked higher up the hill than ever before. In the fading light, I pointed the board downhill, letting gravity take me to the edge of my comfort zone. If there is a higher power, it interjected, tilting my board on edge, and I leaned into the first real turn of my life. Toeside, then heelside, and then toeside again. I linked turns all the way to the bottom. Coming to a stop, I was so excited that I broke a buckle trying to quickly unstrap so I could sneak in another run before dark. From that day, my time on the mountain skiing got shorter and shorter so I could get home and snowboard my local hills.

One day that next summer, I sat at my kitchen table, going through the mail. Jackpot: the Burton catalog had arrived. I opened it to the page that listed all the resorts that allowed snowboarding and saw my home mountain, Stowe, now listed. I jumped out of my chair and did a victory dance around the house. My life had changed—little did I know how much.

The first time I dropped off the top of Stowe, it was Sunrise to Standard. A run I'd skied a thousand times transformed in front of my eyes. The mundane, feature-less groomer turned into a three-dimensional skate park. Every run was like this. I had a totally new mountain, and I couldn't get enough. The only exception was the infamous "Front Four" (Stowe's four double black diamonds)—deemed too hard for snowboarding. We didn't care. Adam was hooked too, and we rode first chair to last no matter what the conditions.

Back then, the sport was so small I could go to the resort and end up riding with all the snowboarders. By now, my brothers and I knew who the best riders were and our goal was to take the lift up with these local heroes so we could ask them questions. The main thing we wanted to know was how they were able to ride every day. We were ecstatic when we discovered they were bartenders, waiters, house painters, and the like. Realizing that people made a living in ski towns and could ride daily changed my life's path. My brothers and I painted houses, washed windows, and worked in the restaurant industry through high school and well into our mid-twenties, so that we could be on the mountain as much as possible.

Academy and Riding on the Cheap

As a parent, I'm impressed my parents accepted my unwavering path to seemingly nowhere, even when the hockey coach called after he realized my name was no longer on the roster. He had been flabbergasted when I told him I just wanted to snowboard. The call ended when he told my dad I was "throwing my life away."

When I was fourteen, I made the decision to really go for it. My mother and I drove to an empty bus station three hours from home. It was November, and a dark-green van waited for me. I loaded two snowboards: a three-year-old Sims Switchblade that had a crack running down the middle of the nose, held together by duct tape, and a Heavy Tools race board with plate bindings. A half dozen other students and I said our goodbyes, and the van took us north to a single building on the edge of a logging road just outside Sugarloaf Mountain. The resort sits on a massive stand-alone peak that towers 3,000 feet above the valley floor. It would be my home for the next four years.

I must have been nervous and scared, but all I remember is thinking, *Holy shit! I'm actually going to be able to ride every day!* I had very little info about Carrabassett Valley Academy (CVA) beforehand and had briefly met only one other student, Bungy. Bungy's dad, Warren Cook, was the reason I was attending. Our fathers were best friends in college. When Warren heard from my dad that I was obsessed with snowboarding and had won and come in third in the only two contests I'd ever entered, he convinced my dad to send me up to Sugarloaf for the winter to attend CVA, then a struggling ski academy trying to make a name for itself. Attendance was roughly sixty kids ranging from eighth grade to postgraduate. One of these kids was an eighteen-year-old snowboarder from New Brunswick, Canada, named Mark Fawcett. I'm not sure if it was out of financial desperation or because of Fawcett's relentless persuasion, but CVA opened its doors to snowboarding. This was at the height of the skier-boarder rift in the early 1980s, and it would be years before

Certified

At 8:30 a.m. on Opening Day in 1986, I stood at the pass office with hopes of getting "certified" by the only snowboard instructor, Lowell Hart. Lowell would determine if I was good and safe enough to ride Stowe. Getting off the lift with him, I had the same focus I carry today into serious terrain. Blow it here, and I'm back to hiking the backyard. I did one run with Lowell and showed him I could link turns and stop. Or, rather, that I knew enough to fall down before going too fast, so I wasn't a hazard. Thankfully, I passed. This clearance made me the first person certified to snowboard Stowe. It had absolutely nothing to do with skill—I've never actually heard of anyone failing the test. I was first because I was frothing so hard the first day of the season to actually snowboard at a resort and to finally be able to take a chairlift instead of hike.

The experience of dropping into my first run on a real mountain I already knew so well from eight years of skiing was surreal. It was like stepping through a portal into a whole new enhanced land, because I was now standing sideways. All the steeps and rollers were magnified and the jumps more pronounced. My home mountain went from mundane to magical. I put my skis away for good that year, and if the lifts were spinning, I was riding: rain, shine, frigid temps, or storms. It didn't matter. I had a new compass that put an abrupt end to traditional sports and altered my life forever. I didn't know how I was going to do it, but one way or another I was going to figure out how to wake up and go snowboarding every day.

another academy would do so. I can only imagine the heated debate with the ski coaches over whether to welcome the knuckle draggers.

Academy life may be thought of as a bunch of entitled and soft rich kids, but my experience was different. For a ski academy to make a name for itself, nothing speaks louder than winning. CVA therefore focused on getting northern New England kids who were just under the radar of the elite Vermont schools. About 98 percent of the kids were on financial aid and wanted to win at all costs. Our day started with a run at 6:15. If you were out the door at 6:15:30, you were assigned dish duty. The first class started at 7:30, and we ended at 5:30. Three hours of dryland training every day and school on Saturdays. Any free time was spent playing pickup sports. The talent level was ridiculous. Some students went on to win gold medals—Bode Miller and Seth Wescott—and others became Olympians or regulars on the World Cup circuit. It was interesting to see who made it and who didn't. Wescott was obvious, Kirsten Clark too, but Bode Miller was not considered the best skier in school. He was fast but loose, crash-prone, and considered uncoachable.

Surprisingly, being the only two snowboarders in school wasn't a big deal. Fawcett and I were so obsessed with riding that, even on the coldest days (and, by cold standards, Sugarloaf hits a level all its own), we never took breaks. Some days, we were literally the only ones riding the mountain. To stay warm required unorthodox methods—wearing two hats, two jackets, two pairs of pants, two neck gaiters, anything extra helped. We were often perplexed about where everyone else on the team was training. Little did we know that the lift shacks doubled as warming huts where the coaches and other kids would watch us doing lap after lap.

On Friday mornings, Mark and I drove three to five hours to New England contests in his white sedan, making sure to arrive in time for some half-pipe laps and to find a place to stay. Whatever mountain we visited, the locals would open their doors to anyone who needed a floor to sleep on. That first year, Fawcett and I competed in thirty-five contests and never once stayed in a hotel or in our car. We also never ate out and were masters of riding on the cheap. I basically subsisted on peanut butter and jelly and spaghetti for years. My parents and the school were oblivious to our fine-tuned dirtbag program, but the results spoke for themselves. Fawcett competed at the pro level and held his own with riders who would soon make it big on the international stage. I was winning every race with ease and fighting for the podium in half-pipe, but never quite winning. At breakfast Monday mornings, the headmaster would congratulate the people who made the podium that weekend. Hearing our names over and over and seeing our commitment on the hill started softening him. Soon the ski coaches were letting us run their courses and even giving us tips on line and form.

Jerry Masterpool, Cross M, and the Turn

Traveling to races, I started seeing a unique, cultlike sticker on the boards of many on the Burton A team, which at the time dominated all aspects of the sport. The sticker was a rough cross with an *M* scrawled underneath. It looked like graffiti of the latest underground punk band. Was it a new brand? A special club? I traced the logo back to a man who I believe was the first professional snowboarding coach, Jerry

Masterpool. Jerry had left the Burton team to start his own team, Cross M, bringing with him Mike Jacoby, Tara Eberhard, Jason Ford, and other non-Burton riders. Fawcett continued to have success at a regional pro level and was dabbling on the US pro tour. Soon he was training with Jerry, and when the pro tour came to Vermont for the Burton US Open, Fawcett introduced me.

An intimidating figure who looked more like a member of Hells Angels than a coach, Jerry had a goatee and long hair. He was a man of few words and absolutely no bullshit. Fawcett arranged for me to take a few training runs in front of Jerry, who rather quickly dissected my flaws. Back then, I just did what felt right and never gave any thought to technique. My approach was basically to put the board on edge and carve the shit out of it. On day one, Jerry explained things that made total sense but that I'd never even imagined, especially about proper turns. When I started on Cross M, the title of "Overall World Champion" was the pinnacle achievement, and Craig Kelly had held the title for three years, later losing it to Mike Jacoby, whom I also trained with.

Ironically, Jerry was not a snowboarder. A seasoned ski coach, he brought racing fundamentals to the snowboard turn and discipline to my life. Jerry made our life much harder with his military-level discipline, but deep down, we knew we needed this because, other than Jerry cracking the whip on the training hill, we were completely on our own, doing whatever we wanted.

As a coach, Jerry was committed to getting the most out of us, not to being our friend. He pushed us to our limits constantly, but I never questioned it because it was working. He broke down the turn like I've never seen before or since. Patience, initiation, drive, angulation, pressure, and upper-body alignment were beat into us. He timed us daily, although he rarely showed us our results. We didn't need to see them because 90 percent of the time Fawcett set the pace. He was consistently in the top five in the World Cup, which was incredibly rare for someone from North America. Another teammate, Jasey-Jay Anderson, who would later win a gold medal as well as more World Cups than anyone else, was a wild card who would catch lightning in a bottle every once in a while and crush us all.

Jerry brought intense discipline and structure to me at a time when I otherwise would have had very little. Show up late and you were hiking the course. Make stupid mistakes and you were hiking. We would have two warm-up runs before training, and the rest of our riding was done in front of Jerry and recorded.

Jerry's wife filmed every run. Jerry placed a radio up top, and he'd give us instructions and stop us at the bottom. Every turn of every run was analyzed in microscopic detail. At the end of the day we would watch film. If a turn was late, early, or half-assed, Jerry would play it over and over in silence. He'd break the embarrassment with something along the lines of "Don't waste my fucking time ever again."

Transitioning to Pro

At sixteen, filled with fear and hope, I boarded a plane in Boston to fly cross-country to California. Mark Fawcett picked me up at the airport, and I pulled out of the start gate at my first pro contest a week later. Turning pro was a decision I wrestled with for almost a year. *Am I too young? Can I compete?* There is no half-step to turning pro this young. I was placing a huge bet on my future. I was officially off the leash and "live without a net." Much to my surprise, I got third. I think I won $900, which was massive. At this point my parents had fallen on hard times, and I was on a full scholarship thanks to Warren Cook. I was paying for snowboarding from my summer job bussing tables. It worked fine for traveling the East Coast, but the $3,000 I'd saved didn't go very far on the pro tour. Being handed cash was eye-opening. How many tables would I have to bus to make $900?

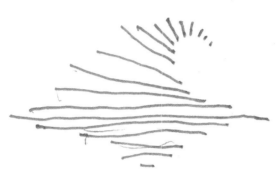

The money allowed me to extend my tour and compete in more pro events. I never saw a podium again, but I was able to recoup entry fees and feed myself. Hotels were still out of the question, but Fawcett had traded his car for an Astrovan that became our home. Without the help of Jerry Masterpool and Fawcett, I have to question if I could have made the transition to pro. There were no team managers back then. I witnessed so many amazing riders struggle with the transition only to head home because of lack of funds, never to be seen on the tour again. There was no time to ease into things. You either won money right away and used it to get to the next event, or

Seth Morrison, Skiing Visionary

I once ran into Seth Morrison at Loveland Ski Area, a smaller front-range resort near Denver, in early November. The resorts had been open for two weeks, but we were relegated to two "white ribbons of death" groomers. Seth was by himself, riding six hours a day, and he was on his fifteenth day in a row. His goal is to get in sixty days by January 1 every year. It's not by luck, or that he was born with superpowers (maybe a few), that Seth revolutionized freeskiing and became one of its biggest names.

Christina Lusti: World-Class Shralpinist

Canadian Christina Lusti is a retired World Cup ski racer turned world-class Shralpinist who has the right amount of gusto, grit, and humility to put down some of the most serious first descents in the world. Now a certified AMGA mountain guide, the former Olympic skier has starred in several ski films. I asked her about how she shifted to backcountry skiing and what her experience as a woman in the sport has been like.

"I moved to Revelstoke twelve years ago. It wasn't my first time backcountry skiing, but it was my first introduction to ski mountaineering. When I was still ski-racing I knew I wanted to ski big lines, but I didn't know much about the how. This lack of backcountry knowledge was my inspiration to pursue the guide program. In 2009 I enrolled in an adventure guide program; it was the start of becoming an ACMG ski guide. All the training leading up to guiding helped balance out my understanding/confidence in the mountains. In 2011 I skied my first first descent (solo), and since then I've been guiding, skiing professionally, and skiing for myself.

"In my early years, I was so keen and eager to get it done that I'd try a line, back off, try again, back off. Maybe now I'm a little more patient, and I'll wait for the right conditions. Turning away from a line is a huge, huge part of ski mountaineering and having a long career in the mountains.

"It's usually awesome being a woman in the mountains. Like most people there, I just put my head down and try to be a solid person in the hills—except I look cute and probably smell better. I have a huge admiration for Hilaree Nelson; she's a mega hero. Strong, humble, and sends so hard it gives the bots FOMO. I love it.

"Of course, there are downsides. Sometimes it's hard to be heard and to find your place. It's still extremely hard to get good technical gear in small sizes. Companies still make female ski boots much softer than men's, and the high-end men's boots often don't go small enough. I haven't had a ski pack that fits me in three years. I'm probably getting paid less too. Fun stuff . . .

"My advice to women who are getting started in serious backcountry skiing:

- Have patience
- Take courses
- Have good partners
- Have great mentors
- Do it because you love the adventure
- Have fun"

you were done. The pressure of every race was every bit the pressure of riding over steep exposure. Riding for gas money and food would leave me dry heaving at the top of a course, wondering if I'd have a good dinner or not. Like exposure, every race was a no-fall zone. I didn't need to win, but I did need a top-fifteen finish to cover costs. This "must make it to the finish line" is not the mentality you want pulling out

Running on Fumes

FROM STOWE, VERMONT, TO NAGANO, JAPAN, 1994

My low point came at the very place I had gotten third at in my first pro race two years earlier, Bear Mountain, California. The morning of the race I woke up with the flu. My entry fee was paid, so I decided to try to race. Somehow I won. I think it was my conservation of energy and carefree attitude, not caring about results. There was no Sizzler steak celebration, though. I was sick, and fading fast, and by that evening I could not breathe very well and had to sleep upright in a lounge chair. I was scheduled to drive east but took my winnings and booked a ticket home the next day. I was so sick by my layover in Dallas that when the flight attendant saw me struggling to walk down the aisle to my seat, she thought I was drunk at first and tried to kick me off the plane. I couldn't talk because my throat had swollen, but she saw the look in my eyes and figured it out when I pointed to my neck.

The next day I was at the doctor in Stowe, Vermont. He looked at the severity of my throat and wanted me immediately checked into a hospital for fear of suffocation. Explaining I didn't have health insurance, I was met with the doctor's empathy. "I want to see you every day." He gave me a box of sample antibiotic packs. A few days later I was on the mend, and I explained to the doctor that I had a trip scheduled to Japan within the week. He didn't like the idea, but gave me more meds, coupled with emergency pills in case the sickness came back.

Ten days later, dead broke, I returned to Logan Airport to meet up with my Japanese classmate from CVA, Aki, and Adam Hostetter. Snowboarding was so big in Japan then that it represented 30 percent of industry sales. Aki had arranged a dream trip, all expenses paid for by Eagle, the biggest snowboard shop in Japan. Adam and I would spend three weeks competing on the Japanese pro tour. Aki did not say much, and whatever the question was, he answered with a pleasant "yes." At the airport I opened my wallet to show him I had no money. As in zero. "Should I be getting on this plane, Aki?" Aki answered in broken English: "Yes, money no problem. Money when we get there."

We knew nothing about Japan or the mountains there, but Aki was right: we were handed envelopes of cash when we got off the plane, but we never needed any as they never let us pay for anything. I was frail and weak from not being able to eat solid food for almost two weeks, but Japan ended up being the perfect place to heal. After a brief Tokyo promo tour, we drove to Aki's family house in the mountains outside of Nagano. Traveling up the road, we could not believe the height of the snowbanks as we got closer. The pow was like nothing we had seen before, and we had the mountain to ourselves. We settled into riding bottomless powder and eating Japanese home cooking at night. Slowly I came back to life.

Going to our first race, it was clear Adam and I were a notch up on the competition. We briefly discussed not pushing it too hard, as there was money to be made. We ended up swapping wins and riding a ton of powder. Three weeks later, we were back at the airport feeling rested and strong again, flush with cash. Handing over the envelopes of cash to be exchanged, I watched in awe as the hundreds started flying, to the tune of $10,000. Prior to the trip, I'd thought for the first time that I couldn't do it anymore. I had just about given up, cried uncle. The physical, mental, and financial toll was too much. I'd dabbled in the World Cup, getting crushed by the Europeans, with very little reason to believe success was in my reach. But now the debt was gone, the door wide open again.

If it hadn't been for that doctor in Vermont and the love and kindness of our Japanese hosts, I'm not sure where I would be today. That summer I signed a deal with Rossignol, which covered my living expenses. I was by no means rich, but I got my driver's license, bought Hostetter's truck, and was able to rent a closet in Tahoe just big enough to hold a few duffels and to sleep in. Glorious.

of a start gate, but I was dealing with no-fall situations—and not because I feared getting hurt. If I fell, I wouldn't be able stay on the tour. I wonder if this pressure played a role in my ability to ride "fall you die lines" with confidence.

Riding with someone better than you every day is the simplest way to improve. Over this nine-year period, I spent more than 250 days a year on snow with Fawcett and the Cross M team, which now included my cousin Adam. If I wasn't training or competing, I was freeriding with Hoss and Fawcett. This much focused time on snow built a strong base for me and had profound effects on my technique. Success came in North America with consistent top-ten finishes, podiums, and occasional wins, but I struggled in Europe. Fawcett developed into one of the only North Americans who could compete with the Europeans. Watching Fawcett's daily commitment to training was inspiring and frustrating. Run after run, year after year, I was consistently a few tenths of a second behind. Mark was never cocky, and although he was one of the fastest riders in the world, he shared my love of freeriding and all things snowboarding. Along with my cousin Adam, Fawcett craved freeriding on days off. Often it was the three of us taking turns driving through the night to catch the first tram on a powder day in Jackson, Wyoming.

Luck and Circumstance

Graduating from high school was one of the most liberating days of my life. College was never in the cards. I finished high school on fumes, barely qualifying for graduation. I told teachers, advisers, and my parents that I had no interest in college. I didn't want to spend the $35 on an SAT test or go through the motions of applying to college. I wanted to go snowboard the best mountains around the world for the rest of my life. This was not met with great encouragement.

The weight of my financial situation took its toll and kept me up at night. I was $10,000 in debt, had no health insurance, and no driver's license. My skill set outside of snowboarding was painting houses, waiting tables, and washing dishes. Climbing out of that much debt would require a lot of dishes. The day after school ended, I threw everything I owned into the back of Adam's pickup truck, and we headed west with a plan to train at Mount Hood in Oregon. We had road-tripping down to a science—one person slept while the other person drove. We averaged fifty thousand miles a winter and, in just a few years, I would cross the country seven times.

This was such a volatile time in my life. I was playing a high-risk game with my future, not to mention my health. Success and failure came down to a few tenths of a second. I had no backup plan at all, which gave me the power to keep going at all costs. Ironically, my schoolmate Bode Miller put himself in a similar situation. He talks about failure not being an option and the power of no plan. It's in these tenuous spots where we see what we're made of. A little bit of luck at the right time doesn't hurt either. Luck, however, often favors hard work.

What I Believe: A Life Manifesto

I believe in karma. Not so much the *I'm going to win the lottery because I helped an old lady with her groceries* version. More the idea that if you keep spreading positivity, keep opening doors (not closing them), keep giving more than you take, then your path in turn will be smoother and happier.

I believe in the power of compounding returns. That implementing small things into my life like a simple morning routine done over and over for years on end can lead to major returns. The same holds true for simple diet changes, staying hydrated, and reading and writing a little every day. Look at your path in life as a series of decisions. I think of those decisions like turns on the mountain. How you weave those decisions together is how you weave through life. Just as 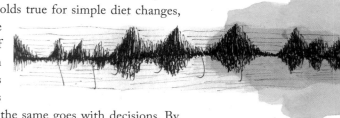 making good turns is a never-ending pursuit, the same goes with decisions. By reading, writing, creating art, surrounding myself with inspiring people, I evolve, and my decisions evolve.

I believe that whom we surround ourselves with matters. I look for the jazzed, knowledge-seeking, positive people who push my mind and body to think big and go big.

I believe in asking for help. Starting the nonprofit Protect Our Winters (POW), as an effort to fight climate change and its adverse effects in the mountains, I had nothing to lose. I knew the only way it would work was if people rallied around it. Asking strangers for help was scary. What if they said no? POW is the result of scientists, athletes, and industry leaders saying yes.

I believe in mentors, both informal and formal. These are people who have more knowledge than me, people who have been down the road ahead of me. Masters of health, wealth, sport, and science from whom, just by hanging out with them, I learn. Some aren't in my daily life. Mostly, these aren't snow mentors but climate and business leaders to whom I reach out with specific questions.

I believe in an "Ode to Progression." Not only is the phrase our product development north star at Jones Snowboards, it also holds true for life in general: "All things can be made better by design or material. Stagnation is not an option."

"Experience is the hardest kind of teacher. It gives you the test first and the lesson afterward." —Oscar Wilde

I believe that fear is the most powerful and detrimental emotion in life and the biggest culprit keeping us from our dreams. For me there are two types of fear. Fear of dying, which is good fear. And fear of failure, which is bad fear. Astonishingly, I've lost more sleep over fear of failure than fear of dying. Understanding the root of your fear and having an intimate relationship with your fear is critical. Fear can keep you alive, but it can also keep you from living.

I believe you only have so many steps on this planet. What are you going to do with them? I choose to use my steps to take me to new places, do new things, and see new landscapes.

I believe that combinations of hard work and doing something more than anyone else in the world will get you 95 percent of the way toward your goals.

I believe there's no such thing as overnight success. Someone once told me if you want something really bad, put your head down for ten years and see where it gets you.

I believe you're born into a society that likes to keep everyone on the same path, and there's very little encouragement to get off that path and forge a new one.

CHAPTER 2

The Resort and Progression

It's a great luxury to hop on a lift and rise effortlessly to the top of a mountain. To strap in and let gravity take you anywhere you please without very much effort. Resorts provide the ultimate freedom to go where you want and to do what you want. On any given day, across the planet, perhaps a few hundred thousand people slide on snow. If you're sliding on snow and are bored, take a look around and realize where you are! If you need powder to have a good day in the mountains, think about getting more creative and push yourself a bit.

"The best person on the mountain is the one having the most fun." My kids scoffed at this cliché, but now they understand it and will point out any random person clearly having the time of their life and spreading the good vibes to the entire resort. Easy to do on a pow day, harder to get excited about when conditions are less than "good." But what does that mean anyway? Many people get caught up in conditions. If it's not at least over the boots and blower, they complain. Seeing an angry expert on the mountain makes me sad; they have lost the plot. Resorts are an amazing resource, a great training ground, and the safest place to ride when avy conditions are high. The terrain is varied, the slopes are controlled, and you can pound your legs into oblivion, getting stronger and more technically polished for those long backcountry treks and more advanced lines. Resorts offer loads of opportunities for skills days to develop, get strong, and work on turns.

Know Thy Turn

Prior to training with Jerry Masterpool, I'd never given turns much thought. I just did it and got away with okay turns. He taught me everything about the turn. Words like *patience, initiation, angulation, driving with the hip, diving with the chest*, and other bons mots were drilled into me over a six-year period. These days, I find myself repeating these same words while teaching my kids the basics of the turn. Most people don't get intense, hands-on coaching at that level. But you can use the same basic discipline to focus on and improve and perfect your turns, using the resort as the ultimate training ground.

Feather and finesse? Carve or slarve? Hippie turns or power hacks? Learn them all and you will rarely fall. It's really what snowboarding is all about. Toe or heel, turns are your toolbox. Hop turns, tight turns, big turns, railed turns, schmeared turns, feathered turns, power hacks. Have purpose and thought in your riding, don't waste fall line, don't waste turns. Practicing different types of turns gives you more tools to work with and lets you venture into a lot of different areas on the mountain with better confidence. Groomed, mellower slopes are the perfect place to work on the perfectly carved turn. The focus should be turn radius, edge hold, diving into the turn, and carving the turn with confidence.

Learning to Carve

Start on low-angle groomers and ride under the lift so you can see your track on your trip back up. Carve turns making just a thin track. See how vertical you can get the board. It's not steep, so go for it. Next step, progress to slightly steeper groomed runs with two to four wide-open sections. The ultimate goal is to ride a sustained, steep groomer (black diamond) and maintain exactly the same radius turn top to bottom. There are very few people in the world who can do this. Watch Olympians Ted Ligety and Mikaela Shiffrin for inspiration. Most people start out carving, and as they pick up speed, their turns grow bigger and bigger, they go faster and faster, and give into the fall line.

> Imagine riding with a coffee cup on your head. Legendary skier Doug Coombs could ride bumpy steeps without spilling a drop.

The key to doing it right is in the initiation, or top, of the turn. Have patience coming across the fall line. When rolling into the new turn, do it with force and commitment. Being aggressively forward and on the front of your ski or board is critical here. Gently move your body weight over the front of the board while feathering the tail through the entire turn. The chest leads the effort. The front foot is heavily weighted, but the back half of your board is feathering or sliding immediately. When done right, you will reach max g's in the middle of the turn, load up your board, and get projected into the next turn. The bottom of the turn should feel weightless. If your board chatters at the end of your turns, you are not getting your direction change done high enough in the turn. When I'm lazy, I find myself getting bounced around and chattering a ton. I snap out of it by thinking about the start of the turn, which makes me initiate earlier—just that simple thought to make sure I turn earlier.

> Feather and finesse? Carve or slarve? Hippie turns or power hacks? Learn them all and you will rarely fall.

Hop Turn for Technical Steeps

The hop turn is a specialty tool, designed for maintaining edge and controlling speed on really steep faces, often in firm snow or on ice. At my home mountain, Palisades in Olympic Valley, we have lots of extra-steep pitches that are great for practicing the hop turn. Find the easiest, steepest pitches on your home mountain. It doesn't need to be long—in fact it's best to start on shorter pitches—but it needs to be steep. These are generally on the walls of chutes or right next to sloping cliffs. Put as many turns as possible in these spots. The firmer the conditions, the harder and better the challenge. This is my equivalent of a hard boulder problem. Done right, I can make two to five turns on a firm, steep flank with total control and little consequence. The harder the snow, the tougher the move. Done wrong,

A Nickel on Your Shin

Shane McConkey and I never did any serious riding together, but on occasion we did hit the hardpack groomers or do some early season touring. He shared my passion for love-of-sport conditions as well as Seth Morrison's commitment to stacking vert early season to build muscle. Like Seth, Shane was an ex-racer and took his technique seriously. One tip that stuck with me as we were lapping with our three-year-old daughters on the bunny hill: "Pretend you have a nickel on your shin. Keep it pressed on the front of the boot and never let it fall." This constant and steady pressure is something I'd never thought of, but watching high-level skiers, it's exactly how they succeed.

I lose my edge and slide into the chute. These are the same turns I may need in Chamonix on a 50-degree slope with 3,000 feet of exposure below. On the East Coast, I'd seek the iciest spots to see if I could hold an edge and then make some turns. Doing hop turns on a 30-degree patch of pure ice is similar to making the same turns on an edgable 50-degree slope.

Again, the hop turn is all about the start. Switching edges is a very explosive move—think box jumps. The upper body and hands lead the way, and the board follows. I think of my hands as my third edge. I want to get them back on the snow as soon as possible. My front hand leads the effort. It is natural to do this going from heel to toe. The real crux is toe to heel. Thinking about your front hand getting back to snow as soon as possible can be a big help in getting you to lead with your upper body. Your hands can give you a little extra hold on the mountain as well. In deep powder this is especially true. You can plunge your hand in like an axe.

Most mistakes in a hop turn happen because the tail catches. You need to be really forward. The front of the board hardly leaves the snow, but the tail does.

Grace and Flow

Now that you have all your basic turns, it is time to put them to work. The ability to flow through a wide variety of terrain—low angle, rollers, bumps, technical steeps, trees, and more—is where you see the biggest difference between a weekend warrior and seasoned pro. To be able to ride the entire mountain in every condition requires a mix of carved turns, hop turns, safety turns, and other moves. I think of it as similar to shifting gears in a standard car transmission. Can you move from first to fifth and back down to third smoothly? In terms of music, being a Grateful Dead fan, I think of how Jerry Garcia moved through complex chord progressions with grace and flow.

> I always plan for the worst and therefore am excited if the snow is softer than I expected, the face is not quite as steep, the outrun not as bumpy, the crust not as thick, or the crux not as hard. Overestimate everything to keep from getting in over your head.

A key to this is anticipating the terrain and snow conditions before you drop in. Head and eyes up, solid on your feet, patient, looking for the clean lines and flow, then diving in, speeding up, and shifting back to a slower pace again, looking for the next line or section. Piecing these lines together as smoothly as possible is the goal, flowing from one terrain feature to the next without stopping, big turns to medium, to small, and back up to big as you flow through the crux. Always turning, occasionally sliding, but never stopping!

Bulletproof: Holding an Edge

I tell my kids, "This is the best ice we've seen in years, we gotta take advantage of it!" to get them out the door in less-than-ideal snow conditions. "Off-piste" may be closed due to the dangers of taking a slide, but I know the steepest groomers that'll be totally glazed over. Instead of just sliding down them, we work on holding an edge. As kids on the East Coast, we used to do this all the time. The "blue ice challenge," we called it. It's amazingly rewarding riding 30-degree bulletproof ice in total control. When conditions are firm or icy, I resharpen my edges every day.

Firm, Chalky Steeps

If it's not teeth-rattling bulletproof ice off-piste, I focus on the steeps. Proper steeps generally are the smoothest. As the mountain flattens out, I look for small airs with steep landings. Being able to slow yourself down after hitting an air in bumpy hardpack is really hard and takes practice. Most snowboarders end up on their butts, chattering on their heels. When the slope is super steep, you often ride with your

hands touching the snow between the actual hop turns. Your hands help give you balance and a little bit of security. Same with my edge. You don't want to overhop your turn—hop only as high as you need to. The goal is to change edges as fast as possible and get the new edge on snow immediately so it can help slow you down. The whole point of a hop turn is to keep a steady, controlled flow. With steep, firm pitches you are just trying to rein in gravity and not accelerate down the hill.

Toe to Heel: The Trickiest Turn

The trickiest and most dangerous turn remains the toe to heel. You're shooting for a complete 180 rotation of the board, edge around to edge, balancing and riding toward the fall line, then repeating. You want to try to reengage your edge as soon as possible, almost perpendicular to the slope. Catching your tail halfway through this turn is extremely dangerous, often causing a fall in the wrong spot. Clear the tail and get the edge back on snow as quickly as possible.

Powder and Keeping the Tip Up

There is an epidemic in snowboarding. Longtime riders frequently have pain issues with their back leg, hip, knee, ankle, and other parts of their body. The root cause is that to ride powder on most snowboards takes an enormous effort to keep the tip above the powder. Making snowboards that I can ride centered, or even front foot, in powder and crust has been at the fore of my snowboard designs. Not only is riding centered or even forward better for your body, it makes you a better rider. The rockered tip and tapered tail date back to the origins of snowboarding, but the freestyle revolution killed it. Everyone ended up on snowboards with big tails so they could ride backward in powder. If you're not riding or landing backward in powder frequently, then you shouldn't be trying to sink a big tail. (It's the same with skis.) Mind you, a freestyle board with a stance moved all the way back can turn a twin tip into a powder board.

The fight to keep the tip up was not just a snowboard thing. It was at the center of Shane McConkey's skis as well. The vast majority of falls on skis or a board come from tip dive, from getting caught up on a crust, deep snow, or a hard transition. Long noses or rocker greatly improved this issue. The greatest effect can be seen in skiing. Skiing powder used to be for the advanced only. Wide, floaty tips with sinkable tails have allowed the average skier to rage powder, crust, and crud that, prior to

> The longer the sidecut, the easier it is to go fast. Big sidecut, big turns at big speeds. Short sidecut, short turns at slower speeds.

this design, was really difficult; these tips make everyone an expert. Equipment and speed provide the key to powder success. Momentum is your friend, especially for snowboarders. Look ahead, get your board straight, and carry speed into the powder to float on top. Make sure to follow someone's track into the entry to build speed, then cut out on your own. Find a track to slide into before the slope flattens out.

The Art of Spineology

There are certain resorts and spots with certain snow levels I go to because I know they have short spines. This allows me to make one to five turns very similar to an Alaskan spine wall but without the risk. You should be able to fall while prac-

ticing without any consequences. Use your entire body, exaggerating the hop rotation with your upper body and waist to get the board around quickly. I've grinded spines with my armpits trying to transfer over. I could easily let gravity do all the work in these same spots or air a small cliff, make one turn where I'm making three, but I'm working on specific skills and trying to get the most out of my mountain. It's why I generally ride smaller boards at the resort—to add length to the mountain. Charging fall line on a bigger board is fun and something I do later

Trust your board, learn your power stance. A power stance is a wide stance that you can hold a ton of g-forces with. Not exactly the stance you would squat heavy weight with, but similar.

in the season, when I know I'll be getting into bigger terrain, but it also means I'm blowing through vert and missing opportunities to interact with terrain and get the most out of my mountain.

Blowing Out the Pipes

When the mountain is empty, I draw big, arcing turns, pop rollers, and work on not getting blown back by the wind when I am in the air. If I catch a good powder cycle before a big trip later in the year, I spend the morning firing lines at top speed to get used to moving really fast through mixed terrain. Speed is something

I work on too. I go out first thing in the morning with the setup I ride bigger peaks on. This is always a little bigger board, because I want to be able to efficiently move through big sections of terrain with speed as well as stomp all my airs. A big board = bigger platform. Size up 4 cm and you are riding 15 miles per hour faster without even realizing it.

Gradually get used to going faster and faster. When going fast, time slows down and your movements must be subtle.

Pica Herry: Chamonix Guide

Pica Herry grew up under the jagged peaks of the Mont Blanc Massif and spends roughly three hundred days each year rock climbing and snowboarding. He continues to pioneer new lines in a range considered void of first descent long ago. We spoke about growing up in exposed situations, the freedom of twin boards, and discovering new routes.

"Riding more often in exposed situations, I quickly understood the advantages of being on your toe edge when negotiating delicate sections, by facing the mountain and being able to use ice axes. So logically half of the delicate traverses should be done on switch stance in order to stay on toe edge, which was my first real interest in riding switch.

"I fell in love with the freedom of twin boards, being able to switch from regular to goofy and vice versa anytime. It brought so much more fun to my everyday riding—every turn or relief became an option for a 180 transition. I found a way to improve my snowboarding and challenge myself without having to go in steeper or gnarlier lines every time. Snowboarding became more creative and comfortable riding both directions, and I find it healthier for my body.

"I discover new lines from photos in books or on the web, but sometimes just from watching the mountain from a different angle. I try to understand these lines by watching them all year round, with and without snow. Then it is just a waiting game to find the right conditions, partner, and snow. Year after year I am still surprised to discover new lines to ride in our local playground. Sometimes you ride it the day after, sometimes you ride it ten years later, sometimes it might just remain a dream line for your entire life!

"Mountaineering skills and imagination are great allies in helping you to ride new lines. Watching these lines at the end of the summer helps you understand if there's fossil or blue ice left somewhere before the first autumn snowfalls, or if there's only rock or permafrost where snow will stick more easily. Then the only way to make sure about what you'll find under your edge is to climb the line before riding it, choosing on the way up the best way to ride down."

The goal is control. Warning! Be aware of your speed, surroundings, other riders, obstacles, and hazards on the mountain. You want to be able to ski the entire mountain in control, at a speed you are comfortable with. Don't bomb crowded runs. The best way to work on building into speed and going fast is to wake up early and get to the hill before everyone else. Cold, fresh groomer mornings work best. Take note if people are on the mountain or not. Find runs where you can see the entire line and let it rip. The faster you go, the more important it is to slow down your body movements, to focus on a balanced stance and trust your board.

Slush Slasher

In the spring, when the slush fest is on, I often go for a surf day. I grab a small surf shape (sometimes my wife's board), tighten my stance, add a bunch of angle on both feet, and turn mogul runs into never-ending snake runs. The smaller board allows me to use the trenches as a mini half-pipe. A narrow stance makes it easier to turn faster. Small board, narrow stance, plus lots of angle allow you to make really short, fast turns. I'd been playing with this concept when I recently had the opportunity to stand in Craig Kelly's bindings on one of his boards. I've always admired his fast turns, upper-body rotation, and overall flow; it blew me away how much forward angle Craig had on both feet and how narrow his stance was. I thought I was really out there with my spring surf stance, but Craig was at a whole new level. A great example of not being tied to preconceived notions and traditional thinking. People get so obsessed with their stance and making a three-degree change. If you're at all bored, really mess with your stance. The first run will feel horrible and weird. By the third run, it'll feel normal.

Skills Days

It's fine to spend a morning or full day cruising the resort, just focused on having a good time. That's a big part of what it's all about. But, with progression, making a point to get better at something, it's helpful to spend some energy focused on different parts of snowboarding. Even if you're an advanced rider, concentrating on getting skills dialed can make a huge difference in your riding, especially when you venture into the backcountry. No two days on a mountain are the same when it comes to conditions. The mountain's always changing, often hour by hour. Some days are better than others, but regardless of conditions, there's always something to be gained from a day exploring. Being able to read the conditions and find the sweet spots on any given day is a skill years in the making.

Switch Tuesday: I pick a day and just ride switch. I use a twin with a duck stance. I spend the majority of the time riding switch. Hit everything you take for granted, switch. Be ready to fall.

The less ideal the conditions, the more rewarding it is to find hidden zones on a day most people stay home. These are what I call love-of-sport days, or skills days. Type 2 fun. These are the days that make others seem easy, build character, and get you ready to rip when conditions are stellar. The more different conditions you ride—

Use Video to Analyze and Improve

Back in the day, it was a mini miracle to shoot video and then watch yourself. These days, most riders have a movie-quality camera in their pocket. Use it. Have your friend video you coming down your favorite line. A video is worth more than a thousand words. You don't need to shoot every run, every turn. A little bit goes a long way. There's nothing more humbling than seeing yourself on video, but it's the simplest way to learn. If you want to improve, get the camera out and analyze. Your mistakes will stand out. Next time you ride, think about your body, the position of your head, chest, hips, and feet. How do you want to look? Envision the form you want, then try again.

powder, ice, windpack, groomers, breakable crust, corn—the better you're going to get. The hard part is motivating for these conditions, but that's what makes the difference. The more "technical" the conditions, the more excited I am. When you can rail bulletproof ice, a firm day becomes a powder day.

There are no shortcuts to strong riding. Like every sport or skill in the world, you need your reps. The more, the better. I think of the resort much like I imagine pro rock climbers think of climbing gyms. It's not my favorite type of climbing, but it can be really fun (empty resort powder days are amazing!), and it's a great way to get in good shape, stay fit, and develop technique. Skills days play an important role in gaining strength, refining technique, and pushing limits. I ride specific areas to strengthen specific skills, working on these almost daily throughout the season. The resort can be punishing though. These days I focus on 60 percent splitboarding/touring and 40 percent resort riding. My resort days are shorter but high intensity. On my standard resort day (80 percent are hardpack), I wake up my body with a few easy groomers. Often this is a top-to-bottom, long, rolling intermediate run, where I slowly increase the amount of force during turns, listening to my body to see how I feel. Once warmed up, I focus on the steeps and smoothing out the chop.

> The senses become heightened, the everyday stresses of life fade with each passing turn, and nothing else matters. We have tapped into a special world.
>
> With dedication, the right mindset, and some creativity, you can ride dream lines your whole life.

The Chairs

Chairlifts have had a huge impact on my riding and life. The more I tour, the more I appreciate riding a chairlift. I now have less of an appetite for the hyped-out sunny

Saturday powder than I used to, but I enjoy the midweek hardpack sessions more than ever. After long backcountry trips carrying heavy packs, I appreciate the lift as much as I did when I was first allowed to ride it. No backpack, no avy danger, no stress. A special thanks to Jake Burton and the others who helped open the lifts to snowboarders in the 1990s. Also to the lifties and lift maintenance operators. You've helped bring so much joy to so many people. As one of my mentors, Alaskan steep-skiing pioneer Jerry Hance, said to me recently: "It never gets old. Every season I feel so lucky when that lift starts up again and I get to hop on it and let it take me to the top." Below I list some of my favorite lifts. I've purposely omitted small resorts out of respect for the locals, but I recommend seeking the obscure.

» **Stowe Quad, Stowe, Vermont.** The lift that set the hook and altered my life's course. The day Stowe first allowed snowboards, I'd been skiing for eight years. I knew the mountain well, but in an instant the trails I'd been skiing turned three-dimensional, as if I'd been sucked into a video game. From that moment, if the lift was spinning, I was riding. Accessing almost 90 percent of the mountain, 2,400 vert, and ten-minute laps, the Stowe Quad has, unsurprisingly, produced many strong skiers and riders.

» **Spillway Chair, Sugarloaf, Maine.** Certainly one of the coldest rides in the world and my vote for best groomer access, Sugarloaf resort boasts 2,800 vert, much of it steep and consistent. Riding this lift daily with a bunch of world-class athletes and future Olympians, it was all about going really fast, sending big roller airs, and arcing perfect turns. (I later realized it was, surprisingly, the optimal training ground for firing Alaska lines.) Strapping into a 183 cm race board, hard boots, and 52-degree angles, my CVA classmates Adam Hostetter and Mark Faw-cett and I were dragging armpits and pulling so many g's that it felt like our goggles were going to roll over our noses and end up on our necks. I learned the fundamentals training every single day at this place.

» **Jackson Tram, Tetons, Jackson Hole, Wyoming.** One ride up this tram at sixteen and my goals of becoming a world champion lost some gusto. Sign me up for dishwashing and dirtbagging. Whatever it took to ride the tram every day. In 1998, I moved to Jackson full-time, the same year the backcountry gates opened. Over a four-year period, I rode the tram all day, every day, and progressed both my technical freeriding and avy skills. There's no other lift in America that can put you into such epic resort, sidecountry, and backcountry terrain.

Dear Chairlift

So many lives changed and thoughts rearranged
Friends found and marriages bound
As the lift soars, the wind roars
Never the same, never a bore
As steady as the sun and moon
Over and over, around and around,
helping people's worries be lost and souls to be found

» **Whistler Peak Chair, Coast Mountains, British Columbia.** In 1992, my brothers, Todd and Steve, along with some Jackson friends, and I made the long drive to Whistler. In proper dirtbag style, we slept in the parking garage of the yet-to-be finished Chateau Whistler and hiked the lower mountain to the upper lifts to avoid the base mountain ticket checkers. The Blackcomb/Whistler combo is worth the hype, and I often wonder how I didn't end up moving there. The Whistler Peak Chair is the crown of the resort. The variety of terrain off that lift is enough to keep you busy for a lifetime. Technical alpine lines, endless tree runs to the valley floor, and the perfect start for leaving resort boundaries and touring into the high-alpine peaks.

» **Marte Chair, Las Leñas, Argentina.** My brother Steve first told me about this chair in a letter he wrote while spending the summer in Argentina. "You wouldn't believe this lift," he wrote. "It goes straight up this crazy, scary face, with the longest, steepest, most technical chutes I've ever seen. The side country is off the charts too. Short hikes get you to big faces, more chutes, more everything." A few years later, while filming for my first ever snowboard movie, rider

Free the Hills

My friend sends a video of a lone skier on a single chair ascending slowly up the mountain as snow falls lightly from the sky. As the skier passes the midstation, the Grateful Dead on the radio grows louder. The lifty and the skier trade a smile and a wave. So peaceful. A winter wonderland I want to be transported to. I need to ride that chair. Experience that serenity. Just watching the video calms me, warms my heart. "Where is that?" I ask. "Mad River Glen."

It hits me that as a snowboarder I cannot ride that chairlift. The realization makes me sad. Something about the peacefulness of the video, coupled with the empty chair. That skier and the lift-op—we are one and the same except I stand sideways on one board and they stand forward on two. Or maybe the lift-op is a mono boarder, in which case the only difference is the sideways part. Focusing on the three remaining lifts in the United States that are off-limits to snowboarders is something I do not put energy into, but it is time to open the doors at Alta, Deer Valley, and Mad River Glen. To say: This mountain is for everyone to enjoy. A place that brings together people of all colors, nationalities, and backgrounds. A place where everyone is welcome. A place of unity, where strangers become friends bound by their love of sliding on snow down a mountain. The world has enough divisiveness in it already. Free the hills—not because you *have* to but because you *want* to. Because a place of inclusion is better than a place of exclusion.

Steve Klassen and I spent a few weeks there. My brother was right. He, however, left out the frequent avalanches that are known to take out the lift and the most extreme winds I've ever experienced.

» **KT-22, Olympic Valley, Lake Tahoe, California.** When I first entered the KT lift line corral in 1992, I felt like I'd entered the snow version of the cantina in *Star Wars*, crazy creatures eyeing me down, shouldering for position and quick to point out your place. At the time, I'd hardly traveled beyond New England, and the awesome mix of purple hair, dirtbags, legendary locals, tattoos, and Tahoe slang was too much for me to handle. Looking around, I counted famous pro after famous pro. Dirty GORE-TEX was more my vibe than baggy pants and neon jackets. At just under 2,000 vert, it had me wondering, *What's all the hype about? Doesn't look that special . . . pretty short.* Fast-forward thirty years and KT has become both my favorite chairlift in the world and the one I've ridden

> "Like other Alpinists of my generation, I turned to lower mountains, where the possibilities for solitude, wildness and discovery were easier to find." —Steve Swenson

KT-22

OLYMPIC VALLEY, LAKE TAHOE, CALIFORNIA

So many memories in one view. My first time in line, age eighteen, seeing all my heroes from the snowboard movies; or at twenty, when Mike Hatchett, the owner of Standard Films, asked if I wanted to film with him on the chair. But some of the worst ones too. Mental and physical soul-tearing wounds that turn into scar tissue that never really heals.

Of all the crazy places I have been, this single view right here has taken more friends than any in the world. Right in front of me is the spot I lost one of my closest friends, MC. The words "MC hit a tree, he is dead, I am so sorry," which my wife sent via a text message on a satellite phone twenty years ago, are still so vivid. I still feel regret for not coming back for the funeral because I was in a remote cabin on the Alaskan border, filming. Farther up the mountain I see the chute where C.R. Johnson hit a rock, bled out, and died on the spot. To my left, the tree that took Erik Roner's life. The building where we memorialized them—and too many others—is behind me.

The good memories are less vivid. So many cliffs stomped and lines ridden in perfect conditions with friends hooting by my side. So many love-of-sport hours spent riding technical steeps in variable conditions and powering through bumpy outruns to build my legs and confidence, so I'd be ready when the stars aligned on the distant trophy lines.

My one and only descent of the iconic spine wall that towers above the valley, McConkeys, takes up space in my memory. Shane McConkey's death was still so fresh when I walked into the lift line early on a powder day. Ski patrol surprised me when they said I had "early ups," because it was the first and only time I had been allowed up early. "The line looks good," said the patroller on the lift. I had missed the memo, but they were letting me up early to ride the line that had been renamed in Shane's honor.

Using the post of the eagle monument that held Shane's ashes, I shimmied onto the face, made a few super-technical turns in a controlled free fall, hit the exit air surrounded by sluff, and stomped the landing.

An emotional avalanche overcame me as I rode out the bottom, so I pulled over into a group of trees and wept.

Surprisingly there are few other memories from almost thirty years and thousands of hours spent on this lift. I think the sparseness of my memories is because I am always so present and forward-thinking on the mountain. No reason to think about yesterday when there is so much to figure out today. "Where's the best snow, what lines are in? Is it a sun-softened east, chalky north kind of day? Are the techy steeps in or is it low-angle gullies, groomers, and cat tracks?" I try to check every box.

The mountain forces us to be present, and I wonder if that is the hook that keeps me coming back day after day, year after year. However, without thought the past does guide. A gentle whisper in my ear run after run helps me charge blind rolls, dance through cruxes, and hit the sweet spot of an air.

So much time, joy, and pain from this single lift. Seasons and days pile together but no two are the same. The steady teacher whose lessons are subtle but collectively significant. Mostly it is the friendships formed here that stick with me. Now it is sharing the mountain with my kids.

Combine the teachings tied to this lift—the joy and the pain, the friendships made, the conversations had, the informal chain of mentorship that naturally gets passed from generation to generation—and you come to understand how powerful a single chairlift is to a community.

the most. The high density of cliffs, ramps, chutes, spines, pillows, and trees gives it the most featured terrain of any single chair that I've ever ascended. Linking up multiple airs of all varieties with serious steeps and clean runouts in a ten-minute lap makes KT the ultimate training ground for freeriding. No surprise, then, that it's produced more Freeride World Tour winners than any other lift in the world.

» **Chair Five, Mount Baker, Washington.** Believe the hype—don't follow the locals! I'll leave it at that.

» **Aiguille du Midi, Chamonix, France.** Most extreme lift in the world. Only the French would have the audacity to put a tram up the north face of the Midi. It would be like putting a tram up the Grand Teton, but you'd have to cover the Grand in glacier ice and make it much steeper and have a sidewalk leading from your apartment to the

"It never gets old. Every season I feel so lucky when that lift starts up again and I get to hop on it and let it take me to the top."
—Jerry Hance

entrance station. Some of the most extreme lines ever ridden in the world sit right under the lift. The Mallory, for example, is 3,000 feet of fall-you-die turns with multiple rappels. The run sees so many tracks these days that moguls form. Descending from the Aiguille du Midi is one of the greatest riding experiences out there—go . . . with a guide!

» **Mont Fort, Verbier, Pennine Alps, Switzerland.** From the top of this tram, the steep rideable terrain is so vast that, depending on which valley you end up in, you might be multiple hours by car from the town you started in. Certainly a lifetime of terrain from a single tram.

» **La Grave la Meije, French Alps, France.** One lift to rule them all. Out of a fairy tale, or a horror movie, depending on its mood and your appetite for steeps and tricky lines. One lift, 7,000 vert, not a single groomed run or sign.

» **Snowbird Tram, Utah.** The fall line is so direct you can drop a basketball off the top of this tram and it'll end up in the parking lot 3,200 feet below. The snow is so dry, and the terrain so rocky, it's essential to follow a local, but good luck keeping up given the number of incredible lines. This is another mecca for producing some of the best in the world, and one of the most fun days you'll ever have when the conditions are firing.

» **Hellbrunner, Mont Blanc, Italy.** This lift reaches up the Italian side of the Mont Blanc Massif and appears to be the more approachable, less extreme, and more freeride version of the Aiguille du Midi's French side. But do not let the huge, rippable flanks catch you off-guard. The terrain accessible from the Hellbrunner has killed too many legends to list, on slopes that they would call "*tranquille.*" If you do ride, get in and get out before the heat turns it into a roaring dragon. It's also a great launch point to the most serious lines on Mont Blanc.

» **Austria—the entire country.** My Swiss friends may disagree, but the Austrian chairlift engineering prowess remains unrivaled. The country is practically linked together by chairs and trams and other ascension devices that must be seen to be believed. Ride from town to town, groomers, touring, powder, with great food along the way.

» **Japan—the entire country.** The land of bottomless powder under the lift. Bring the floatiest craft you can find.

Travel offers important perspective. You realize that the world is a diverse place with diverse views. These days I travel much less, but I stay longer so I'm able to really immerse myself in the community and the environment.

CHAPTER 3

Mistakes, Goals, Mentors, and Partners

Formal goal-setting is something I've shied away from. Maybe it's my fragile ego's fear of putting something out into the universe and failing. Or maybe it's because putting all of my chips into one pot seems cavalier and potentially dangerous. Don't get me wrong, there are so many lines out there I really want to ride. But I don't need to write them down on paper or stake a flag atop a goal. If some wild, once-in-a-decade line comes into form, I'm going to drop everything and do my best to climb and ride it. In those moments, nothing else in the world matters but the step in front of me that leads toward my objective. Link enough steps and you're eventually standing on top of your goal or objective.

However, there are trips like my Nepal expedition in 2013, when I had a single focus to ride the spine wall I would later name Shangri-La. Denali and Mount Timlin were also very much single objectives. In those scenarios, although I'm at peace with maybe not reaching the end vision, I was (and am) incredibly driven to succeed. By embracing the process, doing absolutely everything in my power to succeed, I'm totally at peace if I have to walk away from a goal I've worked so hard to achieve. The journey is the reward.

My approach to business is much the same. Over the years I've developed a life manifesto, a short list of what I believe. Focus on what's in my control, surround myself with the best people, don't cut corners, do more work than the rest. (This is true in snowboarding too—if you do it more than anyone else in the world, you are guaranteed to be in the upper 95 percent. However, getting to the upper *99 percent* takes 50 percent more work!) Also, let the customers decide if we're doing a good job or not. They determine how big or small a company or a movement gets, not a goal written in a PowerPoint presentation. Inspiration for goals remains very personal.

The bigger the goal, the more time I chew on it. Being in the right headspace to let thoughts freely come and go is important. It's when I'm on my bike, walking up a mountain for hours on end, waiting for a wave, or sleeping under stars that my mind quiets and the important things rise to the top. It's those thoughts that rise above over and over again, those which I cannot talk myself out of, that determine where I choose to set my personal compass. In doing so, these goals become integrated into all facets of my life.

The Journey Is the Reward

I came to embrace this sentiment when I went all in on foot-powered snowboarding in 2007. It is not when things are going right that this motto is most important, but when things are seemingly desperate or I've worked really hard on an objective but come up short. Embracing the journey, focusing on things in my control, accepting what I have no control over, acknowledging missteps, doing the best with the hand I am dealt, and focusing on the process not the end result—this is the essential mindset with serious Shralpinism.

Some lessons are in your face. Rocks hurt, stay away from cornices, respect avalanche conditions. And some take years and are more subtle. They are life lessons that come only with time in a range. Learning how to leave your ego at the trailhead, that humility is the best tool, and that being present in the moment is essential.

Mistakes and setbacks are the simplest and most humbling way to learn. Never in my life have I learned as much as when filming my first foot-powered movie, *Deeper*. It became essential to accept as part of the journey such situations as waking up in the middle of the night, climbing for hours on end, getting to the top of our line at sunrise just as unforeseen weather moved in and we were clouded out. Otherwise, we'd have all quit. Certain lines would take up to five attempts. On some lines, like Blanche de Peuterey in the Mont Blanc Massif, I had to accept defeat after multiple attempts over a three-week period. Instead of viewing turning around as a mistake or failed attempt, though, I changed my thinking: *We added another chapter to this line, and it will be that much sweeter if it works out in the future.* Accepting so-called failure as a teachable moment that may help you later in life is at the essence of "the journey is the reward."

Mistakes made: rushing for light, taking stability for granted, not respecting the wind.

I think about the bad back that first laid me up the summer before the 1998 Olympics and forced me to focus full-time on healing. The same injury reared its

The Art of Dealing with Down Days

Down days have never been tough for me. My life off the mountains presents pure chaos. Emails, phone calls, school schedules, shopping, bills, etc. When we're not unplugged, we deal with a lot. It's a luxurious experience when I'm "forced" to stay inside my tent, high in the alpine wilderness, with no connection to the outside world for days on end, even if I don't get to ride. My days are filled with all the things I rarely have time for at home—reading, writing, art, and games of any type.

The more complicated the real world gets, the more we need to have a way to disconnect, unplug, and experience the fun of life.

I'm competitive by nature, always enjoy a contest, but I'd never really thought much about games in the backcountry beyond my portable chess set. Photographer Jeff Hawe made an interesting observation about the importance of games, aside from passing the time, while on an extended trip into the Wrangell and Saint Elias Ranges. As the down days wore on and the storm stretched into the sixth or seventh day, two long-haul board games always appeared out of nowhere: Risk and Monopoly. Maybe it was a way to keep the strategy and risk management thought process active and sharp during the extended days waiting for weather to lift. "Planning and riding lines out there is a game of strategy with a much higher wager than a few Monopoly hundred notes," Jeff said, "but it makes you think how aggressively you should go after the high-rent districts or continent prizes."

On down days it's crucial, for sanity and to prevent fatigue, to get outside the tent or cabin. Getting my body moving, even if this means doing circles around camp, is a great way to flush lactic acid and break up tent life. There's usually something to skin up and ride down, a low-angle mini lap near camp to make a few turns. Even those few turns reset the day and make me feel so much better.

Looking for Opportunity

MOUNT BERTHA, GLACIER BAY NATIONAL PARK, 2021

Embracing the journey is embracing reality and doing with it the most you can. This is essential when dealing with the weather and the snowpack. The spring of 2021, Mother Nature dealt some of the most unique extreme weather circumstances I've ever encountered. The plan was to get dropped off by boat deep in Alaska's Glacier Bay National Park. An ocean blizzard pinned us in the bay, extending our twenty-five-hour boat ride into a six-day crawl. Sneaking into the mountains between storms required an eighteen-hour wobbly death march that put us into camp just before a seven-day wet snow/rainstorm that at times had us digging out every three hours to keep our tents from collapsing.

When the storm finally broke, the sun came out and temps spiked 40 degrees above average. The closest town, Haines, reached 75 degrees. We were poised on a high glacier with north-facing terrain, the perfect setup for mid-April spine riding. This was the first sun we'd seen in two weeks, but instead of hiking and riding, we sat in camp staring at the surrounding slopes. The first day three hundred avalanches ran within view. The second day, two hundred. Our spine paradise, which ranged in elevation from 6,000 to 7,500 feet, was ruined in forty-eight hours.

Rather than wasting time on our desperate situation, my mind shifted to "What opportunity does the situation present?" This takes practice, starting with very small, positive-focused moments back home. "What's good right now?" That opportunity came in the form of a peak one ridge back, the 10,300-foot Mount Bertha. Specifically, the 3,200-foot northeast face that is usually covered in ice and unrideable, except maybe in summer. "What if this warm weather softened the ice? What if the rain that hit camp was snow up that high?"

I shifted my view as soon as it was apparent the entire area we'd been focusing on for months was off the table. There's usually a great outcome if you train your mind to look for one. A few days later, when the mountains had settled, my partners, Griffin Post, Elena Hight, Ed Shanley, and Leslie Hittmeier, and I found the answer: a screaming yes! Perfect conditions up high. Quite possibly the best line of my life, thanks to a heat wave.

head again eight years later and got so bad when I was in my late twenties, I thought I might have to stop snowboarding. My journals from this time certainly do not talk about the journey being the reward—they are bleak, full of self-pity. *I have set up my life around snowboarding. I have the whole world in my hands, but I cannot fix this injury, and doctors are telling me the only way to do so is to stop.* Almost twenty years later, I can say with confidence that my bad back was the best thing that happened to my body. It made me move away from flat landings, saving my knees in the process, and taught me to take my health seriously.

> Time in the mountains is a privilege and a gift. It grounds me and gives me answers to life's toughest questions. It's a place to examine and fine-tune my life's compass.

Sharing Our Mistakes

Somewhere I heard that 95 percent of life is mistakes. They're a huge part of every sport. They're going to happen, no matter what. Thinking otherwise creates all sorts of problems, so it's much better to anticipate them. How you deal with mistakes is actually the most important part of how you live your life. This is a big part of traveling in the mountains, figuring out how to ride better, and learning how to lead a long life exploring.

I used to hide my mistakes, because I didn't want to deal with the critics. There shouldn't be shame in making mistakes, even big ones. You don't *want* to make them, but they will happen. And hopefully, no one will get killed. A bad day in the mountains is way worse than a bad day on a basketball court or in the classroom or boardroom. Great people and teams, championship teams, really embrace a positive culture. I'm a huge Tom Brady fan. Watch him on the field with his team, and after every play, good or bad, big mistake or touchdown, he's always fist-bumping with everyone. Drop a pass, miss a shot, your teammates still

> I am a product of my experiences.

high-five you. *Make a mistake, it's okay, keep going, stay positive.* A positive mindset is the key to progressing, which is an enormous part of riding and learning, and ultimately your art. As a community, backcountry riders need to share our mistakes. Especially if it involves an avalanche. Letting the community know you started an avalanche or have seen one could save someone else's life. The community needs to praise people for sharing this important info and not judge them.

Building Your Team: Partners and Mentors

Everyone's idea of a perfect partner varies, but trust and understanding are vital. You want to be able to talk openly about conditions and what worries you, and agree that it is always okay to turn around—you should not worry about changing plans, and your partners should support it wholeheartedly. If not, find new partners. The single biggest trait I avoid in partners is ego. When dealing with large groups, I like to empower every person regardless of experience level. I want everyone expressing their concerns. The other big trait I look for in partners is love of sport. I want to be around energized people who never complain

> Studies have shown that, in the mountains, a group of men and women is much safer than an all-male group.

Ego Is Not Your Amigo

Ego is one of the most dangerous traits I see in climbers, skiers, snowboarders, mountaineers, and other activities where risk looms. If I see people flexing in the mountains, I avoid them. It's not just overinflated egos I fear. My own biggest mistakes have come from overconfidence and letting my ego get in the way of protocols and warning signs. On the flip side, some of my best riding has come after a close call or a bad crash, because I became hyperfocused on the process.

Skill is a big part of success, obviously, but so is the right mindset and attitude—and keeping egos in check, whether your own or someone else's, is key. For me, the whole experience is what snowboarding is all about: long skin tracks, problem solving, and camping out in the middle of nowhere. I want to ride with people who have the most stoke. Who has a love for riding deep down in their soul? Those not just there to "get the shot" and a paycheck. The ones who can find humor and positivity when things seem dire. Those just happy to explore the mountains regardless of conditions and who recognize how fortunate it is to be healthy, to simply have the great luxury of frolicking in the wild places.

Zahan Billimoria: Finding the Mountains

Zahan is a mountain guide, skier, and climber based in Jackson Hole, Wyoming. He has made ski descents in some of the biggest mountain ranges in the world and has set speed records skiing in the Tetons.

"Honestly, I was no good in school! I always needed a purpose to excel at something. In school it was about conformity, so I couldn't get motivated. But when I found the mountains, I switched on. I went all in as soon as I could. I learned to ice climb up dead trees in the forest near my house and learned to rappel off local highway bridges—all of it was by instinct, with very little education. I used to read the back of the Petzl catalog where it explained how to use the equipment; that's where I learned my first steps. But I just loved being up there—it was all I could think about—so I just kept at it. As dangerous as it was, and as much as I wouldn't recommend kids start that way, I do have great memories of the emotions that accompanied being in the mountains. I loved it.

"My parents didn't come from a mountain culture—mountains equaled risk—so they discouraged it at first. But eventually they realized it wasn't a passing phase, so they hired a guide for me to go out with. His name was Christophe Profit, a legendary French mountain guide, and after my day with him, it was on. I knew what I wanted to do with my life. As I started learning the craft, my parents became supportive, though they always struggled with the 'unnecessary risks.' Even though he was a legend, and I was a clueless kid, he was cool to me. I saw what it could look like to make a life in the mountains, to be a professional. He showed the way for me."

about conditions—the more desperate things get, the better their sense of humor becomes. Nothing bothers me more than riders who complain about conditions. Being in the mountains, regardless, is a gift. Who's the best rider on the mountain? The one having the most fun. Third on the list of traits for good partners is skill set. The more serious the mission, the more I like to stack the deck with the most skilled riders I can find.

A good riding partner also shares the same level of acceptable risk. Having different comfort levels is what leads to the most tension among partners. Respect people's risk tolerances and find the partner who best mirrors yours. However, there are times when different risk levels can be helpful. For example, I like having people around who are a little timid and who ask hard questions about the day's

The person who aces the avy test may not be the smartest person. Survival is a mix of good science and quieting the noise of social distraction, pressures, and expectations. It is knowing yourself and recognizing your mental and physical shortcomings. The same attention must be used for evaluating your partners. Are they going for gold, or afraid of everything?

My first mentors were my brothers, who received their formative studies from the Jackson Hole Air Force. Follow the trail of their mentors, and you quickly get to Bill Briggs, the first to ski the Grand Teton. Briggs's descent was ceiling shattering in the ski mountaineering universe. How he got the gusto to climb up there by himself and do what was thought of as impossible, ignoring the cries of "you will die," I don't know. With unwavering self-confidence, a thirst for the sharp end, and so much time in the Tetons, Briggs saw possibilities others couldn't dream of. It was such a moon shot that people didn't believe he'd actually done it. It wasn't until people saw photos of Briggs's track that they believed him. Add in the fact that his hip was fused and he walked with a limp, and Briggs personifies the power of the mind to overcome fear and pain.

plan. This helps keep me in check because I am often chewing my arm off to hit big lines. The reverse can be the case too: maybe you are conservative and need a nudge to get over your fears.

As for mentors, the key is to not overreach. Find a person you admire who is a few steps higher on the rung of knowledge and then draft. You can move up the ladder, passing people along the way and finding people higher up to learn from, but if you start reaching for the top too soon, it can be overwhelming and you're bound to fall. In the mountains you do not start out in the advanced pro-level course; it's the same for health and fitness. At twenty-three, I wasn't ready to become a vegan who meditates and does two hours of yoga and other workouts a day—that would've been too much.

Recruiting

Finding people who want to go to exotic locations and film movies isn't difficult. Talent is the easy part. There are a lot of incredibly skilled, accomplished riders who can send on demand and have a stomp ratio of 90 percent or higher. What's really hard is finding someone with these abilities who is a team player, doesn't have an ego, doesn't take stupid risks, and can stay positive through ten-day storms, death crust cycles, or travel beatdown.

When I started focusing on longer hiking and camping missions, finding mentally stable and upbeat partners became critical. I learned that some people shine on shorter trips, while others struggle at the start and rise late into a trip when the chips are down. Keeping morale high through the doldrums of weeklong storms or multiple days of moving heavy packs is challenging. Add in those times when the conditions take a turn for the worse, which happens all the time, even with great planning. This happened in Svalbard, Norway, when it rained at the top of the peaks on our first day and then froze. Tough, changing conditions can take a toll on the crew. One depressed soul can bring everyone down, and the team is only as strong as your weakest link. It is easy to gang up on someone who is angry and bitter; it's essential to have people who can build them back up. Finding the energy to inspire and to distract with games, books, and discussions goes a long way.

I'm very picky when it comes to riding partners, and it's definitely not all based on ability. When putting together a crew, I make sure I have skilled people on the mountain, including those with medical knowledge. I also like bringing a rookie along. It's infectious for the entire crew when someone gets amped about experiencing new things like seeing a real glacier or putting on crampons for the first time. The one constant I look for is attitude. If I sense someone taking risks when it's not a time to take risks, they're off the list. Ride with people you like to explore with, who raise your energy level, who make everything more fun. But make sure they have a cool head and, foremost, focus on safety. Riding with people better than you can be exhausting

"The reasonable man adapts to the world; the unreasonable one persists in trying to adapt the world to himself. Therefore, all progress depends on the unreasonable man."
—*George Bernard Shaw*

Andrew McLean: Miles and Smiles

Powder Magazine named him one of the greatest skiers of our time for good reason. He is a master-class Shralpinist who has skied some of the most remote, serious lines in the world. However his thirty-plus years of pioneering steep lines in the Wasatch's complicated snowpack might be his most impressive accomplishment.

"During the past few low-snow seasons, I've been refining my powder-hunting skills to get first tracks in soft snow regardless of the prevailing conditions. I still have a ways to go on that one. Over the years my inspiration and mentors have shifted from the early extreme skiing French icons to people like Ruedi Homberger or Otto from Tahoe—guys that have made skiing a lifelong activity, ski every day, hang around a woodstove with friends at night, and do it again the next day. That's a lot of miles and smiles.

"Lately I've come to really appreciate and learn a lot from touring with people who have decades of experience. They tend to be superefficient, ski with excellent unspoken backcountry travel protocol, have insightful snow observations, and provide an endless trove of crazy skin track stories. It's fun to be sitting on a summit with a group like this and realize how many millions of feet of climbing and years of touring are represented."

and humiliating, but without a doubt it makes you better. This is why I've always tried to surround myself with the best riders in the world.

Find the Masters

For my first ten years as a pro, I was pretty much always the youngest person in the crew. Watching, listening, and asking questions of those way more experienced was very valuable. At first this was hard for me, because I was young and shy, but most experts appreciate younger riders who take an interest, and they love sharing their knowledge. A common question I'm asked is "Who influenced your snowboarding the most?" Some people have taught me more than others, but my riding and style

"Ride to live another day." —Gerry Lopez

come from everyone I've ever spent time with. It started at a young age. My brothers and I always looked for and tried to emulate the best riders on the mountain. It's a great way to learn. Watch them from the chair and ride near or eventually along with them. Learn how they start and move through turns. Learn how they adapt and recover. Watch which lines they take, which airs they hit. There is a lot of learning just through osmosis. So much of what we do in the mountains is subtle but collectively makes a difference.

You will find a few "masters" at every mountain. These are the riders who are out there almost every day. They've spent a lot of time riding both the popular and the obscure lines, every nook and cranny, in all types of conditions, so that, whatever the day, they know the best spots and where to have the most fun. You'll see them on a day most would call bad—too firm, too cold, too rainy, too something. With smiles on their faces these masters share their info: "Right-side trees on the Tumble is going off," or "The Terje hip is perfect right now." They have developed a wealth of knowledge over many years, and if you take the time to approach them, they can help your riding immensely, in the resort and the backcountry. The more time I spend in serious mountains, the more I value the older generation.

The classroom is essential but more so are mentors. I have lived a gifted life as a snowboarder and have been in the mountains with some of the best. I was smart enough to see this opportunity and I took full advantage of it, and that continues today. I am a product of the people I have been surrounded by because I watched, listened, and asked questions.

Sure, you can learn about avalanche safety in classrooms, but when it comes to overall mountain knowledge and how we move up and down the mountains, these lessons are passed along from generation to generation on skin tracks, in lift lines, and while standing by the bonfire. Each generation moves the wand as far as they can before handing the baton to the latest crop of fresh chargers, collectively evolving as a community, generation by generation. Tragically, in this pursuit of progression, each generation experiences loss. It is the sobering price of a sport that is always seeking to go bigger, faster, and higher.

There are no experts in the mountains, but there's no better scorecard than time. The longer someone has been doing this, the more respect I have for them. I watch them closely, ask questions, and listen. A track record matters in the mountains. But, even then, the mountains don't care. Those who are still climbing and riding at seventy usually know what they're doing. If I compare what I've learned from my dozens (and counting) of avy, medical, and mountaineering courses with what I've learned directly from mentors and riding partners, it's not even close.

"It's one big feel-out." —Drake Olson

CHAPTER 4

Risk

Humans can be quite vocal when someone dies doing something different than the norm. Online forums erupt with scathing comments about the selfishness of taking unnecessary risks and causing so much pain for loved ones. These comments hurt because there's some truth to them. Watching and weighing risk is a privilege, to be sure. Fear, humility, and loss are part of any backcountry rider's journey. But there are ways to stack the deck in your favor while pushing the limits.

Raising kids has certainly added weight to my decision-making in the mountains and brought volume to the question: Is what I do irresponsible? If I think about the close calls I've had in the mountains—all avalanches—they all occurred in moderate terrain. Terrain that I hope I'll be riding well into my seventies. A close call on Shangri-La and a fall in northern British Columbia that scarred my face could have carried worse consequences, but they weren't nearly as life threatening as the avalanches I've experienced in moderate terrain. It would be so much simpler if I could just throttle back on the intense lines and take the risk out of everything.

> The impact of my accomplishments is unknown, but it does not matter. I am satisfied and happy.

My appetite for the sharp end has decreased in many ways over the years, but to say I'll eliminate all risk from my snowboarding will probably never be true. In 2013 my daughter, Mia, was eight and my son, Cass, five. I had the opportunity to climb Denali with an amazing group of people ranging in age from thirteen to sixty-three. Conrad Anker and his son Max Lowe organized the trip. Conrad was

The Edge of Life and Death

Riding the edge of life and death takes its toll, and many people have faded away from the mountains. Injuries and substance abuse are far too common among riders. Is it a repercussion of being a global superstar or beating your body up so much that it is in constant pain? But it goes beyond superstars. Suicide rates are on the rise in mountain towns, especially among older riders who get priced out of their community, and it's not just the middle-aged. Especially with the onset of the pandemic, younger riders are also feeling pressures, both on and off the mountain. I don't have answers, but it's a real issue that we need to be aware of. (National Suicide Prevention Lifeline: 800-273-8255)

with Max's biological father, Alex, when he died in a massive avalanche in 1999 while approaching Shishapangma, in south-central Tibet. I was in the middle of shooting *Higher*, and a month earlier I had climbed and ridden one of the biggest faces of my life, Mount Timlin.

Leaving my two little children and wife at home was becoming harder and harder. A video of my son crying and pleading with me, saying, "Why do you have to go, don't go," on the way to the airport to come to Denali made it into *Higher*. As excited as I was to spend time with Conrad, Jon Krakauer, and others, and to learn from them, it was Max I really wanted to get to know. Or, more specifically, to ask him what he thought about his father taking risks in the mountains. Max is one of the most likable, fun, and kind humans I've ever met, so becoming friends with him was easy. He is light-hearted and deep thinking and conscientious. However, bringing up the subject of his dad's death was not easy. Eight days into our climb, we were on poop patrol. (On Denali dealing with poop is taken very seriously. At 14-Camp the protocol puts someone on belay at the edge of a designated crevasse to dump the poop down the sewer.) After doing the dirty work and cleaning and washing our hands, I asked Max about losing Alex.

"I have to ask, as a dad taking risks in the mountains, and you being a kid who has lost their father in the mountains, how do you feel about risk?" Max's response: "It is really sad and I miss him, but it was his life. There was no way we could tell him to stop, it would have killed him." I've heard this thought many times, and it resonates with me deeply. We must be who we're supposed to be. What makes your life most full at any given moment may be selfish. It may hurt others, and there are

> "What surprises me most is 'Man,' because he sacrifices his health in order to make money. Then he sacrifices money to recuperate his health. And then he is so anxious about the future that he doesn't enjoy the present; the result being he doesn't live in the present or the future; he lives as if he's never going to die, and then he dies having never really lived."
> —His Holiness the 14th Dalai Lama

trade-offs and agonies that a lot of people must live with. It's often difficult to find even something close to an answer, but it's vital to think about.

A Privilege

Is the goal to live in a protected room, making it to one hundred without ever really taking any risks? Or to push it as far as you can, no matter what? Or to come stumbling across the finish line battered and bruised, but still going, with stories and experiences that pushed you to the limits, with people and places you love more than anything? It is perhaps the greatest sort of privilege to decide to add risk to your life because it makes you feel alive. Because you can. An insane luxury. We all take up precious resources on this planet; the very least we can do is reach for the stars and appreciate the opportunities we've been given. Your life is your own, often with a great deal of responsibility and demands, but living for some cushy future or not pursuing your dreams creates loads of problems as well.

Is this the key to a happy, long life? Creating strong, loving bonds with people close to you? Getting joy out of simpler things? Life is precious, life is fragile. We all die, but do we all live?

Weighing Risk

I've lost too many friends and cried too many tears—why do I put myself in this position? The list of friends lost to the mountains is dozens of names long. Contrast this to my childhood friends living on Cape Cod who have never been to a funeral for someone under forty and you have to ask the question: Why do we do it?

> The mountains require full attention. Being in the present, living in the now, is key. Outside pressures need to stay in the parking lot.

Part of the reason I've lost so many friends may be because I know so many people from my thirty years of largely living out of a suitcase and traveling the world. The list of friends dying of cancer is sadly on the rise, including most recently Tate MacDowell, who was just thirty-eight when he died. Seeing a friend fight so hard to live and then have their life taken from them is the saddest thing I've ever witnessed. Watching Tate struggle while I was out exploring mountains made my life seem reckless and stupid. The last time I was with him, he was very frail, and it was clear his days were numbered. I pushed his kid into waves while he watched from the beach. He labored up three flights of stairs, going as slow as one could go but achieving his small goal of not stopping.

> *"Fear is like a fire. If you can control it, it can cook for you. It can heat your house. If you can't control it, it will burn everything around you and destroy you. Fear is your friend and your worst enemy."* —Sui Ishida

Witnessing our last sunset together—which produced the most spectacular green flash either of us had ever seen—I mustered up the courage to ask Tate the one thing I really wanted to know: "How do you feel watching people take risks?" He never really answered my question, because it was so obvious to him: eight months earlier he had mustered up the strength in between chemo sessions to make good on climbing the Grand Teton, a goal he'd set when first entering chemo two years earlier. As he walked to his first treatment, he saw a photo of the iconic peak hanging in the hall. "I should probably climb that thing when this is all over," he said to me when he was still relatively healthy and his cancer diagnosis didn't look that serious.

During Tate's treatment my brother Todd connected him with a friend, Brian, going through the same situation in Victor, Idaho. The two men fast became chemo comrades and learned they had the exact same photo hanging on their respective treatment walls. A year later, both men set out to climb the peak; stomach issues forced Tate to turn around, while Brian summited. Todd made a film called *Mountain in the Hallway* about their experiences.

Simple vs. Mellow

The simple is hard. The mellow is intense. My eyes see bigger, more technical lines. They make sense. But the warm-up line gets my blood pumping. I need time. I need to warm up. I am back. I feel it in my soul. It's like the first conversation with a close friend I haven't seen in a while. Is there still chemistry? Do I still have the stomach for this? I don't need to figure it out right now. But it is exciting to be back. The first dance is a success. The terrain progression journey has started.

Jimmy Chin: My Greatest Risk

Jimmy's career combines photography, filmmaking, professional climbing, and skiing. His films include *Meru* and *Free Solo*, while his climbing and skiing adventures have been as ambitious as they come.

"People often ask, 'What's the greatest risk you ever took in life?' They often assume it was a decision on an expedition. For me, it's clear as day what the greatest risk was. Deciding to leave behind all the expectations of my parents, the pressure of what I was 'supposed' to be doing. That was the greatest risk I ever took. My path and career didn't come easy, but I had the one advantage of knowing that I truly loved what I was doing and the people I was surrounded by. That's what got me through."

The seriousness of Tate's illness became clear shortly after his summit attempt. We assumed his goal of standing on top of the Grand would not happen—he was fighting for his life, and it seemed best to settle in for the long haul, but a year later, Tate was attempting the Grand once again. This time it was without the fanfare of a film crew but with the help of a few close friends. He squeezed the climb into a seventy-two-hour break he had from chemo. His doctors had told him not to attempt the climb for fear it would further weaken his already taxed immune system. Tate had double vision from dozens of brain metastases, as well as enormous tumors in his knee bones and clavicle and ribs. And his lungs were spotted with cancer. He had an eyepatch. And a huge backpack. Next time you think you cannot keep going, think of Tate. Tate climbing that peak in his condition was one of the most impressive feats of mountaineering I'd ever heard of. He was so weak and frail, he practically crawled up the mountain. It ended up being a twenty-hour push that started from high camp at 3:30 a.m. Tate fought through a snowstorm, dizziness, and an upset stomach but never wavered.

> Low expectations are a good companion in the mountains.

A year later Tate lost his battle with cancer. I think of Tate and the other friends who are no longer with us when I'm climbing out of my sleeping bag and cramming my feet into frozen boots on cold mornings. It's in the dark hours, moving through the vertical world when others sleep, that I feel closest to them. If they're looking down on us, it would be during these times. The more desperate things get, when I feel I can no longer move on, I think of these friends for motivation. How badly

Flat Irons and The Tusk

CHUGACH MOUNTAINS, ALASKA, 1997

I acknowledge that I lost one or more of my nine lives early on in Alaska. My two older brothers, Steve and Todd, paved the way for me. They survived their own red flag phases and were quick to point that out when I started visiting them in Alaska. I was a classic example of the over-amping, mega risk-taking, "backcountry" snowboarder. I had all the skills I needed to ride serious lines. I was riding 250 days a year, felt super strong and confident, and had successfully ridden some of the heavier lines in the range. I even had my freshly inked Avy Level 2 certificate. But I was only a few years into spending time in truly uncontrolled back-country situations. I'd never lived a season with lingering buried surface hoar or deep instability, had never seen shooting cracks in the snowpack fracture uphill. I simply got dropped off, rode as hard as possible, then got a ride back up top. Even though I'd spent most of my life snowboarding, the backcountry was a different world, and I had not yet come to grips with the red flag I was wearing.

At twenty-four, I considered myself above the law. I rode two Alaskan lines that year that I would not ever repeat. The Tusk, with a super-exposed, sluff-racing crux that had me skipping on my heel edge at warp speed, literally hanging on by a few millimeters of steel for my life, in a "you fall, you die" scenario. The other line was Flat Irons.

My plan on Flat Irons was to sluff the face and then surf the running slide through a tight chute. Dropping in, laser-focused, I clicked into full charge mode. There was a point right before the start of the chute where I could pull up and let my sluff pass by. With total confidence, I passed that point of no return with zero hesitation. There was no sluff check—it would slow me down, and every second counted.

I made huge, arcing turns on the upper face and, as I entered the chute, the sluff crashed off the walls above my head, richocheting, and it felt like getting hit by a dump truck. The force completely annihilated me, and I cartwheeled 800 feet down the rock-lined chute, thankfully never hitting the sides. I ended up finding my feet toward the end of the chute, came flying out of the sluff, and finished by straight running the rest of the face. The footage ended up being the last shot in the biggest snowboard film of the year, "TB 6" by Standard Films, and it launched my movie career. But I knew I had crossed the line.

The Tusk rears up in a pointed summit, so dramatic that, even in a range of sharp summits, it seems out of place, cartoonish. The main line starts off the shoulder of the rock, a long hanging shelf with terminal exposure on its left and a rock wall on its right that becomes narrower and steeper as you drop toward the crux 1,000 vertical feet below. After the crux the line doglegs to the right and continues for another 1,000 feet. The top slope is dead fall line, so the only way to avoid the sluff is to beat it. If you get caught by the sluff or blow the turn, you'll tumble over a couple-hundred-foot cliff band, certain death.

I had identified a safe spot before the crux, if I wanted to wait and let my sluff pour through. Since the snow seemed perfect, I gave little thought to stopping as I approached the crux—but I didn't factor in the snow changing. Until then, I'd had great conditions, so good I didn't have to think about the snow at all. Exactly in the most critical spot, however, the snow was sunbaked. I was traveling about 30 miles per hour, a 100-foot cliff a few feet to the left and, coming up fast, hundreds of feet of sloping cliff below. There really wasn't any place for error, let alone a fall.

Thousands of hours training and my old coach, Jerry Masterpool, saved me that day. I made the most critical high-speed heel turn of my life—one that took all my might to hold on to. Halfway through the crux, the predictable settled powder turned crusty. My board started bouncing and chattering. I needed to make a solid rescue turn while holding massive amounts of g forces. Jerry's voice repeated on loop in my mind: "Balance point, quiet upper body, drive the hip, don't lean in." Due to the proper technique I'd honed over eight years, I held the turn just as a monster sluff roared by on my left, tickling my tail before it cascaded into neverland.

"I don't know about that," my brother Steve said quietly over the radio when the dust finally settled. I didn't either. At the bottom I shook with adrenaline. I had gotten very lucky. With a setting sun, we flew back to town and called it a season.

Fear may be the body's most complex behavior to wrangle. It is surely the most important. How do you know when fear is real and needs to be respected, or when it is mental and needs to be conquered?

would they want to be there suffering under the weight of a heavy pack, trying to reach a distant summit?

Fear, Humility, and Loss

The fear starts creeping in a week or so before the trip. I call it four a.m. fear, because it can wake me from a deep sleep and end my rest in an instant. The fear is the reality that I'll soon be departing for a serious trip or stepping up to a serious line. Zero-mistake snowboarding, where one bad call means I won't be waking up next to my wife or seeing my kids come down the stairs for breakfast ever again. They are with me 90 percent of the time when I'm in the mountains. I carry them as a reminder of what is at stake. Once the crampons go on, and I cross over that line of safety into the "no fall, no fail" twilight zone, I need to compartmentalize my family. I need to be as mentally light as possible,

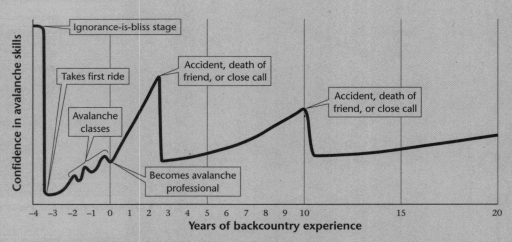

Life Events vs. Confidence

Source: Adapted from a similar graph by Clair Israelson.

As a kid, I laughed at this graph that shows how life events affect your self-confidence when it comes to avalanches. Now I could pretty much place incidents on it like it was my own journey. It is eerily familiar to most of us who spend our lives in the mountains.

Zahan Billimoria: Resilience

"I had two close friends die in separate avalanches, and it pushed me to commit to my passion full-time. I was reminded by their loss that life is short, and that if you want something, you better go get it now, because it might not be there tomorrow. That was a bit scary. I just knew that's what I needed to do, and I trusted myself to find a way to provide for my family, and to stay alive.

"Not everyone gets back out there, and that's okay. To me there's no pride in the fact that I chose to go back to the mountains. It's like an addiction I won't give up. It killed so many of my friends, I've almost lost my life so many times, and I'm still out there. Is that really something I should be proud of? If you have an accident and you decide *That's enough, it's time to start a new chapter, to reinvent myself,* that's awesome."

tuned into what the mountain is telling me, and stay 100 percent focused on the task at hand. I think the emotional tsunami that crashes over me after a serious line is the thought *I will see my wife again; I will see my kids again.* This may sound like I'm rolling the dice with my life, which I assure you I'm not, but being very real with yourself about the risks you're taking is important. Shralpinism is serious business, and we should never be desensitized to the severity of a close call.

When my friend Shane McConkey died ski-BASE jumping in Italy, I was holed up in Alaska waiting for the weather to break so we could embark on our first foot-powered glacier camp. My anxiety was already peaking. I was wondering if I was on the right path and if we could actually ride dream lines completely on foot. The phone call was one I've had too many times, but this one hit especially deep, because I am so close to Shane's wife and daughter. I made it home for the funeral, and Sherry and Ayla moved into our house through the process. Watching and reflecting on the pain they went through because of Shane was surreal and sobering. Saying goodbye to them after a couple of days and returning to Alaska to continue my expedition was one of the hardest things I've ever done. This was an important trip, a turning point in my life. Documenting foot-powered, high-end snowboarding at a similar level to helicopter-focused trips had never been attempted before, and we still didn't know what was possible. Yet driving back to the airport, I was literally gagging and dry heaving as tears ran down my face. I couldn't imagine traveling, hiking, riding exposed lines, or doing anything risky at all. What I was doing could end in death, drastically changing the lives of my wife and children.

Stepping into the mountains a few days later, I still felt like the whole world was going to come down on me. This is a feeling that arises every time I lose someone close to me in the mountains. It brings me down to ground zero. Not only do I *not* want to go into the mountains, I actually look at them with anger. Somehow, after a while, I'm always compelled to go back, to explore again despite all the tragedy and risk. This does not mean I'm reckless or fearless. I'm on a constant quest to hone my skills and to increase my knowledge so I can come home every day. Spending a life in the mountains pushing my limits, surrounded by other people who do the same, is a dangerous pursuit, pure and simple.

My humility in the mountains comes more from friends lost than from the close calls I've had. I can honestly say, however, that I've probably used up a handful of my nine lives. What makes close calls and bad accidents so sickening is the large gaps between occurrences. You can never let your guard down. Exploring the mountains requires constant awareness and a very wide berth for any error. This is why I never consider myself an expert and, quite frankly, why I was reluctant to write this book.

Regaining Confidence

In 2013, when we were dropped off at the bottom of the biggest lines I've ever attempted in the eastern Alaska Range, two days after learning my very experienced friend Joe Timlin had died with four others in a Colorado avalanche, I was literally afraid to leave the landing strip. The gigantic, steep, unnamed face loomed above and was so terrifying I couldn't even look at it.

Death knocks your confidence down to zero. Having this level of humility hurts, but it's a far better mental state than overflowing with confidence and ego. The balance remains tricky and is constantly changing. Stepping up to big mountains and lines is a zero-mistake game. Every single mistake I've made in the mountains stems from overconfidence coupled with complacency. So how do you push forward and keep your head on straight? Break big goals into small steps in order to end up standing on top of the line of your life and making it down safely. The first step is the hardest step. Start small, go slowly, do your training and research, and be humble. Look at the simplest and safest line, gain knowledge, and keep progressing up the ladder, gaining confidence along the way. Realize and accept that there's always risk.

"There comes a time when one must risk something or sit forever with one's dreams."
–Trevor Petersen

It took us two weeks to get comfortable enough to start looking at the unnamed face and think it might be rideable. Setting out at dawn on our eighteenth day, my partner Ed Shanley and I finally managed to regain our confidence after many baby steps—first with binoculars, then with cautious approaches and feel-outs. When we finally crossed the bergschrund to navigate upward, it was our fifth time on the face.

We'd gone through many ideas and setbacks. At one point I made it to within 400 feet of the summit, but I encountered such firm ice that it ripped the crampons off my feet four times. On another aborted attempt I hit similar ice on my way down as I crept off a crown line and landed on my heel edge on bed surface that was bulletproof ice. I rapidly picked up speed and my ice axe was ripped out of my hand when I tried to self-arrest. Even though I was only a few feet from softer snow, I could not get my heel edge to hold on to the ice enough to get me to it. I switched to my toes and was able to get just enough purchase to move across the bed surface and get to the soft snow on the other side. It was the fastest I have ever gone from being in full control, creeping on my snowboard, to accelerating out of control high on a big face that had a significant cliff lower down. This was a humbling experience, but I had time. When I did reach the soft snow I took some breaths, regrouped, and—knowing how precious sun is in Alaska and how much we had already endured—decided to climb the 2,000-foot spine that I was now at the bottom of for a redemption lap. And I used the time to reevaluate our route. That night we decided on a new route up the face that we had never considered. In very early morning light, Ed and I left camp to climb the biggest face of our lives.

> Some lessons leave a mark. The season-ending injury, the friend who never made it home . . .

Turning Around *Is* Success

When considering any line with consequences, I never say, "I am going to ride that line." Instead, I always say, "I'm going to take a look at the line," or "I'm going to start up and see how it goes." This difference may seem minor, but it puts everyone on the same page that the line or summit will only be achieved if everything lines up. Turning around is okay. Making it down safely, no matter what, is always the goal over everything else. Many mountaineers, after putting everything into a huge effort, almost summiting, and then having to turn around, will lament, "That was my greatest failure". Bullshit. Old-school. Failure is not coming home. Failure is getting hurt. Losing a friend. Making a mistake due to over eagerness or hubris. Getting close to a goal you've put your entire effort into and having the guts and mindset to turn around because the danger scale has tipped is something to be proud of and should be celebrated. This outlook and mindset is gradually changing. We need to talk more about accidents and actions rather than condemn mistakes. Mistakes do happen. A lot.

> The mountains are powerful places. They can give you the best day of your life or the last day.

From the moment one steps into the mountains, it is an investigation into the possible hazards that may be lurking out there.

This mentality is really the Art of Shralpinism and big mountain riding. To be able to push through the hard times and have total commitment to your goal, but also to recognize when to turn around on something you've wanted more than anything in the world, something you have put every ounce of mental and physical energy into, and to really let it go. Getting to this sort of mindset takes time and a great deal of grounding in the present. If this mindset is the art, then the science is using methods and tools to know when the window opens or closes. When that window opens, I can tell you, I do not need an alarm to wake up. The more complex the face, the rarer it is for that window to open. The higher the consequences, the more certainty you need. When I head up serious lines, I am constantly looking for reasons to turn around. I break it down one step, one section, at a time. I have to convince myself at many, many points along the way that "yes" is the correct answer to "*Should I keep going*?" My mantra: "If it's not a screaming yes, it's a no."

Five hours after leaving camp, and with the help of verts, axes, and crampons, Ed and I climbed 3,800 vertical feet up the center of the face and stood on one of

Xavier De Le Rue: Cultivating Fear

Xavier and I have traveled the world together climbing and riding some of the most serious lines I have ever done. When it comes to technical Shralpinism, he is on a different level. His "mellow" is my "extreme." Countless times I have seen him doing things on a snowboard I did not think possible. He is also a three-time freeride world champion.

"I have learned the hard way that fear needs to be really taken into consideration when riding and having to make decisions in the mountains. I would even say that it needs to be cultivated, because it is actually so hard not to ignore it when you are having an amazing pow day with your best mates, the sun is shining, and the snow is blower. The danger can come from so many different directions, and especially when riding pow, that you need to force yourself to have a bit of fear in you so that you can keep alert and aware to all the potential dangers and happenings around you.

"Don't get me wrong: it really sucks and it takes a lot of the fun away from snowboarding. But from what I have seen and learned throughout the years, it has always been, for me, the only way to continue to ride lines with an acceptable level of risk. I have considered this as the price to pay to continue to charge throughout the years."

the biggest spine walls of my life. Dropping in, we felt very little fear. We knew almost every foot of the face, what the snow would do, what would happen if we needed to exit, how we'd communicate with one another, and where we would make our turns. We rode the line with confidence and joy, after many, many yesses along the way. Soon after, the wind turned and stripped the face. A local pilot flies by it every year. He says he has never seen it rideable again. The only skier in the area, the owner of the lodge we stayed at before the trip, assumed we'd gotten skunked. His lodge is 50 miles from there and the mountains all around it get ruined by the wind. The storm that hit us with 7 feet of snow was only 10 inches near him.

It's hard not to use the word *miracle* when the stars align on the complex faces. You cannot plan for it, cannot force it or will it to happen. Embarking up a mountain that can kill you is an intimate conversation with few words spoken. What are the mountains telling us? Are we listening? Humility and patience allow me to better understand and communicate with a mountain, a range, a season.

Jon Krakauer: Minimizing Risk

Jon might be known for his writing, but he is also an undercover Shralpinist and one of the few people I trust enough to ride with in his home range, the avy-prone Rocky Mountains.

"Many times after skinning for hours into the high country, I'll determine that conditions are unreasonably hazardous, decide not to ride the line I'd hoped to ride, and just go meadow skipping instead. Often I'll remain in ski mode and never even put my board together. Splitboard touring through low-angle terrain is something that gives me tremendous joy and is a much safer option. Which isn't to say that I know how to avoid all risk. That's impossible. I do what I can to minimize it, but I acknowledge there's a chance I might get killed anyway."

Stacking the Deck

Do everything you can to set yourself up for success, defang the danger, and harness the tailwind. This might mean setting a skin track to the base of your line to help you navigate tomorrow's predawn hours or putting a fixed line over the bergschrund to help speed up a bottleneck. Maybe simply hiking another 100 meters to get to a better vantage point or rappelling over an edge so you can see a little more of the blind roll or choke.

"I am lightened by low expectations."
—Steve House

Just a few examples of little things that can, when combined during a trip expedition or season, increase the chances of achieving goals and coming home safely.

You can also stack the deck mentally, a big advantage when it comes to the mountains. The right mindset can greatly reduce anxiety and doubt and prevent you from getting caught up with emotions or the expectations of a mission. It's important

Elyse Saugstad: Lessons from Tunnel Creek

Elyse is one of the hardest-charging freeskiers in the world and has racked up every possible major award in the freeskiing universe. She has also helped develop one of the most approachable and relatable women's backcountry safety clinics, known as SAFE AS (Skiers Advocating and Fostering Education for Avalanche and Snow Safety). I asked her about what might have changed the outcome of the Tunnel Creek avalanche.

"On this particular day [February 19, 2012], I did not show up prepared like a good, reliable backcountry partner should, as I had not read the avalanche forecast. For several reasons (but none worthy), I had checked out mentally that day and relied on what these guys had to say. Basically all that was discussed was the avalanche danger rating—which was 'high' on most high-elevation aspects but at 'considerable' for the aspect we were planning to ski. None of the detailed discussion came into the conversation.

"After the incident, when I went back to look at the forecast discussion, I noticed there were obvious potential red flags, but since I hadn't read the report, those details went unnoticed. I have no idea if my buddies had gone beyond looking at the danger rating, but I hold myself at fault for putting myself in that position. Every single member in a group needs to read the avalanche forecast and come prepared to chat it over.

"One major hurdle that exacerbated the situation was the group size was way too large. This breaks down communication and lends a group to staying on course once a decision is made, regardless of seeing red flag signs that should deter or alter the decision.

"It's a black-and-white issue for me to wear an airbag, just like a transceiver, shovel, and probe. Without a doubt I survived the Tunnel Creek avalanche because I was wearing an airbag and deployed it. Yes, especially back then, there was a sense of machoism in waiting to pull your airbag, which is plain stupid. That's what it's there for!

"At the top of the list of how I have changed is learning the power of no: *No, I'm not going to ski this today if things don't seem to add up.* The mountains aren't going anywhere, and I'd rather give myself the option to ski another day over pressing my luck.

"Another powerful thing that has changed within me is finding my voice. It's not that I wasn't speaking up before this incident per se, but because moving through the mountains safely is a fairly black-and-white issue to me, I became more apt to vocalizing my thoughts, questions, and/or concerns, even if it goes against the grain of a group. This is also enriched by not blindly relying on partners that seem way more experienced. It's best to always be a part of the conversation."

not to carry the weight of success on your shoulders. It makes backing down much easier. To defuse summit fever, I expect that the last few noes, high on the mountain, will be the toughest ones to turn into yeses. Tahoe-based ski mountaineer Cody Townsend has a mantra: "It takes a hundred yeses to make it to the top and one no to turn around." When I do make it to the top of a complicated line, I'm elated because, mentally, I was half expecting to be turned around a while ago, but the reason never came. *Holy shit, I can't believe I made it to the top!* as opposed to *Fuck! I need to turn around!*

Real vs. Boogeyman Fear

Understanding the origins of fear is very important. Is the fear truly justified? Or is it just "boogeyman fear" in the form of strange noises at night coming from a serac fall you're nowhere near, or some airy steps high on a face when you have secure crampons and an ice axe in your hand—you're totally glued to the mountain—but you simply feel the exposure and height? It's important to evaluate yourself and understand if you get paralyzed by fears that won't hurt you, or if you're an overamper who has a hard time backing down from something once you've started. Being able to quiet the noise, to not get swept up in emotions, good or bad, and see them for what they are, is critical. It isn't just about you either. You want to have a good understanding of your partners' fear and risk thresholds. I'm more guilty of overamping than of boogeyman fear. So having a partner who's more conservative than me, who needs to be talked into a line and not out of a line, is better for me.

Teamwork

You must learn a lot about protocols, preparation, and group dynamics. You go into hostile territory as a team, where a mistake can mean death; lives are in one another's hands. You can control how difficult of an environment you want to go into. The biggest tragedies come when people let their guards down. This is where getting into the habit of following established protocols can greatly reduce mistakes and damage. The more you take away fear and add room for error, the better and stronger the mental game. Systems help. Just listen to expert skier Elyse Saugstad, who survived the devastating Tunnel Creek avalanche in 2012, talk about the power of no, listening to fear, and finding one's voice.

Set Goals and Boundaries

Establish personal boundaries and follow them. "I don't mess with deep instability" or "I never ride over secondary exposure" are two simple protocols that significantly reduce your odds of a bad scenario. Add in riding one at a time, clean terrain, and well-trained partners and the tailwind blowing you toward success starts to become significant. To stack the deck in your favor, you must understand your goals. I love riding steep, featured lines, but I hate complex snowpacks. This is one of the reasons why I live in the Sierra and have focused most of my snowboarding on coastal snowpacks, traditionally less complex than interior snowpacks. The downside is that this region doesn't have the consistent, all-elevation, all-aspect powder that lasts for weeks such as you find in places like the Wasatch Range, the Tetons, or the Rockies. But I really like to stack the deck, so I'm willing to live with that, because it removes a lot of risk from the start.

When it comes to travel, I've focused primarily on Alaska, due to these same traits: maritime snow and a generally less complex snowpack. This isn't to say I don't venture to other places; I just wait for a simpler/safer snowpack that I'm more comfortable dealing with in those places. "Your luck is really good, this is the best our snowpack has been in years" has been said to me dozens of times—chance had nothing to do with it.

White Moments

So often the endorphins, an adrenaline surge, and focus come together on the perfect day, at the perfect spot, and we are taken to a special place that Russian weight lifter Yuri Vlason has called the "white moment."

I am lucky enough to have achieved a few white moments. Most of them were tied to great risk. Where I knew I was in a no-fall zone but just let go and let the moment and my board take over. Where I grinded the edge of life and death, hanging on by a thread but so confident with my movements that I had zero concern with the consequences. Those runs that I know I could never repeat, because I now understand how seat-of-my-pants I needed to be to beat my sluff or hit my landings.

The release of energy from a run like this is so strong I could lift up a car, and the emotions so strong they leave me screaming with joy; but as I get older, I try to focus on getting this same high without the same risks.

The Mountains Are Whispering to Us

Brain waves and senses wide open and alert to pick up the words, moods, and lights the mountains are whispering to us. At first our minds are cluttered and noisy. We struggle to hear their whispers.

With patience and openness we start a conversation. What are they telling us? Agendas and egos muddle their words. An open and quiet mind, coupled with low expectations and acceptance of the mountains, is the key to a long life dancing in these untamed and unruly environments.

Understanding when to dig in and push through the hard times. To be totally committed to a goal, charging into the dark unknown past your comfort zone and past the boogey man, but just as easily turning your back on the goal without hesitation when the door gets slammed shut. That is the dance. That is Shralpinism.

Pushing the Limits

But why? Why would you ever do this? What I do in the mountains feels right. I often wonder if I lived in a cabin, removed from the rest of the world, would I have so much fear? Reading about accidents is important—it's how we learn—but it also builds emotional scar tissue. How much does this scar tissue hold us back?

My friend Shane McConkey passed in 2009. I feel the weight at every dance recital, birthday, holiday, and Mother's Day. The sadness has eased somewhat, but the biggest change is that my sadness is no longer for his wife, Sherry, and daughter, Ayla. Shane left them in a position for success. They are surrounded by unbounded love from our friends. In many ways Shane did his job. He provided for his family, and his daughter can do anything she wants in this world. My sadness is that Shane isn't here sitting next to me every time his daughter takes the stage, rides KT-22, or blows out her birthday candles. When Shane left on his final trip, he was conflicted. He was at the top of his game, but I knew he struggled with the risks. These sports and mountains give us so much. They make us who we are. They give us our highest highs, but also our lowest lows.

"At the peak of tremendous and victorious effort, while the blood is pounding in your head, all suddenly comes quiet within you. Everything seems clearer and whiter than ever before, as if great spotlights had been turned on. At that moment, you have the conviction that you contain all the power in the world, that you are capable of everything, that you have wings. There is no more precise moment in life than this, the WHITE MOMENT, and you will work hard for years, just to taste it again."
—*Yuri Vlason*

Getting paid to push the limits is taxing. More than once, usually after something serious happens or someone close to me has died, I get the feeling I've painted myself into a corner. Coming home after being in an avalanche with photographer

Sucking the Marrow

RED SLATE MOUNTAIN, SIERRA NEVADA, MARCH 2018

DAY ONE

At my feet towers Red Slate Mountain, one of the giants in the northern Sierra. Premier descent on all sides; a snowboarder's paradise. If I could only snowboard one mountain the rest of my life, this might be it. I wonder how many years it would take for me to cross one of my tracks?

The light has gone from yellow to red to purple, my tent serving as the perfect frame, watching the shadow climb the west face. The smaller peaks have gone to bed, quietly sleeping in the gray light. It is at this time of day that the master of the range stands out and steals all the glory. To be the master comes with burden and responsibility which the smaller peaks are happy to relinquish. For it is in these upper reaches, now glowing red, where the wind howls the hardest, the storms stay the longest, and nature releases its full fury.

We are the only audience bearing witness to this spectacular painting—a great reward for our efforts hauling heavy packs ten hours today to lie at the base of this legend.

DAY TWO

Too tired to write, but too good of a day not to—a day to tell my grandkids about, a day that will undoubtedly be a memory for eternity. At my feet, the North Couloir perfectly splits Red Slate, a Sierra glory line due to its size and consistent pitch that holds its angle from top to bottom. This morning we opted for an upper-side entry. As I rounded the corner into the main vein, the turns got bigger and faster, and I came out the bottom at top speed, holding on for dear life! I rolled to a stop and fell to my knees, doubled over, yelling and gasping for breath. A White Moment. My first in some time, and something I wasn't expecting sixty seconds earlier.

Back at camp, we refuel and redistribute our heavy packs: one load with unneeded gear gets shuttled to the upper saddle; the lighter load for tomorrow when we head west. After two hours of climbing, we are rewarded with our first proper view of the western line. We have no real destination but try to quickly digest the sea of fresh peaks in the waning light. With our extra gear stashed for the night, we continue upward, working the endless west ridge and one false summit after another. Finally, I see Nick Schneider on the highest point, the full moon on the rise a few feet above him. We are on the highest peak we can see. Another fluorescent sky with black jagged peaks poking into it. No wind, no noise, complete solitude—perfection.

We ride under the moonlight without headlamps, the best snow of the day. Rolling, hooting, gliding side by side in the massive bowl. Ten minutes later we are back at camp, speechless from the Red Slate Double Down.

DAY THREE

I am officially off belay, walking through mountains I have never seen before. My house is 147 miles away, and everything I need for ten days is on my back. Stripped down to the bare essentials: food, shelter, crampons, snowboard.

This particular valley is tight. You can't see into it even from the two tallest peaks. Dumb luck didn't bring me here though: I used the same method as in other parts of the world. Go for the thickest part of the range near big peaks where the hidden gems generally lie. Obscured by the giants and out of the spotlight of the frontcountry, they sit quietly and peacefully, enjoying their solitude.

A few hours later we gain the distant pass. "Last chance to not know what is on the other side of this mountain," I joke. Surprise! More granite, more chutes, more towers, more ramps, and more mountains. The saddle is no more than 40 feet across, bookended by towering peaks. We are shocked at the lack of wind and pause for twenty minutes to see if we just caught a lull (more than three hundred days a year this pass is inhospitable due to ferocious winds). We seize the opportunity and set up camp at 11,600 feet. This was not part of the plan, but you take what you get, and today we get to have our cake and eat it too.

The sun does its dance once again, reds and yellows to the north, blues and purples to the south, followed by the moon. Colors in constant flow, gradients I dream of while painting.

I feel myself getting into the rhythm and flow of the land. This is the highest camp I have ever had in the Sierra. To my left is the ridge to our morning line, to my right the evening line. I am smack dab in the middle of the mountains, and I am now going to sleep . . .

We are starting to get into the surreal, dream-state stage of the trip. We find our pace: wake in the twilight hours, ease into the day with coffee, wait for sun to reach camp, pack our gear, then start walking and riding until we run out of daylight. We deliberately move slowly; on long trips I never like to rush the pace. Every line has an estimated drop-in time, and I pad the schedule so we don't burn too much energy and limit our ability to climb all day. But this morning's climb to our high camp goes quickly, and we gain the upper plateau in half the time anticipated. The snow on our intended line needs more time to soften, so we take the opportunity to climb the broad snowcapped peak to our left.

The view shakes me. It is like getting a lightning bolt to my soul. A proud, stand-alone peak with a steep northeast face falling from its summit explodes from the infinite landscape. The hundreds of other peaks now mean nothing. I see nothing else. It is like spotting your eternal soulmate in an ocean of people. Perfectly triangular, perfectly sized—a just plain perfect peak. When Elena Hight and Nick join me, I let them spot it on their own. It doesn't take long! And after looking at the map, within ten minutes our plan for tomorrow has changed. We have a new objective, new camp, new drainage, and new path.

Focus on today regained, we spread out on the large open bowl below us, hooting and howling while descending an unnamed 11,000-foot peak. The fact that it is unnamed is not unusual in this landscape; the majority of these Sierra peaks remain nameless. Looking north I see Mount Dana barely visible 80 miles away. Between Dana and me the named peaks are easy to spot: Red Slate, Bloody, Banner, Mammoth,

and Ritter all rise above the masses. But they are the outliers.

Not that winter exploration or big traverses in the Sierra are new. These lands have seen footprints for thousands of years. Native Americans, prospectors, sheep herders, early explorers. John Muir opened up some of the higher peaks, Snowshoe Thompson traversed the range in winter, Norman Clyde explored the more vertical realms, and Dave Brower and friends started making turns down the snowy flanks in springtime. Then in the early 80s Allan Bard and his partners skied long traverses of the range in winter, culminating in their roughly 200-mile crossing called the "Redline Traverse." They stayed as high as possible on the crest, and it's not hard to imagine they pitched camp at our Red Slate or saddle camp. But did they take time out of their already ambitious itinerary to burn calories riding the steep faces of the lesser peaks I am now walking towards?

I can't say. The younger me would have wanted to stake a claim, get that attention. But I now see the value of keeping things fresh and unknown for the next generation. For me, getting on a western slope a few days from the car is where my focus has been the last few years. I think of it in terms of travel. I can either sit on an airplane and travel across the globe to an untracked remote range—or drive three hours south and carry a pack for two days. The end result is the same.

This line of thinking has had me planted in the Sierra since my Himalayan expedition three years ago. My main sponsor thought I made a mistake when I submitted my travel receipts last year. The $1,118 sum was far below my allotted $30K. I had to assure them, yes, I'm still actively snowboarding! Little do they know that I am as commit-ted—perhaps more committed—as ever to pushing my personal boundaries.

DAY SEVEN

Sucked every last drop of marrow out of the day.

and filmmaker Jimmy Chin in 2011, I remember walking into my house and seeing photos and paintings of mountains on the wall and wanting to tear them all down. With tears in my eyes, I went to see my three-year-old daughter, and above her were photos of mountains. My nightstand was filled with books and magazine articles about the mountain life. *Why have I done this?* As hard as it has been to lose friends, the avalanche with Jimmy has impacted me more than anything else because it could so easily have been me.

Always Back to the Beginning

I have to assume that if I was turning 10 feet farther to my right, I would've caused the same slide that took Jimmy in the Tetons that day. And if I was taken, I probably would have died. Walking out, the weight of failure hit me, and it became challenging to push on. Our group didn't have a full burial, but we'd come very close to a death, mine or Jimmy's. I couldn't stop thinking about never seeing my wife, Tiffany, and kids, Mia and Cass, again. I felt like a jerk.

> One bad call can erase a lifetime of good calls.

A total asshole, for potentially adding more loss to a community that had already suffered a lot of death in a very short period of time. It made me angry—at myself, at the mountains, at my partners and my friends for letting me continue to do this. I hadn't had a close call in at least ten years. I thought those days were over, that I had it all figured out, that I was done with the danger zone. It'd be so much simpler if close calls always happened in serious terrain. In places where it's easy to identify the danger. The reality is that, more times than not, my close calls have happened in terrain that I hope to be riding for the rest of my life.

So how do you regroup and get back on track when your passion revolves around the mountains? Jimmy canceled his Lhotse climbing trip and headed to the beach for a month. I was midway through shooting the film *Further*. It was mid-March, the start of prime time for me, and I couldn't retreat to waves. It took longer than usual, but I did what I've always done after close calls or losing a friend. After a short break at home, I crawled my way back in, starting with nonavalanche zones, expecting everything to slide. Back to the beginning. Back to learning.

I called up my close friend Jim Zellers, followed him around for a while, and talked it out on the skin track. Not only has Jim been doing this much longer than me, which means he has lost more friends, he also has no problem scaling his riding back to rolling, relaxed terrain. Jim has been through it all, so I assume he knew what I was feeling. He listened and didn't judge our decisions. He asked details not to be a critic but to learn from the incident so he wouldn't make the same mistake. Always learning, curious. This, coupled with his high stoke for just being outside, helped me take my first steps back into the sacred mountains that had betrayed my trust.

> I embrace the simplicity of staying properly fed, well-rested, and hydrated so I can spend my days exploring the fresh canvas.

Of course, hindsight brings clarity and, as obscure as it was to have an avalanche that day, Jimmy and I obviously made a mistake—one that's burned into my inner soul. I won't make it again.

My "Live to Ride Another Day" List

When April rolled around one season long ago, I arrived in Alaska fat on humble pie and hoping for some better days. The first person I saw returning from a day in the mountains looked like they had just seen a ghost. "Three out of four in my crew got hurt," he told me. "Super sketchy, dangerous. Be careful, it's gnarly—good luck." Unfortunately, that was only the beginning. By the end of the month the injury toll was in double digits, and the close calls were many. Despite the fact that the conditions were some of the worst I'd ever seen, I used my more than ten years of Alaska experience and the season's earlier beatdowns to help me do some of my best riding.

At the start of the trip, I wrote "live to ride another day" on a piece of paper and pinned it to a wall in my hotel room. Over the weeks the list grew longer, and before heading out to ride each day, I'd give it a once-over. These are simple things that I've said to myself in the past, but I felt I needed a reminder—and I still do.

1. **Live to ride another day.** Maybe you didn't get the line you wanted or just weren't feeling the flow. Forget about it and come home safe. There's always tomorrow.

2. **Don't take an agenda into the mountains.** Ride what the mountain gives you and don't force it. The mountains dictate what's rideable, and it changes every day.

3. **Listen to your gut.** Don't let outside pressures cloud your vision. Your gut always knows; you just need to listen.

4. **Don't rush things—slow down.** Haste is very dangerous and causes most accidents.

5. **Respect every line.** Often it's the mellow, moderate line where bad things happen, because you let your guard down.

6. **One mistake is too many.** A lifetime of good calls is easily erased by one bad call.

7. **Triple-check every line.** Go over a line in your head (as well as with photos) over and over and over again, so that once you drop in, you can be totally confident of where you're going.

8. **Expect it to slide.** Even though you have determined a line is safe to ride, *always* have a plan in case it does slide. Know your exits.

9. **Pay extra attention to outruns.** Outruns dictate how fast you can ride a line. Many times someone rips a line, only to hurt themselves falling into old avy debris in the outrun.

10. **Just say no.** Whether it's friends charging you on or a heli circling above with filmers, if it doesn't feel right—for any reason, at any time—don't go.

11. **Do whatever it takes to get a view of your line.** Climb a tree or hike far down a ridge if necessary to get a better view of a line. Know where you're going!

12. **Avoid cornices.** Cornices kill. One of the greatest hazards in the mountains.

13. **Respect no-fall zones.** Avoid them as much as possible. Know where you can risk a fall.

Post-Traumatic Stoke Disorder

The real good trips put you on a different plane. One where you become immune to the little problems of home life. Missing a flight, getting a parking ticket or a flat tire bounce off without so much as a shrug. After a really long expedition, just getting water from a faucet, walking into a store, or going to a restaurant can feel otherworldly. There's a lot to digest after these trips. I'll find myself sitting in silence, staring out into space, reflecting on all that's happened. The thousand-mile gaze can be hard on your family. Gradually, over time, the magic wears off, and inserting yourself back into society can be difficult. There's a void that can't be filled by the treadmill of life, and it's hard not to miss the simplicity of a trip, where your attention is focused solely on moving through mountains, the snowpack layers, keeping your tent from collapsing, and staying nourished and warm.

So another day full on humble pie. This one will take a while to digest.

Reentering life again with Tiff, Mia, and Cass happens fast. To be back on the sideline, bare feet in the grass, sitting with other parents cheering our kids on is really special. It could make me wonder why I'd ever risk my life on cheap thrills from the mountains. This is the mental dance all backcountry riders play.

A big shift for me as I've gotten older is my ability to get more satisfaction out of the ordinary. Just the realization of how lucky I am to be sitting on a chairlift or walking up a mountain. My ongoing quest to get more out of less and to have lower hurdles to jump stems from the question: *Do I really need to be on the edge of life and death to get excited?* A well-tuned board and fresh groomers, chalky wind buff, January corn, or linking the perfect multipeak tour can get me howling at the moon, powder not required. The ultimate goal is to obtain *The Power of Now* author Eckhart Tolle's level. That book opens with Tolle sitting on a park bench, taking in a tree, and becoming so in the present moment and in tune with the tree that his mind and body become electrified.

"It's One Big Feel-Out"

Understanding how rare it is when everything actually aligns is critical. Riding big, steep lines in powder is the ultimate game of patience. The norm isn't going out on a sunny Saturday and going for it because it's your one day off. The norm is staying out of any terrain with consequence and riding variable snow conditions to stay safe. In a good year, sunny, steep, stable

Christina Lusti: Humbling Moments

"Seeking out big, challenging lines has become a passion project and something that keeps me motivated. Every year I learn something new about the process; I'm constantly being humbled by the complexity of it all.

"I handle fear with calculated decisions. Humbling moments lead to reflection of our actions. Reflection of our actions leads to growth and knowledge."

pow on big terrain may line up only a handful of times, and often the window is only a few hours long. As legendary Alaskan backcountry pilot Drake Olson said: "It's one big feel-out."

Tactics will get you only so far. Equally important are the mental teachings of the masters. Being present, focused, mindful, becoming aligned with nature, and embracing the process are just as important as the tactical tools. Always tinker with and refine the rubric: this mix of discipline and protocols combined with hyperpresence, combined with the science of snow, matched with perfect terrain selection. This allows you to understand when you're able to safely navigate high-consequence terrain, open the valves, and dance with the dragon. All of this combined, making it happen, becomes the Art of Shralpinism.

PART TWO

Science

There are no shortcuts to the summit of your dreams. Before you can be a Shralpinist and truly gain the experience and spirit of riding, you need the basics. You ride, you fall, you figure out why . . . and you do it again and again and again, experimenting, learning a little bit more each time. Approaching mountains requires a lot of knowledge, which develops every time you step into the skin track or slide down a hill. If you want to spend a lifetime snowboarding, you need to take a slow systematic approach and celebrate every step along the way. This is the science of riding, dedicating yourself to the learning component.

You need to develop a strong baseline of how to actually ride down a mountain. Other important areas to develop are knowledge around mountain and avalanche safety, health and fitness (which includes the mental game), and gear. These can be taught to a large extent, although each sphere requires a lot of research and instruction, gained from reading, talking with experts and friends, taking classes, and getting out into the elements to try it all out. This process can seem overwhelming, but a strong understanding of the basics is key to building a foundation.

CHAPTER 5

Mountains

Looking out from my snow-covered tent, seeing fluted mountain walls rising from the glacier, I'm amazed. There are many paths to camping in the middle of the largest wilderness area in North America or on the edge of a spine wall in the Himalaya. How did I end up here? It is a privilege to be able to explore these wild places. Never take that for granted. Often, it is the people who had to work the hardest just to get to the mountain who seem to go the furthest.

The Right Mindset

We take what the mountains give us—keep expectations loose, travel light, eyes wide open. Be humble. No walls, no boundaries. Open up, set your imagination free, dream big, and get moving. But how do we organize and think about this risk so that we can get out there? What are the initial steps?

First, start with the right mindset. Walking into the mountains is walking into a world that does not care who you are, what your plans are, or how much training you have had. Mountains do not tolerate ego; it is the single biggest trap. This goes for me as well. Most of my close calls have happened when I was rolling high, with my ego inflated. Success in the mountains is a double-edged sword. Nailing line after line, making all the right calls, avoiding close calls—we strive for these achievements above all else. But too much success can lead to overconfidence, which is very dangerous when risks abound.

Mindset is the most controllable, useful tool we have. It is also the most trainable—a before, during, and after program. It's taking a quiet breath at the trailhead and acknowledging what you're about to do. Turn off and tune in. When I step off the road and onto the trail, I'm entering a truly sacred place—one that plays for keeps but provides infinite reward. At the root of almost every mistake I've ever made is mind-drift, an agenda based on preconceived assumptions, or an inflated ego that clouded my judgment.

> Rules and preconceived notions are dangerous.

Dissecting mistakes is where the real learning begins. Mistakes are equal parts tactical and mental. Being honest and asking what mindset I was in when I made a mistake, broke a protocol, missed signs, or chose a poor line is a simple way to greatly improve safety and success. Many studies have shown that acknowledging mistakes and taking the time to think and learn from them paves the way for greater future success. There are three ways to avoid the traps that most often lead to mistakes:

Be present. "Mountains speak, wise men listen," John Muir said. The mountains demand your full attention. If you aren't present, you miss signs that keep you alive. This is why I like to do my most serious riding unconnected and removed from the outside world. It's in this backcountry state that I become most connected. My most serious riding goes down when I've slept at the bottom of a mountain's face, staring at the line, sometimes for weeks. In this state, the level of connection becomes very intimate. You can feel the mountain's moods, feel its breath and energy.

Have patience. Throw the calendar out the window. You cannot force a summit or descent. You cannot make decisions simply based on "It's the last day of my trip, I've worked really hard, weather's moving in, so now's the time." The mountains don't care. They're ready only on their own terms. Always listen and be ready to bail. When I look at my mistakes, so often it was early in a trip or just after a storm cleared, where my froth was at a fever pitch and I skipped steps, lost my patience and awareness. Developing and refining your own personal protocols is a never-ending process. In this book I try to break down some of my mental and tactical methods. Develop your protocols, and then stick to them.

Just say no. The goal is to live to ride another day. I repeat this mantra over and over. Realize today might not be the day, and it's okay to say no. Be present enough to make these calls. Don't get too emotionally attached to an objective. Avoid summit fever. Celebrate backing down.

Assessing Risk and Staying Safe

As backcountry riders, we're not trying to outsmart the mountains. The game starts from the moment we step onto the snow; it's an investigation into the puzzle of potential problems as well as the opportunities. On any given day, there may be many hazards, and, throughout the day, the hazards may all change. It's your job to decipher which issues you can manage safely, adjusting for the risks as much as possible, so you can head home when the fun is done.

So how do you stay safe? It helps to understand what risks are out there. Then you can get into levels of risk, what's acceptable and what's not. I have a steady internal conversation going with myself as well as an open dialogue with my riding partners. Being real about the risks, and talking about worst-case scenarios, is vital. As frank as: "If I blow this turn, I die. If this slope slides, I die. I don't want to die. I am freaking scared right now! Why am I scared? Is it boogey man fear or real fear?" Risk can be divided into two main groups: objective hazards and subjective hazards.

Objective Hazards

These are things that can happen anywhere, anytime to anyone just by leaving the safety of home . . . and there's not much you can do about them. Wrong place, wrong time type situations. Lightning, earthquakes, and occasionally random events like rockfall and serac or cornice fall fit into this category. Objective hazards occur whether you're there or not. You can lower this risk by choosing not to go. But then you would probably never even ride at a resort, let alone in the backcountry. Route-finding can eliminate some of these hazards.

The Art of Shralpinism

The ability to recognize when the window to safely climb and ride a line opens, dropping everything and committing to it with all your might—but not getting so committed that you miss other signs. You can turn around at a moment's notice with ease and not sweat the decision. It's when the stars align and the valve opens, when you tickle the edge and maximize the opportunities that conditions permit.

Easier said than done. All we can do is give it our best, have a clear head, not get caught up in the moment, and do what feels right. Be tapped into your gut, and listen to it.

Himalaya: So Much Unknown

SHANGRI-LA, NEPAL, 2013

We've been at it hard for over three weeks and have only ridden two lines.
There's still so much unknown. So much to figure out. Hopefully the weather
forecast is accurate, and we get three days to figure out the face and
hopefully ride it. A-plus sunset tonight lifted everyone's spirits. Sun has
been at a premium this week.

There is not a breath of wind. I'm alone. High camp is a mile away.
It's noon, I've just woken from a nap. I watch as a different type of
cloud builds. Flying saucer-type. But it sits behind Shangri-La—the wall
looks perfect. I look to the peak where yesterday I sat for three-and-a-
half hours, waiting for a break in the clouds that never came. They were
different clouds than today. They were the only clouds in the range and
they sat on Shangri-La like a big brother covering a little brother with a
blanket and refusing to let him go. Everest was to my left, not a cloud on
it. Behind me Makalu, Lhotse, Baruntse. All spotless. All day.

I gain a new perspective that only comes from long periods of time off
the grid and disconnected. There's a lightness to my step and my mood.
Senses improve. Awareness sharpens. Since arriving in Nepal, there has been
an ever-present danger that has either been at my fingertips or on my
mind for almost a month. It creates a subtle edge that never completely
leaves the brain. It is not talked about much, but I know I'm playing a
dangerous game in an uncontrolled world. Every move is calculated and well
thought out, but when breaking new ground, there's that constant threat
of a missed call or a missed step. My wife and kids are close to me as
I approach the glacier. Walking through the crevasse-covered glacier, my
mind transitions from family and free thinking to the dangers ahead.

Two hours into my day, as the sun lights up my world, I cross the
bergschrund. There is no longer room for any distant thoughts of family.
I'm now in the vertical world. Danger above and below. It is time to be
present. The mind is clear, my senses are clear and sharp. I'm on the
edge of the world, sticking to it with the help of an axe and two crampons,
five points. I enjoy it. I am free. I am out there.

Subjective Hazards

These are caused by us—things we can control. Setting off an avalanche, forgetting to turn on a beacon, not placing rope protection properly: these are human related, based on our own decisions. You can help lower these risks through practice, experience, conditioning, training, and education.

Many hazards, especially when climbing and riding, fall into both worlds—not great for people who like to ride mountains.

Xavier De Le Rue and I once almost plummeted hundreds of feet into the sea as a huge chunk of shoreline broke away beside us. Five days into an Antarctica trip, we were riding steep lines day after day, lost in a dream at the bottom of the world. The previous morning, we'd ridden one of the best lines of our lives and were brimming with confidence. We then faced a line requiring an ice climb directly out of the boat then across an ice shelf to the base of the line. As we moved, the ground shook and just to our left the whole shelf, about the size of a basketball court, collapsed into the sea. It created a wave that swept seals off their ice floes.

> Hanging on for dear life to the side of a mountain so you feel alive deserves some questioning.

We looked at one another like we had just seen a ghost. As random as the shelf collapsing seemed, it was low tide and the waterline was a few inches below the shelf, so it was no longer supported by the ocean water. We knew we had just used up one of our lives and, although the hazard was no longer there, we decided to spend the day walking the shore and hanging out with penguins. I'm not proud of these experiences, and I often hid them from my wife and did not put them in our films, because I didn't want my family to worry any more than they already did. I did not want to be seen as the guy who constantly

My risk tolerance is far less than it used to be. This is a good thing. But I still have an appetite for the sharp end. The ingredients need to be perfect for me. Is this selfish, irresponsible?

takes crazy risks. If experience doesn't kill you or seriously hurt you, it certainly leaves a mark, and the lessons learned become chiseled in, ensuring you won't (hopefully) make the same mistake twice. The goal is to start understanding the dangers and building your personal systems to first recognize and then deal with the hazards. Developing a personal protocol (like avoiding snowpacks with persistent weak layers) and following the same steps every time are important.

Starting Out, Find Your People

It's a wonderful time to be a backcountry rider of any level. So many resources are available, with a community of formal and informal teachers for any level of rider. An abundance of books and online videos, websites, and articles are at your fingertips. Get plugged in. Show up to any and all outdoor activity gatherings. Attend adventure slideshows, screenings of ski and snowboard movies, expert talks, and backcountry skills courses; join a climbing gym or a regular mountain bike tour; take avy classes and learn how to read the daily avy report; and hike the local trails. Keep showing up, and eventually you'll start finding your people, and you'll learn a lot along the way. Perhaps more than anything, you want to trust the people you ride with, and spending time with them builds that trust. Ideally, find people who are doing what you want to do and get them to take you out on trips that match your ability level. Even just going for a short tour builds a lot of knowledge.

Do not simply charge out on your own and get in over your head. Learn the basics and, as your experience grows and you move into lengthier and more expensive courses, spend the time to find the right teachers—ideally local experts from your home range. Everyone has a different idea of a perfect partner. The most important things are trust and understanding. You want to be able to talk openly about conditions, what worries you, and agree that it is always okay to turn around—you should not worry about changing plans, and your partners should support doing so wholeheartedly. If not, find new partners.

Everyone's brain works differently, so everyone's approach to investigating the mountains will vary to some degree.

Be Prepared and Take Courses

You can find most of the basic science and planning courses in your nearest mountain town. Many people dedicate their lives to teaching mountain skills. Take an intro to the backcountry course. Then take the next level. Develop more awareness by adding intro avalanche courses. There is a concerning trend of people accelerating their learning without putting in the real-time experience. I still sign up for specialized avy rescue and refresher courses every year to make sure I am ready—and I always learn more. These courses vary from learning about the latest snow studies and snowpits to new rescue, shoveling, and emergency medicine techniques. Every few years, I take a step back and spend half a day going over the basics of terrain choice and backcountry travel as well: subjects I learned in an Avy Level 1 class. When you take the time to learn again, you realize how important the basics are, and the basics form 90 percent of decision-making.

"I don't like a partner who is just 100 percent in for himself, who doesn't recognize that my partner is my friend. If you go with a friend, you want to share it with your friend, and you want them to have the experience and think always how hard it is."
—Ruedi Beglinger

Tech and Social Media

As with most good things in life, there is a shadow side as well. Innovations in tech and the ever-presence of social media exemplify this positive-negative split.

The good. Avy centers provide daily online forecasts and observations. A full report is one simple click away. In addition, the fact that most riders have a camera in their pocket at all times may be the single biggest improvement to avy information covering popular backcountry zones. Photos of recent avalanches and snowpack breakdowns are priceless. You can see exactly where and how slides are occurring in a specific spot. Avalanches are usually consistent throughout a range, generally occurring on similar terrain and aspects, and at similar elevations. As a community, if we post photos of avy activity as soon as we can, with the elevation and aspect, we learn valuable info about the snowpack.

Even more important, if we are involved in an avy situation, it's critical to report the incident immediately, posting on social media and tagging the avy center. (This is the only scenario when you should be posting while in the mountains!) In the past, I would try and keep close calls quiet to avoid possible shaming or my wife hearing about it. However, I've totally changed my views on this subject. I now understand that the information may save someone's life. My hope is that avy centers evolve to a point where timely posting of notable conditions and debriefs with photos become the main point of reports and alerts.

The bad. Beware of FOMO (the fear of missing out)! It's scientifically proven that posting photos on social media that garner a lot of likes gives you an endorphin high similar to drugs. This lure can turn into more than a bad addiction and become fatal when people hype

Have a Plan, but Be Fluid

Language is important. Saying "let's go take a look" instead of "we are going to climb and ride," or suggesting "I am going to start up the widowmaker" instead of "I am going to climb and ride the widowmaker" subtly signals to everyone that our goals for the day will only happen if everything falls perfectly into place. Everyone is clear that we can turn around at a moment's notice if something does not feel right.

> I have a general direction but like to stay open-minded, supple, and in tune with what the mountains are telling me.

And being okay when things do not go as planned is equally important. This is why "the journey is the reward" is my mantra. Most days start out with a basic plan, but plans change and things can go sideways. You get lost finding the trailhead, a pole breaks, you lose the track, or you're having too much fun and go for another lap until after dark. Or maybe it's more serious: a broken binding or a broken femur, and panic or negative thoughts get in the way of successfully dealing with the situation. This is what we train for, why we practice: the unexpected.

backcountry lines during dangerous avy cycles. Images can negatively impact your decision-making. Just because someone gets away with riding a face in dangerous conditions and gets a lot of likes does not mean it is safe. Some people can fall into the trap of "getting the shot."

> Understanding backcountry travel requires time. The key is not getting yourself killed as you learn.

Wanting to be out riding when others are posting pics of amazing snow and lines despite risky avy conditions is understandable. Letting go of this need to always be out there, pushing harder than everyone else, is difficult but vital. I learned this lesson when I first started making films—to ride for myself, not the camera. Daily media overexposure definitely tests our abilities to regulate ourselves and risk.

Time and Experience

There is no replacing time. You can't rush it, you can't buy it, and you can't learn it. Time is essential when it comes to backcountry riding. We participate for the long haul. Taking courses is helpful in learning how to travel safely in avalanche terrain, but courses do not replace the simple lessons gained from a lot of time in the mountains, even basic weekend trips. I trust a twenty-year backcountry rider with no classroom time to navigate safely in serious terrain over someone who has taken numerous avy classes but has only logged a couple of years in the backcountry.

I point this out because there's an ever-growing, newly minted crop of backcountry chargers out there, recently avy-educated and super fit, who can shred lines at the pro level. I call them the "red flag guys." I was one of them. This attitude—"I am going to do things that have never been done before"—is not necessarily bad, but it should be recognized. These people seemingly have everything they need to push the limits of the sport but are missing one key ingredient: time in the backcountry.

The mountains follow their own rules, which we must learn in order to ride safely. Learning these rules requires a lot of experience, hours and hours, years and years of going out and coming back, and going out again in every different condition imaginable, focusing on how it all fits together. The instincts and feel you gain over time are just as important as the knowledge gained in a classroom or riding technique developed at the resort.

There are many ways to navigate safely in the mountains, and I've been very fortunate in getting to witness the approach of some of the best in the world. There are people like Exum mountain guide Zahan Billimoria, a master of snow science, who has a profound understanding of snow crystals, temperature gradients, and the latest snowpit analyses. On the other end of the spectrum, there's Jerry Hance. His

approach is totally unorthodox. I'm not sure if Jerry has ever taken an avy class, dug a traditional pit, or looked at a snow crystal with a magnifying glass. But his hands are always in the snow, and watching him feel his way through the mountains is amazing.

Two totally different yet effective approaches. And when it comes to sizing up the stability on a serious line, no one is better than these guys. My avy toolbox is more of a middle-of-the-road mix of feel and science. The more time I spend in serious mountains, the more I value the older generation. The longer someone has been doing this, the more respect I have for them. I watch closely, ask questions, and listen. Your track record matters in the mountains. But, even then, the mountains don't care. Whether you are seventeen or seventy, every day is a new day, and one bad call can erase a lifetime of good calls.

> I learned early on that I wanted to ride the best lines in primo conditions for as long as I lived. And in order to live a long life, I needed to get educated.

Terrain Progression

Ideally, take your first trips into the backcountry with a guide, mentor, or experienced friends and when the avy danger is low, without much new snow. But even more experienced riders should adopt the concept of "terrain progression." It's not just a beginner approach, but an ethos to work your way through the mountains: start small and safe, then build up to bigger or more consequential terrain. For a beginner, terrain progression should take avy danger completely out of the equation. Experts should

Old Man Figs

He is at home in the mountains. Steady and unflinching.
A deep but simple thinker. His school is his eyes. So much time
   in the vertical world walking, gliding, climbing, and being.
Days turn into years, years turn into decades.
The happy pessimist untrusting of the snowpack.
Finding joy in harvesting the local wind buff, or noodling the
   low angle fields of pow as he patiently waits for simplicity in
   the snowpack.
Every day, every season.
Not cutting edge or boundary breaking most of the time.
An elite, seemingly casual journeyman with a large and growing
   number of cutting edge descents around the world.

test small sections of avy terrain, looking at aspects and elevation. It's another way to evaluate snow, especially just after a storm or if you don't know the local pack. You can gain more knowledge by cutting a small cornice or dropping in on a small slope to see how the snow reacts than by digging a snow pit. New snow or big winds? You start over, terrain progressing again.

First Steps: Intro Terrain

Embrace the process, start out slow, work your way up, and have low expectations. Start with short approaches via open, low-angle slopes, less than 25 degrees. Travel in nonavalanche terrain with nothing above you that can slide. I call this meadow skipping, great for beginners and pros alike. Terrain should have clean outruns so if a slope slides, the rider won't hit anything and the debris will fan out shallow rather than deep.

Once you're comfortable with your gear and basic routefinding, progress to moderate terrain (slopes of 25 to 30 degrees). These backcountry areas may be popular, well-trafficked slopes close to town that can get bumped out. Although riding tracked-out backcountry is not what you're ultimately after, it's a good way to log time and gain experience with relative safety.

Getting the right cocktail of stability and soft snow on the high peaks seems to happen about four to eight times a year.

Terrain Progression

The tenets of terrain progression

» Have a known starter slope that you can get to the top of without putting yourself in avalanche terrain danger.

» Target a particular aspect and elevation you want to progress in. Stability on NE side doesn't mean stability on SW.

» Find a slope with a clean outrun so if you do get caught in an avalanche you will not be pushed into a terrain trap but instead into a flat open slope that will allow the avy debris to fan out.

» The slope should be short and steep with easy islands of safety that allow you to safely do a slope cut.

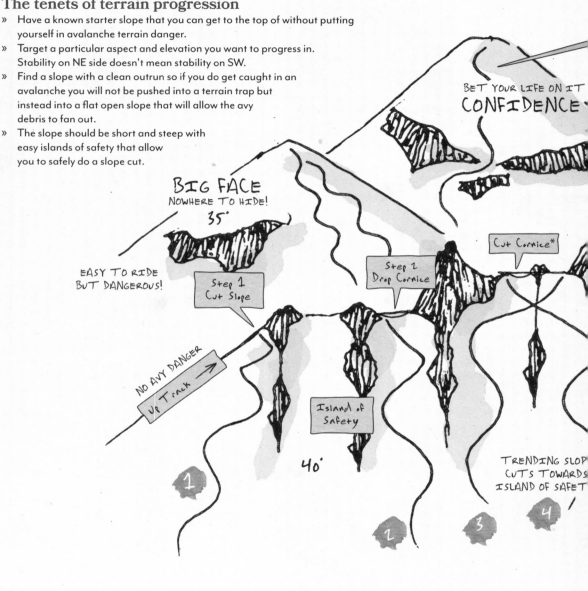

BET YOUR LIFE ON IT
CONFIDENCE

BIG FACE
NOWHERE TO HIDE!
35°

Cut Cornice*

EASY TO RIDE
BUT DANGEROUS!

Step 1
Cut Slope

Step 2
Drop Cornice

NO AVY DANGER
Up Track

Island of Safety

40°

TRENDING SLOP
CUTS TOWARDS
ISLAND OF SAFET

1

2

3

4

*Cornice too big to cut

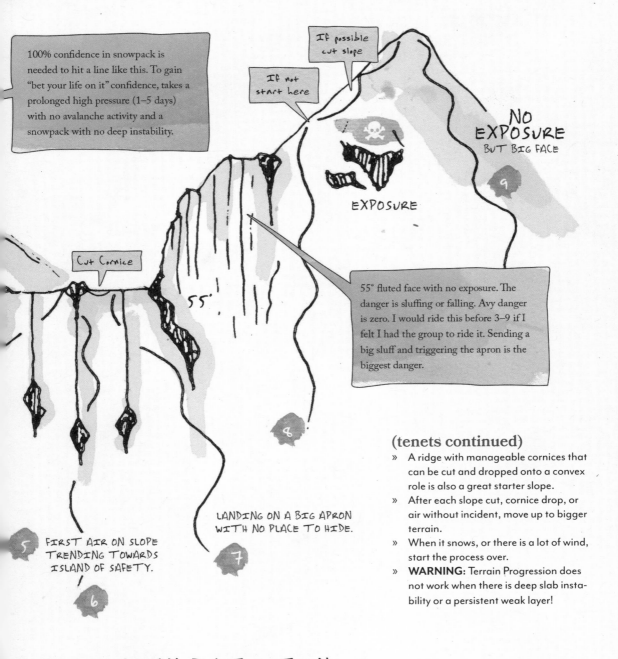

100% confidence in snowpack is needed to hit a line like this. To gain "bet your life on it" confidence, takes a prolonged high pressure (1–5 days) with no avalanche activity and a snowpack with no deep instability.

If possible cut slope

If not start here

NO EXPOSURE
BUT BIG FACE

9

EXPOSURE

Cut Cornice

55°

55° fluted face with no exposure. The danger is sluffing or falling. Avy danger is zero. I would ride this before 3–9 if I felt I had the group to ride it. Sending a big sluff and triggering the apron is the biggest danger.

8

(tenets continued)

» A ridge with manageable cornices that can be cut and dropped onto a convex role is also a great starter slope.
» After each slope cut, cornice drop, or air without incident, move up to bigger terrain.
» When it snows, or there is a lot of wind, start the process over.
» **WARNING:** Terrain Progression does not work when there is deep slab instability or a persistent weak layer!

LANDING ON A BIG APRON WITH NO PLACE TO HIDE.

7

5

FIRST AIR ON SLOPE TRENDING TOWARDS ISLAND OF SAFETY.

6

CLEAN/FLAT OUTRUN

If you are caught in an avalanche, you will not hit a tree/cliff and have a high chance of not being buried.

Inbounds

In resort terrain, well-worn tracks and bootpacks often lead to great areas. Do not veer from these paths, however, and beware of "sucker tracks"—one or two tracks that divert from the main path, as these often lead to large cornices or impassable cliffs (i.e., experts-only terrain). I've learned this lesson too many times, especially in places where I'm not super dialed, and the talent level is really high. Don't get fooled into the untouched pow. No matter how inviting, there's usually a good reason the locals avoided that perfect panel. And, if you do feel you are getting into a bad situation, stop and walk back up your track. I have done this dozens of times, and it's better than the alternative.

Sidecountry

Sliding through resort boundary gates into the sidecountry should not be taken lightly. These areas, right next door to the controlled resort, offer great riding with only basic or even no touring gear needed, but with all the risk of the real backcountry. No matter your ability, when you head outside of the resort boundary for the first time, you're a beginner!

Unlike starting at a normal backcountry trailhead, these higher access points can put you into serious terrain right away. And while resort snow and backcountry snow look similar, they can differ incredibly, because the resort is controlled by ski patrol daily. The areas just beyond Jackson Hole's access gates are a good example. If you head out the south gate off the top and get too low on a mundane traverse, the beautiful rolling fields of low-angle powder slowly increase in pitch, eventually dead-ending above a large, mostly impassable cliff band—which I found out the hard way when I was twenty-three. *Why traverse when I can ride these barely tracked powder fields?*

I took the walk of shame back to where I started—the only option—as I had no idea where to go but back up. This particular area has killed more people than anywhere else in the range. A shocking stat, considering hundreds of tracks a year get laid down on "you fall, you die" lines like the Grand Teton. Many other resorts provide similar gates that lead straight to avy terrain. The snow looks the same, but it can differ significantly, since ski patrol does not control it every day as in the resort.

> Beware of the friend who knows just enough to get you into trouble. This is usually a friend of a friend who knows more than everyone and plays the role of expert but is still very inexperienced. If all of your friends lack experience, it's a good idea to find additional teachers.

Risk-taking, Timing, and Playing the Season

I am much more timid early season. I hold back and think about training for the long season ahead. Mid-winter is all about stacking days and building your base. In spring, I focus on fewer but much bigger days. Sending season comes in late spring, when there are fewer rocks and more base. The snowpack is traditionally much safer and simpler then due to the high sun angle.

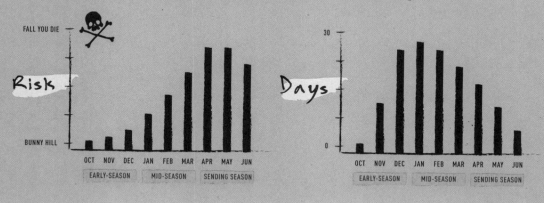

Backcountry

Backcountry riding remains the ultimate goal and is what I enjoy the most. There are so many elements involved, and it's a complex puzzle to sort out, one that's always changing. But that brings its own rewards, hard to find within resort boundaries. The best backcountry riding comes when there's good powder and you set your own course up and down. These conditions usually happen mid-winter, but they bring with them the need for avy awareness and evaluation skills, which can take a long time to develop.

Spring is by far the safest time to ride in most ranges. It is not by chance that the most serious lines I ride are generally in this season. The avalanche danger is generally low. Start with the known trailheads. Get up early, hike on frozen corn snow. And try to time your descent for when the surface transitions from frozen to soft snow.

Being excited to get up before the sun and put on your boots when everyone else is heading to the beach or biking can be hard, but spring opens up much more terrain, due to generally much lower avy danger. Risks still exist, though. Starting early when the snow is firm might require

"You don't get points in this life for doing dangerous and selfish things, but you do get satisfaction from it. So we should see it for what it is—personal enjoyment, that's all. We aren't out there curing cancer or making the world better for anyone else, so enjoy the journey and do what fills your cup, but don't get trapped by an obligation to do risky things." —Zahan Billimoria

Terrain and Time of Year

The avy danger rating plays a huge role in terrain selection and your risk. When avy danger is high, focus on low-risk, mellower terrain. When the avy danger is low, it's your chance to target steeper, more complex terrain.

The dots here show what I'm riding, given the conditions: low-angled terrain when avy danger is high and steep terrain when avy danger is low. The trickiest calls to make are the dots in the box.

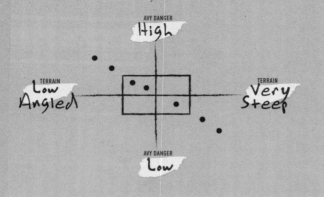

crampons and ice axes and great technique. Beware of falling or sliding on ice, stay away from exposure, and start tagging peaks. New powder on top of hard surfaces presents other challenges, namely avalanches as the sun warms the recent snow. The biggest hazards include big temperature changes, which can cause slides and cornice collapses.

Conditions and Surfing the Range

Surfers have been on the forefront of forecasting and reading weather conditions: picking the right spot, at the right time of day, that optimizes tide, swell, and wind direction—the difference between scoring or not. In the backcountry, nailing the conditions is not as critical. The peaks get blanketed with snow, and you can pretty much ride anywhere that is safe. However, there's often a huge variation in snow type and quality, depending on elevation, aspect, wind exposure, time of year, and temperature.

I think about a mountain range like it's a coastline. Our surf spots are mountains, our swell is the new snow, and wind direction and speed can turn a good swell bad and a bad swell good. We have tides too. Low snowfall equals low tide, high snowfall equals high tide. Knowing what cocktail of conditions creates fun, safe riding in a particular spot, or where to go that might be great, is the goal. Unlike surfing, temperature and sun play huge factors in the mountains. What elevation has the right temps, what aspects have the right amount of sun? For cold winter snow, we focus on the shaded, northerly aspects. Every range gets the dreaded north-to-northeast wind events that will shut down these powder sanctuaries. This is when we set our focus on sun-softened corn snow on the south aspects.

Every day and each year is different. I think of it as the ultimate treasure hunt. Nine times out of ten you can ride a soft, smooth surface if you know where to look. Every range follows the same basic principles: What has the snow been

Laird Hamilton: The Ever-Evolving Waterman

Laird pushes the boundaries in all things water. He is also an accomplished fitness machine. I spoke with him recently about his approach to surfing, aging, and living.

"I've been willing to do things that weren't necessarily directly connected to surfing just to subsidize my surfing. I'm going to do whatever I can, be whatever I need to be to get on the water. In a way, I think that's the essence of surfing: the ability to do whatever you need to to make it. I'm using that metaphor in my life.

"There's something to be said for the early stage of development and I can become slightly addicted to the process of the creativity: *Hey, here is an idea. Wonder how that would work. Let's try it.* And then, *Okay, that doesn't work. Let's try this way.* I like that process.

"I don't want to be defined by my equipment. That's why I like the term *waterman* rather than *surfer*, because *waterman* can include surfing, swimming, sailing—whatever you can do to engage with the medium. The most critical thing is to be interested in what you're doing. If you're not interested, it's going to be hard to be any good. You have to have some real desire. Is it for them, or is it for you? Regardless of how it might look from the outside, I've always been about the long haul. I'm always looking at the old gray-haired guy in the place who the young guys come to talk to. I might be that guy a little sooner than I thought. One of my favorite phrases is 'victory through attrition.'

"I have to be careful about falling victim to my ego and going back out to do something I've already done just because I'm good at it. I don't need to do it again. I'd rather do things I haven't done before. It's just a lot more interesting. Another great saying is 'Never let your memories be bigger than your dreams.' If you're living off of stuff that you did back when, that's bad.

"The greater the consequences of trying something new, the greater the fulfillment when you succeed. But there are three ways you can get into doing really dangerous things. One is that you're ignorant. Another one is that you're in denial. The third option is that you have experience and can rely on that. In truth, there's probably a combination of all three in every situation: a little denial, a little ignorance, a lot of experience. Or—less good—maybe a little experience and lots of ignorance and denial. I think it's important to be scared. I question the sanity of anyone who says they don't have a level of fear, they're not scared in the situations that they should be. Either they're lying because they're scared and they think somehow that's weakness, or they're not assessing the situation correctly. When you're scared, listen. Harness what you feel because when you tap into that scared feeling, that fear, it makes you powerful. It makes antelopes outrun the fastest animals in the world. It ramps up your vision, your hearing, your depth perception. I always say it's the scared mom who lifts the car off of her kid. You get superpowers. You get superstrength when you tap into that fear and are able to use it."

exposed to? What aspect and elevation holds the best conditions? When is the optimal window to ride the line you are after? Knowing when these windows open and close is the key to big mountain riding. Learning these spots takes time.

In my home range, California's Sierra Nevada, the window for optimal riding changes quickly. Wind, a temp warm-up, sun, rain, or a blizzard usually affect many aspects at once. The powder race in Tahoe is manic at times. It's five-star for a couple of days if we're lucky, then everything changes and only a few spots hold the best snow. A blown call on aspect, elevation, or time of day, and you could be riding one-star conditions, while just around the corner or an hour earlier or later you could be riding the best pow in the range. As you leave the coastal ranges and get into the interior, temperature affecting conditions becomes less of an issue, making it common to find good snow on multiple aspects and at all elevations.

My home range is the Sierra. It was not love at first sight. I loved the 450 inches of annual snow, the 300 days of sun, and the lift service access to technical terrain. But true love and devotion take more than a few bottomless days lapping KT-22. True love comes with time.

Snow Stability: Gatekeeper to the Winter Kingdom

When the whole range lights up with a solid base and stable snow, I focus on the most obscure lines, those hardest to get in good conditions. Sometimes I wait years

Storm Days

Big storms are exciting. It's what I live for. But the bigger the storms, particularly in Tahoe, the bigger the issue with roads, getting the lifts open, and avy danger. Too many mornings, with too many cups of coffee and too many texts to my plow guy, I can get stressed over something that should make me happier than anything else in the world. And I am not alone. The lift line froth on a powder day can be amazing. It can also turn sour.

My approach has totally changed over the years. I used to drive to the resort early and wait it out, but as the storms grow bigger, resorts are having a harder time opening lifts. This backup can lead to hours in traffic and closed lifts or long lines. Thus I've simplified my approach and attitude on the big storm days. I know that if I'm struggling to get out of my driveway, it means the roads are a mess, the resorts are struggling to open, and odds are the avy danger is high. It also means my backyard is good for pow surfing. When the rare breaks are breaking, ride them.

before they open up again. Riding the more out-of-the-way zones is a good way to keep your go-to areas fresh for when conditions return to normal.

Riding through a Drought

A drought year really emphasizes the need to know terrain. Searching for places to ride powder with only a 12- to 18-inch base in a range of dirt, it became clear which areas boosted 3 inches of new snow into 18 inches. We were looking for areas that benefited from orographic precipitation, areas where the mountains help lift air and moisture, creating new clouds that help enhance snowfall. Formations such as box canyons, high-elevation lakes, thick parts of the range near taller peaks are all good places to find sweet spots. They are the first to grab a storm cloud and the last to let it go. I also look for the snow patches that last the longest into the early summer months. These are usually north-facing and take a long time to melt out. Also, larger trees and moss on rocks and trunks mean you are in a good wet spot in a range. But finding good snow is only half the equation. We must also contend with avalanches. Riding steeper lines where the snow accumulates the most also means visiting areas most prone to avy danger. More snow = bigger avalanches.

Snow stability is the gatekeeper to the winter kingdom. Without proper stability and safe conditions, snow quality becomes irrelevant. We're constantly seeking those times that good snow lines up with good stability. I organize my life around these magic windows. When everything lines up, I'm ready to go. If I'm lucky, this magic window of perfect powder, stable enough for riding serious lines, opens three to five times a year. Often stability and good snow on steep terrain stay perfect only in the morning, so the magic window may be less than fifteen hours a year. As the year progresses, the snowpack stability generally improves, increasing the window, which is why I completely block off my days in March and April.

I set my alarm for a few hours before sunrise, but I usually do not need it because I am so amped. Sleep becomes limited, because these are the days I step up to serious lines. The calendar vanishes, emails and phone calls go ignored, and my life becomes singularly focused on the mountain. This window of quality snow and stability does not take place immediately after a storm clears, so I've learned to take it slow on the first sunny day.

Getting the Goods: Thoughts on Technique

To go down, you must first climb up. Much harder than it sounds, a huge part of getting out there is figuring out the safest, most efficient route up the mountain. These decisions can make or break a descent.

To climb the line or go around? This is often the question. The short answer: do whatever is safest. If you're worried about avalanches when hiking or skinning up, go around. If you're worried about routefinding or hidden ice or pockets of bad snow on the line that could cause you to slide off the face, then climb it directly when avy safety allows. But it's often not that simple. I've lost too many friends based on this decision alone.

When to Go Around

If the slope is safe from avy danger, hike or skin up. If you're worried about the slope sliding, don't climb it—maybe even bail altogether. Going "top down" is my preferred method because it means that you are only on the slope for minutes, not hours, greatly reducing your risk of getting swept off. It is also easier to evaluate avy conditions and test the slope by dropping a cornice, or slope cutting it. The hard decisions come when the slope seems safe, but small slabs or sluffs may flush you down. Failing to spot these problems has happened to me twice. Both times I'd been riding the same area for multiple days, hiking and riding with zero avalanche activity. The first time I was with Alaskan Ryland Bell on my first foot-powered trip in the Fairweather Range. We were hiking a clean line above camp when a small pocket pulled out and flushed us a long way on top of the snow to the bottom. It was a fresh wind slab that had formed overnight while we were sleeping. We were humbled, shocked, but totally fine—the slide was confined to the new, top wind slab layer. If the terrain hadn't been free of cliffs and rocks below, we would have been dead.

Sierra locals Kip Garre and Allison Kreutzen had a similar experience in 2011, but sadly it claimed their lives. They were climbing up the Split Couloir, a 2,000+-vertical-foot, ultra-classic chute down the center of 14,058-foot Split Mountain in the Eastern Sierra. It's one of the most picturesque lines I've ever seen. Unfortunately, the bottom of the line has about a 100-foot waterfall/cliff, making it one of the few lines in the Sierra that requires a rappel. The conventional wisdom is to climb the line so you can preset your rap anchor for the downclimb. That way, you can ride right into it and move through the crux fast. Kip and Allison were topping out when a small wind slab broke, and they were swept back down the chute.

Serious terrain with a very small avalanche ended their lives. This same scenario happens over and over again. Kip was an early mentor of mine when I embraced foot-powered snowboarding. It wasn't the fact that he was fast or that he loved the steeps that drew me toward him—it was his humility, kindness, and willingness to share knowledge. He was elite but acted like he was just a normal, average skier and he always had time for a talk as he was lapping people on the skin track. I'm not sure if I will ever ride Split Mountain. It would have to be happenstance to find myself in the Sierra, with the perfect people and the perfect conditions. If that day comes, I assume I'll be dropping in from the top.

The second time a small slab knocked me off a mountain was in the Saint Elias Range in Alaska. Along with the film crew for *Further*, I was eight days into a remarkable high-pressure system, clear skies and cold temps. We'd ridden everything in sight without incident. There was a slight increase in wind, 5 miles per hour, but no big warm-ups, no new snow. I hiked three-quarters of the way up a 50-degree, unnamed face when a picnic table–sized slab, only 10 inches thick, broke beneath me. I immediately fell onto my chest and accelerated downhill. I was a thousand feet up the clean slope, but at the bottom of it was a 50-foot bergschrund. A survivable fall but one that would certainly injure me.

I train for moments like this, and with all the energy I could muster, I fought and fought to stay upright. Chest into the mountain and feet downhill, I was able to get my ice axe in front of me and self-arrested after about a 200-foot sliding fall. The slab was so unremarkable that, if it had happened while I was snowboarding down the face, I probably would have simply absorbed the break and kept riding. But on the climb up, it caught me at a vulnerable spot. This shows how much more complex hiking lines can be than just dropping into them. Add in that you may be exposed on a face for hours instead of minutes, which makes the chance much higher of an objective hazard—cornice collapse or rockfall—taking you out.

When to Hike the Line

So why would you ever hike up a chute? Sometimes it's impossible to go around or enter another way, and sometimes it's actually safer to hike the face. You get to better

assess the snow quality and know what you're dealing with. If you're concerned about hitting ice on the way down or whether crux sections are rideable, hiking can be very important. The list of names of those swept off their feet to their deaths from hitting hidden ice is long. Ice just below the surface, or ice in areas you ride into blind, is the number one killer of steep skiers and riders in Chamonix, France. It wasn't until I spent time in Chamonix with Xavier De Le Rue that I really understood the dangers of glacier ice lurking under a few inches of snow. The ice is so hard, there is zero chance of stopping unless you have an axe, and it takes great expertise if a fall occurs. This is why riding with two axes is standard in Chamonix and for other steep areas.

My love for the sharp end, for getting way off the deck on a steep face with nothing holding me to the mountain other than my crampon points and ice axe, has grown over the years to the point where on some lines the climb excites me as much as or more than the descent. The combination of endorphins and a prolonged adrenaline buzz from being on the slope for hours, not minutes, is a powerful and addicting cocktail that if left unchecked can be dangerous. It wasn't only hidden ice that opened my eyes to the importance of hiking a line. One of my first alpine starts was in Utah's Wasatch Range, filming for *Deeper*. I did not ascend the exact line, but did solo climb a 3,000-foot chute nearby to access the objective, which gave me a great read on the conditions and stability.

After four hours booting up in the pre-dawn dark, I dropped into Hypodermic Needle, just as the sun was lighting up the 1,500-foot chute. It's a line I had dreamed of riding for years, and I had so much energy pumping through my body, I think I could have run through a wall. Tight turns on the upper steep section gave way to larger turns halfway down, and when I saw the exit, I pointed to it and let gravity take me. I was higher up than I realized, however. When I came out the bottom, I was absolutely flying, maybe 60 or 70 miles an hour. Way too fast. Climbing a different route up, I'd never actually gotten a great look at the exit. The bottom runout bench was not as flat as I'd anticipated, and it was clear I was not going to be able to dump enough speed before a boulder field a few hundred yards after the bench, and it was approaching fast.

I had to throw my chute, basically laying it down and forcing myself to crash. Olympian Bode Miller describes crashing in a downhill race like jumping out of a car onto the freeway, and I can confirm that is exactly what it felt like. Doing this voluntarily, and making the decision in a split second, is something I've never had to do again and never hope to, because I'm not sure how many of those crashes I could survive. I tried to lie down like a starfish, but my body hooked up as soon as I touched and sent me into a violent tomahawk. My goggle lenses disappeared, my gloves were actually ripped off, and my backpack straps broke. The divot from my first flip was the size of a hot tub, even though the fresh snow was only ankle-boot deep. A minor concussion, a very tweaked neck, and a full-body beatdown were the rewards for pinning a chute into the unknown.

Optimizing the Down: Picking a Line

At its worst, the down can be a humiliating wrestling match against the mountain. At its best, riding transforms into art. Staring at a blank canvas can be overwhelming. Break it down. The slope's outrun dictates everything, so start by envisioning that. *I can take this long panel over to that small ridge, then that line, and the other to the right—all lead easily into the clean outrun. If conditions are not what I thought they were or something goes wrong—avalanche, ice—I put myself above the clean exit so, if I do get swept off the face, I am over my exit.* When riding in deep snow, where sluffing is a concern, it is important to leave your exit clean until the very end of the line.

Ride the best snow. This sets you up for success. Be hyperaware of surface textures. Some days pool table–smooth snow is soft and the spot to be, while other days smooth may be unedgable ice. Same with textured snow. Sometimes I search for it, while other days I avoid it. How much sun an aspect gets and timing it right are other keys. If there's a crust, it is often the case you want that snow warmed up as much as possible to soften it. Cold powder you probably want in the shade or just when it gets the first rays of light. Cold powder that starts to get warm too fast can become very dangerous.

> There is no end game, no total mastery in Shralpinism. Moments occur in one's life where it all comes together, the portal opens, and we enter a completely different world. Mihály Csíkszentmihályi describes this as the flow state.

My favorite conditions develop when the north faces waiting in the dark all winter start getting cross-light in the spring for a few minutes early or late in the day. I wait until they have just enough light on the face to be rideable with decent visibility. This means I'm riding snow that has been in the shade all winter. To see the crystals sparkle for the first time and to feel that fast, cold smokey pow under you and around you is the pinnacle of snow quality.

To realize consistent proficiency and art form is achievable. Reaching this level requires a high degree of understanding of technique, snow science, meteorology, and geography, as well as the ability to stay present and mindful for long periods of time so you understand nature's subtle signs. To optimize the down, you need the power of a weight lifter to be able to hold significant forces, the soft touch of a ballerina to finesse edges through different surfaces, the explosiveness of a

Gears

THREE WAYS TO TAKE A SECTION

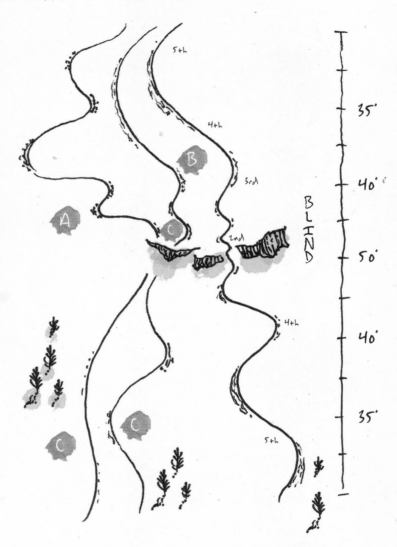

A. Coming into air from the side allows you to get a glimpse of the air

B. Anticipate blind spots. Look for markers like trees or pillars.

C. Approaching the air, look for gaps in trees that put you on your landing path.

D. Smoothly slow down through smaller and smaller turns. Avoid stopping or sideslipping!

The goal with descending down mountainsides is to utilize gravity, interact with the landscape, and get the most out of the current snow surface. Doing this in a wide-open bowl is simple. Moving through complex terrain with grace and flow is a different story. I think of it as moving through gears on a car. We want to avoid abrupt transitions or stopping at all costs.

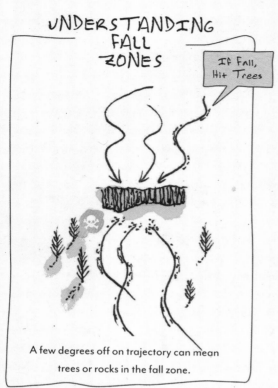

A few degrees off on trajectory can mean trees or rocks in the fall zone.

Understanding Fall Zones

Understanding where you can fall and where you can't is essential. A slight change of trajectory of an air or placement of a turn is often the difference between getting seriously hurt or just bruising your ego.

Stomping Airs

Make your first turn after an air a toe turn. You can handle chatter better on your toes. Trying to slow down on your heels often leads to falling on your butt.

Flowing through Terrain: Defining the Gears

Have a plan, break a line down into specific sections, anticipate blind spots or technical spots, know where you can fall and where you can't, and how fast you can go into the outrun. I think of what gear I can ride each section in.

» First gear: very slow, no-fall zone, serious ice or crust; 1–5 mph
» Second gear: 5–10 mph
» Third gear: 10–25 mph
» Fourth gear: 25–45 mph
» Fifth gear: 45–55 mph
» Fifth gear, wide open: 55 mph and up

Shifting smoothly through the gears, anticipating and executing, is the ultimate goal. To move smoothly through complex terrain is where riding transforms from simply navigating a way down to becoming a musician who flows through different tempos and chord progressions with grace and fluidity.

basketball player to spring off terrain features, the flexibility and spatial awareness of a gymnast for airs, and the overall strength to take football-level impacts when falling. You need elite endurance nutrition so you can walk all day, day after day, withstand the elements, and still have energy to enjoy the down and make it back home safely. With the perfect cocktail of mental gusto and humility while being a good communicator with diverse groups, the sky is the limit!

Know Your Outruns

The outrun dictates everything. How fast you ride, how much risk you take. This is why when scoping terrain, I start with the exit. For example, in the remote ranges of Alaska, it is overwhelming to search the massive faces for a dream line that I will commit my next month to trying to climb and ride. At first it seems endless—line after dream line in the form of fluted spine walls and mega faces! But pretty quickly I realize that the majority of the outruns are crevasse-riddled and unrideable. If you could see my eyes on these searching flights, you'd see I am mostly looking down for flat, clean glaciers.

A clean outrun is only part of the equation. What are the snow textures like, how firm is the debris? This will dictate if you can come into the outrun in fifth gear, wide open, or if you need to shut it down. I first saw the consequences of going blindly into an outrun in 1998 when I was filming with my cousin Adam Hostetter in Valdez for TGR's third film, *Uprising*. We'd flown up via heli, scoped the slope

Breaking Protocol

WRANGELL AND SAINT ELIAS RANGES, 2012

Deep into the Wrangell and Saint Elias Ranges, I dropped into one of the most serious faces I've ever ridden, just as the sun was setting. The line had secondary exposure in the form of a massive bergschrund below, and cameraman Chris Figenshau and I were 6 miles from camp. We were shooting for my film "Further," and our safety guide Ed Shanley was stationed with our stashed overnight kit and medical supplies in the saddle connecting the two locations.

The approach and climb had taken much longer than expected, and nightfall was coming. If something did go wrong, and we were not able to walk, we would be forced to spend the night out away from base camp and with minimum supplies. Relief washed over me as I rolled into the flats below the bergschrund, but it was only partial—Chris still needed to ride down. It's a team effort, and you never want anything to go wrong, especially when night is coming on soon. Chris skied the line cautiously and controlled and crossed the bergschrund in the twilight. We had broken protocol, and it worked out, but I did not take it lightly. It was not the first, or the last, time I would break protocols. The important thing is to acknowledge when that's what you're doing. Chris and I skinned up and over the saddle under the stars, arriving back at camp at midnight in high spirits but with the emotional weight that we had broken protocol and made our margin of error razor thin.

from the sky. It looked fine, just some small avy debris way at the bottom. I was on the ridge with Adam when he dropped in. It was the first run of the day, conditions were perfect, and we were two weeks into our Alaska trip, amping with energy.

Adam made a few turns and then disappeared behind a blind roll. He didn't exit out, and the worry came. Finally, he mumbled into the radio that his femur was broken. I frantically descended the perfect flank, thinking there was no way he'd broken his leg. As I rounded the corner and entered the outrun, I couldn't believe my eyes. The small debris pile we'd seen from above was actually huge chunks of frozen snow that had shed from a southwest face and crossed into our outrun. It was unrideable; Adam sent it into the equivalent of a boulder field at 50 miles per hour, broke his femur, and was lucky to be alive.

Thankfully he was in the flats, it was early in the day, and we had a helicopter. Within thirty minutes he was packaged up and in the air en route to the hospital. Over the years, I saw this story play out again and again. It has happened to me as well. People nail their lines but get into trouble with the outruns or crossing over the bergschrund. After Adam was hauled away, I sat in the debris pile in disbelief. My best friend was hurt, and I had to wonder if it was me who'd dropped first, would I have had a similar outcome? We had never discussed the outrun, had never even mentioned it. From that day forward, I put a ton of attention into the outruns. It's like pointing hills on a skateboard: you need to know how much speed you can handle going into the bottom. How long and smooth? What's the snow like? Any ice or debris? How wide is the bergschrund? When scouting for camp zones, I also look at outruns. If we have clean outruns, I know we can find interesting lines that feed into them and ride right to the tents.

Dark Start: Get Hurt in the Morning

Beating the sun always hurts, but an alpine start is always worth it. The dark hours are free hours: Moving without the energy zap of the sun. Mind easing into the day with the growing dawn. Body invigorated by the cold temps. A slow and steady plod into the dark abyss. Focused on the few feet in front of you illuminated by your headlamp. No distant horizon to deflate your aspirations. Moving and doing while the rest of the world sleeps. There's not much difference between four and five a.m. or two and three a.m.

Beware the traps of an alpine start, however. Countless times I've been fired up and ready to put my head down to skin and hike for a few hours only to get thirty minutes into the mission and have to backtrack, because I was lost. Pay extra attention during the dark hours of travel, especially if there's no moon. Invest in a really good headlamp. Not being able to see more than five feet ahead is harder than you think. I've bumbled around and lost time even while on trails I know well. Ideally you put in a skin track, or at least get eyes on the route, the day before.

Dark starts out of a high-alpine camp present a different set of issues. Steep, frozen slopes, crevasses, and bergschrunds can take much longer to navigate. The dark seems to amplify sounds as well as fear. Countless times I've set out on the same skin track used during the day before and made it to the bergschrund, only to scrap the agenda and turn around after hearing distant, thundering serac falls or spindrifts coming down the face we wanted to climb. There is nothing more deflating than turning around and getting back to camp just as the sun is rising, lighting up your objective, and seeing your tracks in the perfect spot, but you were afraid to push on. It happens. The pull of a warm sleeping bag vs. the unknown is very real. We are all afraid of the dark.

Ideally, if you are going to get hurt, do it during a high-pressure cycle and in the morning. You can never really choose, but it helps to take a conservative approach and leave a lot of room for error. You want to give yourself the best possible chance and as much time as possible if things go wrong. This is why I primarily focus on northeast aspects that get sun in the morning. I will ride northwest faces in evening light, but I am much more conservative because an injury late in the day is much more serious. Be sure you have good communications within your group, so you'll know exactly who to call if the shit hits the fan.

There are countless stories of someone getting a simple injury like a tib or fib break late in the day or in cloudy weather, making a heli evacuation impossible, and the person ending up dying from hypothermia. Nat Patridge, owner of Exum Mountain Guides, almost suffered this fate right under the cable car in Chamonix, France, when he broke his leg. In clear weather the rescue service would have been there in under twenty minutes, but it was a cloudy afternoon so that was not possible. Thankfully a team of experienced mountain guides and riders were able to move him down to the midstation by the middle of the night. Nat still ended up in a coma for three days and barely survived the incident.

TGR follows strict protocols along these lines: no serious riding an hour before sunset, allowing at least two hours to evacuate someone. Mind you, these measures stand when filming, with a full crew and a heli. For foot-powered backcountry riding, I build in way more time. Injuries, broken gear, and other issues take time to deal with. A full evacuation for something more serious can last many hours. Climbs take longer than expected, and we're often still navigating serious terrain, exiting from deep in the range, as the sun goes down. It's important for the team to acknowledge when we're pushing protocols and the risk of getting caught out increases. Always carry a first-aid kit, proper avy gear, and headlamps. Know where you can get cell phone service, and know the equivalent of 911 wherever you are. For expeditions we have a satellite phone and know exactly who to call if a rescue is needed. Keep in mind that there's no cell service in a range like the Sierra so it's critical to have a SPOT device, inReach, or Somewear in most mountain locations.

Cornice Cutting and Black Belt Moves

In a recent class with Jackson Hole's Zahan Billimoria—one of the most scientific snow-nerd guides out there—he laid it down: "What we're doing is basically witchcraft. We'll look back at this time ten, twenty years from now and shake our heads at how we evaluated the mountain and the risks we took." Recognizing that our current mountain protocols are the best we have but that we can always improve is crucial. The goal is to safely ride mountains, not get caught in avalanches, and to come home every day. Most of the time we do, but forecasters, patrollers, expert skiers, guides, and veteran riders die every year. We do not have this all figured out! A growth mindset is a must.

Under Alaskan guide Jim Conway's mentorship, I learned how to step into serious lines really fast. Jim developed a reliable system for managing risk in remote mountain locations where there's little to no sensing data for weather or snowpack. This system formed the foundation of the TGR risk management program. In many ways, Jim approaches mountain risk and safety very, very conservatively, but he has an open mind and is always thinking of new methods and advancements. This attitude is important.

In Alaska and elsewhere, cornices present one of the biggest dangers when accessing terrain. Lots of great lines, but also massive, terrifying cornices right where you want to drop in. Dealing with cornices is one of the most dangerous parts of mountaineering, almost a sure death sentence if you end up on top of one. And, even if you can safely access the ridge, dropping in may be impossible without getting rid of the cornice in the first place. Jim developed specially modified poles, saws, and weighted ropes to safely and efficiently cut these beasts. Cornice cutting is a black belt move and should only be done when you know with certainty there's no one around. If done right, it will put a lot of weight on a slope, test the stability, and often start an avalanche—that's the whole point—but DO NOT cut cornices when riding populated backcountry areas!

Wrestling with the Boogeyman

METEORITE MOUNTAIN, VALDEZ, ALASKA, 2019

We're all afraid of the dark. Was that an avalanche? Or just the wind over the ridge? A cornice fall? Maybe we should turn around. I call this "boogeyman fear". It's easy to laugh about in daylight, but I have turned around many times due to unjustified boogeyman fear.

When Tahoe-based ski mountaineer Cody Townsend and I first scoped Meteorite Mountain, outside Valdez, Alaska, from the road, all our attention focused on the approach. Alaska is known for its open, glaciated terrain above treeline, but starting from the road we were forced to battle jungle—alders, willows, devil's club—and two river crossings, requiring precise navigation to make it to the peak's shoulder, where we would find cleaner going above. All during the early morning darkness. Due to countless botched alpine-start bushwhacks, I knew proper planning included a few scouting days to try to dial in our approach. Cody arrived in Valdez a day before me precisely just to get ready to recon.

"How is it?" I asked when we met up. "Well, I just bought flagging, machetes, and three cans of bear spray," Cody replied with a laugh, although his eyes were serious, a bit of worry creeping through. "I think it might be a little rough." We spent the entire next day finding a "route." Forward and backward, sideways, and, at times, on our hands and knees, we generally crawled our way toward the bottom snow. Cairns were vital at the river crossings, where the water was flowing fast and ice-cold, and it was almost impossible to gauge the depth of the river without probing. We chopped and flagged a ragged, narrow trail through the brush, then put in a skin track up to an alpine meadow. Full body and brain workout. We were exhausted.

The next morning, Cody and I left the trailhead at 1:45 a.m. and brainlessly and mostly efficiently navigated the dark hours. Without proper prep there was no way we would have accomplished even reaching the bottom snowfields by dawn.

CORNICES ◆◆◆ KILL ◆◆◆

CORNICE LAW NEVER WALK BLINDLY TO A CORNICED RIDGE

1 GO ROCK TO ROCK WALKING CORNICE RIDGE

2 NEVER WALK BLINDLY TO EDGE

How far back are you?

Hat On Probe

3 USE SPOTTER TO LINE UP GAPS IN THE CORNICE

Hat on a probe helps spotter to see you.
Throw snowballs over the edge to confirm location.

4 ACCEPT DEFEAT!
Riding down your up track because you can't find a gap in the cornice is common!

CUTTING CORNICE TO TEST SLOPE

EVALUATE RESULTS:
How good was the test?
Was the weight heavier than a rider's weight?
Did the cornice put pressure on the avy start zone?

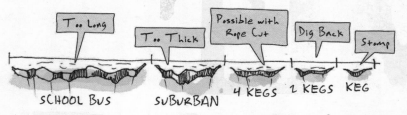

Too Long   Too Thick   Possible with Rope Cut   Dig Back   Stomp

SCHOOL BUS   SUBURBAN   4 KEGS   2 KEGS   KEG

CORNICE TUNNELING TO CREATE AN ENTRANCE ON A SLOPE GUARDED BY CORNICES

Cornice can't be tall or overhanging.

START DIGGING AT THE BACK
(belay recommended)

Less than 3 feet   3 feet or more

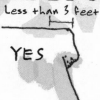

YES   NO

PRYING A CORNICE

1 PUT CORNICE CUTTER ON BELAY

2 CUT NOTCH WITH BOARD, SKI, SAW, OR SHOVEL FOR ROPE TO SIT IN

Be in tune with the state of the cornice.
It's possible to predict the "shed cycle" within a few days.

para cord with knots

If you know your range well, you should have a good step-in slope that you can approach safely from the back, something that has small, manageable cornices that you can cut and drop onto a face. A proper cornice drop done right will tell you more about the snow stability than a snowpit.

I generally start with smaller cornices first. It's important to evaluate if the weight of the cornice you're dropping will load the slope with more force than when you're actually riding it. In a perfect scenario you drop a car-sized cornice that free-falls a few feet, hits the slope with a *thump*, and rolls down the slope. If done right, this technique is more effective than a bomb, because as the big chunk rolls, it places continuous stress pressure down the entire slope.

An open mind, an embracing of the journey, a thirst for the unknown, and letting go of preconceived notions.

My first memory of letting a cornice loose was with Jim just after a five-day storm had cleared, and we were starting back at ground zero as far as knowing the snowpack. We spotted a steep, 50-yard-wide ramp with a convex roll that fanned into a wide, clean outrun. Former racer and Alaska speed demon Jeremy Nobis and I were talking about how we could probably cut the top of the slope and just straight run it to the flats if something broke off. Jim said he wanted to drop a part of the cornice to see what would happen. When the cornice landed, it released the whole slope. Nobis and I looked at each other in awe at the magnitude and speed of the avalanche. Watching something like that rocks your soul. So much power and destruction just a few feet away. Countless times after releasing slides with cornice drops, I've said: "I'm glad I wasn't in that."

Tricks for Finding Cornice Entries

Attach a hat, shirt, or similar item to a probe and stick it high into the air so someone from across the way can see where you are and direct you. This is mainly for when we are shooting, using radios, and have a cameraman on an opposing peak. But you can also do this with someone on an outcropping from the ridge, though it's trickier. Snowballs help here too. Every step, confirm you are in the right place. Going on belay with a spotter is also helpful. We will bring a rope out if we know we are trying to find tricky entries. The rope helps with small cornices but will do very little if you break a big cornice.

Cornice Lesson

TEMPLE BASIN, NEW ZEALAND, 1996

Spend enough time in the mountains and, unfortunately, you will have your own cornice story. My first cornice collapse came early. I was twenty-one, filming for TGR's second film, "Harvest." We were riding a "nutcracker" rope tow club field in New Zealand. Before setting off to like a 1,500-foot face, my brother Todd said: "Watch out for the cornices. The sun will be heating up the backs of them. Stay on rocks."

Two hours later, I found myself negotiating a couple-hundred-yard ridge to find my drop-in spot. I would go from one rock to the next, making big arcs away from the ridge in between outcroppings. Almost to my line, I did the same thing. I was tired, the next rock was 11 feet away. I was walking 6 to 8 feet back, halfway between the two rocks, when the cornice broke on my outside foot. The wind sucked me over the edge, and I floated through the air in disbelief for what felt like forever. When I hit, an avalanche immediately engulfed me. My life flashed in front of me. Literally. Like a movie on fast-forward.

"Time to deal, you got this!" I yelled to myself. I was able to stay upright and turn my feet downhill. I managed a slight view of the sky, prepared for potential cliffs, and tried to conserve energy while fighting to stay upright. As the slide slowed, I swam as hard as I could toward the surface. I was only buried to my waist, thanks to the fact that the outrun was clean and the debris fanned. I was dragged 1,500 feet in about fifteen seconds. The cornice fractured so far back because of the sun, and it was above an eight-foot-wide chute.

When I fell, my board was in my left hand. I had dropped it, and the track revealed that it had glided thousands of feet down the other side of the ridge. My ice axe had hit me in the head, bloodying my face, but otherwise I was fine. The hardest part may have been looking into my friends' faces when I reconnected with them an hour later. Pure horror, like they were addressing a ghost, and embarrassment that I had been so foolish yet so lucky. When something this dramatic happens, you have to

> Have protocols. They can save your ass when the unexpected happens. That's why I always try to take the safest path through the mountains regardless of how stable things seem.

own up to the mistakes that were made. Let them keep you up at night. They should leave scar tissue and make you sick to your stomach. My cornice lesson should have killed me but has actually saved my life a hundred times over. I've hiked to the top of mountains countless times only to turn around and ride the bootpack back down, because I could not find a safe way to find an entry on a corniced ridge.

Cornices Kill

Anyone who has spent significant time in the mountains has their own "cornice story." The moment when the world falls away in an elevator drop of wind drift and blindness. If lucky, you live to tell your mistake. The saddest cornice story I've heard happened not far from my house near Lake Tahoe. It breaks my heart to tell, but I hope it terrifies you enough to never walk near a blind ridge ever again.

Jamil Khan was a young phenom snowboarder who showed up on the East Coast contest scene in the mid-1990s with a big smile, a bag of tricks well beyond his age, and style for miles. He was one of the youngest tagged for the infamous Burton A team. At twenty-three, Jamil was out West and about to start filming for his first major movie part. Arriving at Tahoe's Donner Pass backcountry, the site of dozens of groundbreaking movies and hundreds of magazine photos, he set his sights on the closest feature from the parking lot and hiked the well-trodden bootpack to the flats just above the face. Twenty minutes from the car, Jamil walked out toward the edge to find his line. *Crack!* The cornice broke 10 *feet* back from the edge, and Jamil fell with the collapse and died from trauma.

Searching for Spines

You see spines all over every ski movie: a combination of enormous amounts of snow on slopes 50 degrees or steeper. Resembling a fluted shower curtain and requiring a unique set of circumstances to form, they are mostly found on glaciated north faces in the northern coastal ranges.

My love for riding spines developed in Haines, Alaska, during the early 2000s, and it was there that I learned spines required a whole different mindset. Getting into the mountains after a big storm is mentally and tactically hard. The conventional wisdom was to go to mellow runs, dig pits, and slowly step up to more serious terrain. This is great if you have prolonged high pressure, but you do not become the spine capital of the world with prolonged high-pressure systems and clear skies. Spines take otherworldly amounts of snow, wind, and the perfect moisture content to form. Ten-day storms that literally swallow 30-foot cliff bands are common.

"You are always in the right place, exactly at the right time, and you always have been." —Ethan Hawke

Some springs you could count the sunny days in Haines on one hand. To spend the day noodling 25-degree slopes and digging pits does not make for good movies. One day we were lapping the mellow lines, and I stared across the valley at a heavily fluted face showing signs of significant sluffing. Anyone who has seen a chart depicting avalanche frequency as it relates to steepness has seen that the likelihood of avalanches on slopes below 30 degrees is very low. What's usually missing on that same chart is that avalanches are equally as rare on slopes of 55 degrees or steeper, because they usually slide during or right after a storm. In most ranges, these slopes are irrelevant, because there are no slopes that steep that snow sticks to, so they aren't rideable.

Haines, however, is riddled with steep walls and spines that hold stable snow, despite the intense steepness. "What about that one," I said to our guide, Jim Conway, pointing to a section of 60-degree fluted face. "From an avy perspective, it's safe," he said. And just like that everything changed. Over the next few years, I developed a growing list of starter runs that were 55 degrees or steeper, on heavily fluted faces. Possibly the heaviest line I rode in Haines was called "Hotel Room." We were stuck hanging in our hotel rooms for five days of constant rain and snow.

Decoding Spines

Nature always makes sense once you see it. The hard part is decoding why. Take spines, for example. They are the most elusive snow feature in the mountains. Their beauty, complexity, and rareness have led to a spine obsession that has overtaken my snowboarding, ever since legends Noah Salasnek and Doug Coombs first rode Super Spines outside of Valdez. For years, searching for spines felt like an Easter egg hunt with no rhyme or reason, but I kept looking and eventually found a few eggs.

I learned the largest quantities of snow can be found in thicker sections of heavily glaciated mountain ranges that sit within 30 miles of salt water—this gives you a good starting point. Look for north-facing terrain in tightly stacked terrain on the leeward side of high peaks with high glaciers—there's a really good chance you'll find spines.

Then, miraculously, a short afternoon clearing opened up over a particularly craggy and blank section of the range.

Finding mid-elevation lines among huge peaks is hard, because the eyes are naturally drawn upward. With the help of the sun's rays streaming through the clouds, this mid-elevation spine wall glowed in the distance. We couldn't find a safe warm-up run, so Jeremy Nobis and I were dropped straight onto the peak via heli. The most difficult part of the spine game is figuring out where you are on the wall and managing your sluff. Nobis and I were fighting back nausea on the peak due to the blind rollover; dropping in felt like I was falling off the edge of the world. It is really hard to commit in these situations, to trust that you know exactly where you are on the mountain even though you can only see a few feet in front of you. Sluff management is critical. I ended up entering my exit spine, the only clean way off the face, too high and got flushed onto the apron below before regaining control. A big fall but no exposure.

The safest, most stable conditions line up in spring, in Alaska and elsewhere. For Tahoe, the magic happens in late March and April, the High Sierra in May, the Rockies in April and May, and Chamonix in June. Keeping your head in the game when the flowers start blooming in town can be hard. Your window to ride stable trophy lines can be quite small; knowing when the portal opens and closes is essential.

Harvesting Corn

Scoring perfect corn snow is an art form. What is the right amount of heat and sun? I generally go for max heat. Get the snow as soft as possible before it gets sticky. The unicorn of all snow conditions is catching corn as it is refreezing. Sun-softened snow with a touch of refreeze makes for a fast surface with a soft bottom. Corn needs clear, below-freezing nights, above-freezing days, and prolonged high pressure to form. This makes nailing corn especially sweet, because you get powder-type conditions long after there's actual powder. Good corn is every bit as fun as powder, hence the name "powder's ugly twin brother." All the brains without the sparkly good looks.

Getting the Most Out of Your Guides

When TGR started using guides for bigger missions into unknown territory, I realized we were tapping into an incredible resource. I got to spend long periods of time with an expert. It dawned on me that I should learn as much as possible from each guide I met. I made a point of soaking it all in, to examine every snowpit and technique and to establish a strong working and learning relationship with them. I've taken dozens of avy and first-aid courses, but this is how I've learned the most.

Your Guide Is God

When you go to established huts or cat or heli operations, you will be assigned a guide. Your guide is all-powerful. They hold the keys to the kingdom, and they will dictate where you ride and how aggressive your lines will be. Sometimes this setup can be really hard to deal with. Because of their inherent control, some guides can develop massive egos. Humility, following directions, making good judgments, and time are the only way to gain the guide's trust. If they tell you to be 2 feet from their track, be 2 feet from their track.

> What happens on a trip stays on the trip. On long expeditions, especially if the conditions are challenging, the mood can become tense and sometimes tempers flare. Don't let a tough trip end a friendship.

Twenty years ago, I was at a Rossignol photo shoot at a British Columbia cat operation that illustrates the perfect example of what *not* to do. The cat dropped us off at a high saddle with short, steep lines on either side. Two riders who had grown up in Chamonix and had never been guided before jumped out the back door and started racing up the ridge without talking to the guide first. He didn't realize they had left until they were a few hundred yards uphill. He shouted at them to come back down. A lot of yelling ensued. The French riders could not understand the problem. After three runs of constant battling, the guide had had enough. He put them in the cat, locked the door from the outside, and sent them back to the lodge, cursing, fists pounding the window as they crawled back down the mountain.

Get some friends together
and hire a guide to take you
into the mountains. Treat it
like a personal avy class. Ask
questions and soak up as much
info as you can.

Guides as Safety Managers

These days, guides have evolved more into safety managers, especially for filming. Filming foot-powered snowboarding in remote mountains is a thousand times more dangerous than with helis. It's not just the riders at risk. Getting a cameraman up an opposing ridge so they can get the shot requires travel through avalanche terrain or over glaciers. The guides oversee and direct all these details.

Guides dig pits and assess riding conditions. They usually make a general assessment, and the discussion continues from there. The guides position themselves to assist a rider if an avalanche cracks off. This is typically on the shoulder to the side of the line. For some guides this presents a problem, because then they do not get to ride, which is why I make a point to get everyone—including guides—riding once we figure out the snowpack.

When to use a guide. If I venture somewhere new where I have zero experience with the terrain and snowpack, I usually hire a local guide to show me around the first few days. I get up to speed on the season's snowpack history, and get a lay of the land regarding what the layers are doing, what might be suspect, and other insider knowledge that comes from being a local. This approach also works well in your home range—especially if you've been away, have a complex snowpack, and want to take a closer look and learn more. Get your riding partners together, hire a guide, and have them break down the snowpack and do a live avy course. If you have the means and you want a complex snowpack where you can tag good lines, guides are a huge asset. Pay attention and ask questions!

Picking the right guide. First off, do your research. The guide is a key decision for your trip. Talk with friends or others who have someone they recommend, see if the outfit has any online reviews, and speak to the head of the company and tell them what you're looking for in a guide. For years I've worked with Alaskan guide Jim Conway, who earned the nickname "Conserveway." He is very conservative, and that's why my brothers and I hired him. Jim's nickname later evolved into "Sarge" because of his military seriousness and tone. I've always viewed his disposition as a good thing. I've never needed any prodding to drop into serious lines. Seeing a steep face in good condition has me angling any way to ride it. Many times our heli guides would defer to us, thinking, *These guys are pro, I'm just going to sit back and watch, be there if something goes wrong.* But not Jim. He makes me think about what I was doing.

CHAPTER 6

Avalanche Safety

The most important question to ask yourself is, "What happens if this slope slides?" Be honest with your answer. Would you stake your life on your knowledge? Depending on the snowpack, this is what a lot of people do. When you evaluate terrain, going up or down, you must ask a bunch of questions: Where are my islands of safety? Will I get taken into a terrain trap? Will I go over cliffs, get pushed into a stand of trees, or get raked over rocks? How deep will the slab be? How much might it propagate? By looking at recent avalanche activity in the area, including reports on local sites or personal observations, you can get a really good understanding of what you are dealing with, and then you can start making some decisions.

I could show you dozens of shots of me dropping into a slope and kicking off a small, low-depth avalanche and riding with it. I only consider this small-slide scenario in clean, short terrain with good outruns, when I am only worried about the *new* snow, the top few inches, sliding and sluffing, without any real consequences if the slide does take me for a ride. I bring this up not to encourage you, but as an example that the answer to the question "What if it slides?" is not always death.

It's important to recognize that there's so much that we do not know about avalanche science. Add in the erratic and extreme weather patterns amplified by climate change, and we find ourselves in very unpredictable and unprecedented times. As the economist Morgan Housel wrote, "Things that have never happened before happen all of the time." Understanding the size of the dragon we're dancing with is a key part of decision-making, and being honest about the consequences is vital.

Snow Science and Terrain Selection

Experienced backcountry riders use snow science to analyze and help predict if layers of snow will stick together enough to allow them to walk up a slope and ride back down without triggering an avalanche. Depending on how much stress you put on the slope, and where you put that stress, those layers may or may not stay together. Unlike other sciences on which you stake your life without any thought—say, driving 75 miles per hour using cruise control or getting a valve inserted in your heart—snow science remains mysterious, ephemeral, and in its infancy. I wish this wasn't the case. I want the snow scientists and experts to figure it all out. I wish you could simply go to school, learn the science, apply it to your day, and be totally safe. At times, it can feel like the science is really well understood. You go out and make ten thousand right calls, and the snow does exactly what you think it will. But then *bam*! A lifetime of making the right calls is erased in an instant.

The mountains don't give a shit about science, how many avy classes you have taken, the number of pits you've dug, or how rad you got yesterday. The key to survival

"What we are doing is basically witchcraft. We will look back at this time ten, twenty years from now and shake our heads at how we evaluated the mountain and the risks we took." —Zahan Billimoria

Elyse Saugstad: Communication is Key

"The last few years things have started to change (wahoo!) in regards to being the only female in a group, and I find myself having the opportunity to work with more women (but never a female-only crew—it's more like one other woman in a group of six). With that in mind, I have spent most of my career being the sole female in a ski/snowboard crew. Like most athletes, over time my working relationships have positively evolved as my experience, knowledge, and confidence have grown in the mountains, and this in turn has helped gain respect from my peers. I think there are a few key factors that I have learned over time when working with men or women. First,

coming to the table prepared and ready to participate in decision-making, paying attention to avalanche and weather conditions, having thoughtful opinions, and being able to speak up have all been beneficial. Second, being mindful when I communicate that it's non-threatening, so I don't come off as judgmental or off-putting, but rather constructive. Unfortunately, women walk a finer line than men when it comes to communicating in our society; it's a bit of a double standard so to speak. Third, I have also found it's easier to communicate and achieve the group's goals by skiing with crews that have the same risk tolerance as myself."

Things to Do When There Is a Persistent Weak Layer or Deep Slab Instability

- » Ride the resort
- » Go pow surfing or meadow skipping (terrain under 30 degrees that is not connected to steeper terrain above)
- » Ride a different slope aspect (generally south-facing)
- » Clean the garage

is leaving a lot of room for mistakes. Your science and decision-making must embrace a large margin of error. Snow science is good but far from exact. And it's applied without guidelines or rules. Ask the best riders in the world about their approach, and maybe 60 percent will cross over in their answers. The science works, but it is not a go/no-go tool. It gives us some info but not enough to stake your life on.

Almost every day during February 2021, we heard of more avy deaths and wondered how this could be happening. Thirty-seven people died that season, one of the worst on record in the United States. Risk of avalanches was very high, and the avy centers were doing a fantastic job of warning people, spreading information about current conditions and issues, but people still triggered slides and many died. So what was missing from the equation? What choices did people make that didn't work out using the science?

For one, we had a widespread, deep, persistent weak layer throughout the western United States. A persistent weak layer, or deep slab instability, is when a layer of snow takes much longer to bond and stabilize than other layers. Weak layers are most commonly created by faceted snow, depth hoar, and surface hoar. A weak layer can often lie dormant under the snowpack for long periods of time, giving a false sense of stability. They are often hard to trigger but, once triggered, produce massive avalanches. Don Sharaf, an avalanche forecaster, guide, and instructor, summed it up in a course of his when he said, "I will trust that layer when it is in the river."

I have lost many friends and mentors to avalanches that have occurred on a persistent weak layer; I noted earlier my personal protocol to never travel to a snowpack with this issue, and this is why. If I hear that an area has a weak layer, I take it off the list for that year. This kind of instability is much rarer in a coastal snowpack, which is why so much of my snowboarding is done in coastal ranges. When we do have this issue in the Sierra, I avoid the aspect and elevation it is lingering on.

Nat Patridge at Exum likes to say, "Good terrain choice can erase poor decisions." I keep coming back to this point. You have more power over terrain selection and how you travel through the mountains than you do over the snow. We can't control how the snow reacts, but we can control terrain selection.

Assessing Slope Angle: 30 Degrees Is the Magic Number

If you ride interior ranges in Colorado or Utah, or parts of the Alps where deep, persistent weak layers linger throughout the year, or when your region has a weak layer that's not very predictable, slope angle is generally the *most* important factor to consider when selecting where to go. In order to do that, though, you have to be able to recognize slope steepness. There are many measurement and mapping tools that help assess slope angle. Even if you know the angle, however, situations exist when it's not clear how wide an avalanche zone will break or how far down the mountain it will travel. These problems present greater concerns, and they require much more conservative planning and goals.

In most cases, if the avy danger is higher than "moderate," choose slopes 30 degrees or less. Conversely, slopes 55 degrees or steeper are also very unlikely to slide, but other than in Alaska, few places have terrain this steep that is rideable. And,

> Things to do when avy danger changes the plans: rest day! Pow surf, ride resort, cross-country ski, gym workout, snowshoe, watch movies, shovel, hot tub, read, paint, play chess, play music, or visit friends.

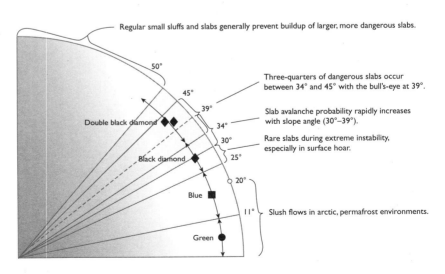

Avalanche activity relative to steepness (Source: Staying Alive in Avalanche Terrain*)*

even if it is, oftentimes the angle backs off, making the lower aprons of the slope prime angle for avalanches. A lot of research shows that the vast majority of avalanches happen on slopes that are between 34 to 45 degrees. If you are at all in doubt about a day's snow stability, keep it under 30 degrees. Unless there's extreme avy danger or horrific deep instability, staying below this slope angle will reduce the avy danger. To make sure, use a slope inclinometer to know exactly what you're dealing with. Use your phone for a quick, easy reading. Lay a ski pole or other flat edge on the slope. Place your phone with level view on the pole to get the slope angle. The difference between a 30-degree slope and a 34-degree slope can be fatal.

"Good terrain choice can erase poor decisions." —Nat Patridge

Understanding what's above you is critical in these scenarios. A Loveland Pass, Colorado, avalanche that killed five people in 2013 is a tragic example of friends skinning across only a 5-degree slope, but under a massive bowl a few thousand feet above and a mile away. Standing where they got caught, it is astonishing to realize that they kicked off an avalanche from such a seemingly safe distance. Season to season the weather is becoming more extreme with global warming and climate changes, creating unprecedented weak layers. This causes avalanches in places that previously seemed impossible. Multiple fatalities in the 2020–2021 season occurred on low-angle terrain hit by avalanches set off from far below and seemingly out of reach.

Meadow Skipping

I live to ride big, steep lines, but they're not the only game in town. When the avy danger spikes, I focus on mellow terrain. We call it meadow skipping. With the right equipment, rolling through low-angle meadows can be super fun. I pow surf my neighborhood's 25-degree slopes a lot. Pow surfing is done on a board without bindings that is often shorter, wider, and built to float really well in low-angle powder. Embrace what you can work with while focusing on staying safe and staying alive. A big part of being a complete rider is welcoming all forms of recreating and knowing the appropriate gear for the conditions. Learn to love everything the weather and mountains throw at you, get the most out of it, and be okay with down days and easy sliding in the meadows.

Have a backcountry setup that makes meadow skipping fun, like wide, fast-gliding skis or a board that floats really well in soft snow.

On a recent cycle with a deep, persistent weak layer, my friends and I simply took north-facing steep terrain completely off the table for over a month. This measure is very rare in the Sierra, and even though there had not been a ton of avy activity, there were a handful of natural avalanches breaking large and wide that would have meant certain death. A classic case of the "spooky moderate" rating more commonly found in the interior ranges. We traveled to our normal zones, near these perfect, unridden steep faces glistening in the sun, but we hardly even looked at them. I did not dig a single snowpit during this cycle. It might have talked me into riding something that could have killed me. To stake my life on a single pit is something I don't mess with, especially when dealing with weak layers such as buried facets and depth hoar.

> Listen to your gut: it is the best and last line of defense. "It just doesn't feel right" is reason enough to turn around.

One of the really cool things about dangerous avy cycles is that they force you to be creative. You start poking around in safe zones that you never realized offered great, unique terrain. This past season I rode a lot of boot-top pow on top of a firmer surface, which made for very fast riding, allowing me to carry speed through low-angle old-growth forests throughout Tahoe, aspects and places I'd never ridden because I'm usually focused on the steeps.

Before You Ride: Develop Protocols

Again, *only* using snow science—a hasty pit, a complete avy pit analysis, or an extended column test—to make a decision on whether to ski a slope can lead to big mistakes. You must understand that pits and tests are only a small part of your decision-making. If you think you can outsmart an unstable snowpack, you're going to end up in a slide someday. Statistically, educated and experienced riders have a higher risk of being caught in an avalanche than beginners. There are no experts or avy masters who have it all figured out. People who think they are experts are, too often, the ones found dead in an avalanche.

It's much better to develop a basic system of protocols, one that uses a mix of snow science; a daily dose of observations; discussions about terrain selection before, during, and after; and the ability to change plans and say no at any time. Make it a goal to know what is happening to the snowpack throughout the season, what's making things dangerous, what's making things safe. Know when and how the snowpack is changing over the months. Talk to riders as much as you can to find out about backcountry conditions and info, and share your knowledge. Look at what is sliding at your local resort. Doing all of these things, incorporating them as much

Five Safety Protocols

1. Always bring your beacon, shovel, probe, and brain.
2. Know the snowpack history.
3. Know your terrain.
4. Know your partners.
5. Have a rescue plan.

as you can into your lifestyle, provides continuous data for good decision-making. You'll be able to anticipate what might likely happen based on what you know.

Consume Avy Info

Read the local avy and weather report every day to understand what has happened, what is happening, and what might happen. Find and use your local avalanche center's resources; its website and social media should always be open on your computer during winter. These centers post updated reports and warnings for the local snowpack. Not only can you learn the base level of risk but also the history of the snowpack, how it's changing, recent events, and what to watch out for. Learning and understanding the report is vital for backcountry travel.

Start with the daily advisory for where you ride. I also keep an eye on areas I think I may be traveling to later in the season. Keep it simple. Read the daily report, and if there are any incidents or avalanche activities, get as much info on the situation as possible. Seek out and really look at photos of avy activity. For me, a picture of a recent slide is much more informative than a written report, but read the descriptions too. Try to understand what's happening with the snowpack and how that affects your plans and risk assessment. If I am really concerned, I'll view snowpit videos. Watching video of a pro forecaster go through snowpits is very helpful and takes only a few minutes. Follow guides and riders who are out there every day via their websites, blogs, or social media. Every year, amazing content is produced on every medium that breaks down avy incidents or highlights new concepts.

Cross Off Terrain—*Before* You Hit the Mountain

Mountain guide Zahan Billimoria makes his own avalanche compass rose, marking what elevation and aspect all reported slides occurred on. It is amazing to see the consistency of avalanche activity. This makes it obvious what aspects should be avoided. I'd love to see avy centers feature this. I don't make a compass rose, but I do look for consistency of aspect and elevation that avalanches are occurring at. When I see that consistency, I cross it off the list of my riding options before I set foot into the mountains: "No NE aspect between 7,000 and 8,000 feet," for example. Weirdly, it's often the terrain that I've just crossed off that I'm most drawn to because it's glowing in the sun and looking prime. Make sure you follow your protocols and listen to your gut.

The Aftermath

Train every year with purpose—it may save your friend's life. A 200-foot convex roll with a horizontal crown across the entire face and only a volleyball court—sized debris field was the site of one of the closest calls I've ever had in the mountains. So many little things needed to line up perfectly to experience the first complete burial incident in my twenty-five years of backcountry riding. Ironically, this incident happened during our crew's annual get-together to do rescue scenarios, bone up on CPR and first aid, and go over things learned during the past year.

We were riding featured, broken terrain (no big, connected flat slopes), with the biggest convex roll only 200 feet long and with a fairly clean out-run. There had been no reported avalanches in the Tahoe area recently. A nearby bowl showed approximately thirty to forty tracks laid down the day before. A small, unreported natural avalanche that had appeared toward the end of the last storm was not seen until a day later. We skinned from a hut to the type of terrain I personally do most of my riding in, what I call broken terrain. Lots of ridges, spines, open panels, waves, rock formations, cliffs, and small chutes. The slope angle ranged from 45-degree steep pitches to small, almost flat benches with interspersed trees. Basically, the opposite of a big, open bowl with nowhere to hide if the slope slides. Most important, there was a clean outrun, so if any part of the slope did slide and someone was caught, they would not hurtle over a big cliff, be dragged over sloping rocks or into a stand of trees, or get pushed into a gully where deep debris could bury them.

To be clear, the mountain face we rode was avalanche terrain, but it was survivable avalanche terrain. Especially since we were dealing with only about a foot of new snow. We skinned up a safe route, linking together islands of safety. Nothing moved. No signs at all. Eight riders had ridden the face before the avalanche. Riding one at a time, slashing waves, hitting cliffs, popping rollers with no signs of avy activity. No snowpack settling at all, no fractures, slabs, or any other obvious signs of weakness in the snowpack.

Jones Snowboards filmer Greg Weaver dropped into the slope, slashed some ridges, glided across a flat spot, and came charging down the bottom third of the face. It was definitely the biggest connected slope on the face, and on each turn he sunk deep into the snowpack, throwing spray like a small bomb going off, especially because he was a big guy and was carrying a big pack. At the bottom of the slope he made a hard turn on a small rollover, triggering the whole slope to spiderweb and crumble all at once. He was turning right, the wrong direction, pointing toward a rock spire at the bottom of the slope when he realized he had started the avalanche. If he had been facing left, he could have pointed it into the flats and would have most likely ridden out of it.

Because he had to slow down as he headed toward the rock spire, the slide caught him as he finished making an abrupt turn. It pushed him downward headfirst, and his pack pinned him. Greg slid roughly 100 feet and then came to a stop, face forward, under the snow, with his arms behind him. If this was a bigger face, or if it went into a stand of trees, it would have been a much worse outcome. If he had been carried feet first, going downhill in a white-water rapid position, he most likely would have been able to sit up and have his head or hand out of the snow. I've taken many rides much longer than Greg's with much more snow, tumbling but correcting my position before the slide stopped and either riding out of it or only being buried up to my waist. Greg's ride was so short there was no chance for him to correct himself. He ended up in the deepest part of a debris pile, deep enough to bury him. The fracture was roughly 20 feet wide and 60 feet long, and the debris was roughly 3 feet deep in its deepest spot. The debris was half the depth a few feet on either side of him.

Andrew Miller came down from the top of the slope to start a beacon search, while Nick Russell, Harry Kearney, Marissa Krawczak, and Jimmy Goodman came from the bottom. They were already in touring mode, which allowed them to cover the 100 vertical feet very

fast and to start a beacon search immediately. Nick's beacon found Greg's transceiver signal right away, and Nick ran toward him. Harry was behind Nick by a few feet; he knew Nick was good with a beacon, so he started getting out his probe. He reached Nick just as the numbers on his beacon were getting low and handed him the probe. Nick hit a successful probe strike on his third attempt. Jimmy, Andrew, and Marissa had started getting out their shovels on their way to the scene and began to dig.

They hit Greg's backpack first. He was facing downhill and his head was buried deepest. His feet were maybe a foot under the snow, while his head was roughly three to four feet down. Greg looked like he had dived into a pool headfirst and the water had frozen around him and turned to snow. He was conscious when they got to him, but he said he had been in and out. It took less than four minutes to shovel away the snow so Greg could breathe.

The Aftermath Analysis

As the story told in "The Aftermath" so thoroughly illustrates, you never know when you're going to have to put your training into real use. We were lucky that day, but we'd also set ourselves up to be lucky. And as important as practicing searching and shoveling are, it's also critical to review how things went after the fact.

What we did right

» We had one person on the slope at a time with other riders in the right spots to stay safe and to get to Greg fast.

» The rescue highlights how important choosing partners is—we all need to be on the same page, ready to go, ready to save someone.

» Having people in uphill mode was key to getting Greg out. This step was unusual but an interesting takeaway. The only reason we were in this situation is we had a big crew. Greg was the ninth person down the slope. The snow was epic and our plan was to session the 600-foot face. As each rider finished their line, they switched over and headed back up the slope. I was the eighth rider down the slope and decided to take it one more bench down because there were so many people in the area. I wanted to naturally space out the crew so we were not all getting to the top at the same time.

What we did wrong

» Although Greg could see three-quarters of the face; he did not know the terrain well. The plan was for him to figure-eight my track, but he got excited and veered off to a different area.

» We let Greg ride a convex roll with a heavy pack on. It was the most complex line on the face. There were dozens of fun ridges and waves to ride that, if we had recommended them, Greg would have happily ridden.

> If riding with a heavy pack, pick mellower lines and dial back the charging.

» Greg and his gear combined weighed in at over 250 pounds. He hit the perfect spot on the slope when he landed with a ton of force. I do not think a rider moving fast and light over the convex roll would have started the slide. Forrest rode to the rider's left of the roll without incident. Over the next couple days, we rode similar, small rolls without incident.

» Once Greg was in the slide, his heavy pack made it hard for him to make a quick escape or swimming moves. Once he was in the slide, the pack pinned him face forward and downhill.

Takeaways

After the avalanche, instructor Nick Bliss and I evaluated the snow, looking closely at the layer it slid on. We dug pits looking around for the weak layer in different areas on the slope. The only reason I could find the weak layer was because I knew where it was. The pit wall looked perfectly smooth and my hand hardness test showed nothing. With a microscope we could see signs of decomposing surface hoar. But it was minimal at best. I've stood in hundreds of pits and seen more obvious weak layers dozens of times and still ridden terrain much bigger and more serious than this.

The Sierra Avalanche Center forecasters came out the day after to evaluate the slide and reached no conclusive results. They found traces of surface hoar in spots and graupel in others, but their pits were unreactive and inconsistent. After reviewing the snowpit, we continued to ride the zone, with the same protocols we followed on the first run. Over two days we probably put a total of fifty tracks in the area without further incident. There were no avalanches reported on that layer the rest of the season.

Part of me wishes the snowpit had shown obvious weaknesses, that I could chalk the incident up to a simple oversight. We had had no prolonged cold spells. I'd been in the range every day leading up to this, riding this aspect, and hadn't

Practice! How to Do Your Own Training

It's important to continue your education outside of classes. Actually practice beacon work and strategic shoveling technique as much as possible. Most people don't. Do this one thing: At the beginning of the season, spend half a day doing mock searching, probing, and digging scenarios. Make sure you practice with people you ride with. The systems you develop in your small group may save your life someday. It may sound like a lot of work, but practicing this at the start of the season helps lower risk and increase fun.

1. **Get a group of your friends.** Split into groups of two to five. I like to go to a resort and traverse to a zone that sees little traffic. Stop in at the patrol shack and let them know you are training.
2. **Treat it like a normal day.** No pregame talks or rescue preparations. Someone goes down and buries a beacon. While waiting, do not talk about the rescue, who will do what, etc.
3. **Make it as real as possible.** Someone yells, "Avalanche!" "Holy shit! Johnny's buried!" Train with purpose.
4. **Bury the beacon at least a few feet down.** This is really important. It's one thing to do a search and get a probe strike, it's another to actually dig your friend out. Studies of fatalities show the beacon search and probe strike are generally quick. It's the digging that takes the majority of the time and effort.
5. **Repeat the drill three to six times.** Once the beacon is found, the person who buried it will pretend they are hurt. Do at least one practice situation that requires stabilizing and moving the person.
6. **Practice strategic shoveling.** Not every drill has to be a deep burial, but I like to dig to the base of the probe a few feet down. Early season it can be hard to find deep spots. Search for wind drifts and give it all you have. In general digging five feet down with five people takes five minutes, which is very sobering.

seen any surface hoar. This was the first time buried surface hoar was mentioned in the avy report all year. It had formed during a three- to four-hour break in the storm that happened in the middle of the night. Knowing this, I would have possibly told Greg to avoid the convex roll, but he was supposed to stay on my line, which avoided it. I had very little experience with Greg in the mountains up to that point. I remember watching him drop in and being surprised at how hard he was charging, considering how heavy his pack was. His line was one of the most aggressive of the trip. I love amping cameramen, but the pack weight changes everything. Looking back at my twenty years of filming, the number of avalanches cameramen have been in is greater than that of riders. I never realized that until Greg's slide. There's always risk, no matter what you think is happening. It may be very large, or very small, but you must always be prepared for the risk to become reality.

The Five Red Flags (and One More)

"It's a good day to forget your boots," I jokingly say after big storms. So many times I have rushed out as soon as a storm has cleared, only to assess the day, dig a snowpit, and become terrified of the avalanche situation. I should've just stayed home. Alaskan guide Jim Conway introduced me to the Five Red Flags. I now list them on my poles, jackets, packs—everywhere—because I can trace most of the mistakes I've made back to not respecting or paying attention to these red flags. They are visual clues that point to potential avalanche danger. Although they won't help identify a consistent weak layer, I use these simple observation techniques more than anything else to judge possible avalanche conditions.

It starts from the second I wake up. When I look out the window on a powder day, I see my

The Five Red Flags + One More

- ☐ New snow
- ☐ Signs of recent avalanches
- ☐ Collapsing or cracking in the snowpack
- ☐ Rapid rise in temperature
- ☐ Strong winds: blowing and drifting snow
- ☐ Terrain selection

first red flag: new snow. If I see the trees outside sway in the wind, I now have two red flags: new snow and wind-transported snow. Seeing recent avalanche activity on the side of the road driving to the trailhead: three red flags. Watching cracks shoot off from my tips while skinning up or small slabs peel off as I bootpack: four. And any time the weather forecast shows a big temp change during the day, that's a fifth flag. Often, even before I get to the trailhead, I use the red flags to help make decisions

Rapid Heating in the Selkirks

THE SELKIRKS, FEBRUARY 24, 2020

Rapid heating is pretty obvious. It's the subtle increase in temps that can catch you off-guard. On my seventh day of touring in the Selkirks with ski guide Ruedi Beglinger, we were getting after and riding serious terrain. Halfway up our second run of the day, Ruedi became alarmed. The sun was not out and we were not overheating, but for the first time in two weeks the temps increased a few degrees. Daily highs had been around 25 degrees F. This afternoon it maybe spiked to 28 degrees in a short period. Ruedi felt it and started climbing on steep rolls above the skin track. At first the surface was just cracking. He got on the radio and warned all his guides. Within twenty minutes the cracks turned into car-sized slabs.

"We are done for the day," he radioed. Next he called Joe Vosburgh, a heli guide in the same range, on his sat phone to see if Joe was dealing with the same thing. "We just kicked off an avalanche," Joe said. "We're pulling the plug." Two to three degrees of temperature change took what had been a bomber snowpack for the past few weeks and made it really dangerous within one hour.

as to where I can safely go that day (or to not ride at all). As the red flags add up, my terrain plans continue to change. Digging a snowpit to analyze the snowpack is valuable, but taking note of red flags takes no time and provides tons of info, usually enough to make a decision.

New Snow

During or within twenty-four hours of a storm, 90 percent of avalanches happen. Give new storm snow the utmost respect and assume high to extreme avy danger during this window. Follow this rule, and you will significantly reduce your risk of getting caught in an avalanche. New snow is the only red flag I do not have a really close call for, because I treat it so seriously. We all love powder, but sometimes it's okay to wait to ride the steeps. With new snow and increased avy danger, I ride heavily treed runs, smaller slopes, broken terrain, clean outruns, and slopes 30 degrees or less.

Signs of Recent Avalanches

If you see signs of recent, natural avalanches—such as crown lines (where the snow has broken away from the slope), avy debris, broken trees, or sluffs—this means avalanches are happening, and the avy danger should be taken very seriously. Use extra caution if the natural avalanches have occurred at a similar elevation, on the same aspect, or at the same slope angle as the slope you want to ride. I'd rather have a single photo of a recent avalanche than five pages of snow science that talks about the potential weakness in the snowpack. Nature is consistent. If you scan an entire range after a big storm cycle that produces a lot of avalanches, it becomes obvious which slopes to avoid. The consistency of elevation, aspect, slope angle, and terrain type stares you in the face. Huge red flag.

Ski areas are also really good places to see how the new snow is sticking. Every morning that it snows, resorts dispatch dozens of patrollers armed with bombs to test every starting zone at the resort. What they don't hit with a bomb they ski cut. A bomb is not the same as a human trigger, but I learn a lot from what slides or doesn't at resorts. If I see massive, large propagating slabs triggered by bombs, I'm concerned about the backcountry. You have to factor in the rider compaction and previous control work, and the fact that the snow has fallen on tracks. Because of this, I do not gain much confidence at a resort if nothing slides. But a resort littered with huge slides, usually on a similar aspect and terrain type and at a similar elevation, provides valuable information.

Collapsing or Cracking in Snowpack

If you hear *whumphing* sounds or feel the slope settle or collapse under your feet or when skinning, this is a sign of unstable layers in the snowpack. Cracks may shoot out from your skis or board as you skin or ride—more signs of dangerous layers. If you have never heard the sound of a slope collapsing, it's terrifying. On big settlements it can sound like an explosion going off. This is the sound of layers in the snowpack failing, breaking, and collapsing, and an entire slope settling into a new position. Thankfully, the only time I've heard this is on low-angle terrain. If you hear and feel this settlement, and you're in avalanche terrain, pull your airbag and get ready for a serious ride.

Cracking is more common with wind slabs on the surface. This is generally new snow, and the cracks shoot out ahead as you move, skinning or riding on steep slopes. Skinning up is a great way to evaluate a slope, assuming it's not in a big avalanche path. Sometimes, if the snow is really sensitive, you'll see cracking between or off the tips of your skis or board. I'll purposefully seek out small convex rolls on my way up and jump on the slope. Putting a kick turn on a steep roll isolates the slope. If a beach towel– or picnic table–sized slab breaks off, I can expect a much bigger slope with similar characteristics to do the same.

Rapid Rise in Temperature

No matter the starting temperature, any rapid warm-up is dangerous, because the snowpack does not have time to adjust to the temperature change. Take extra precautions on the first warm day after a storm cycle.

Strong Winds: Blowing and Drifting Snow

If the wind is strong enough to transport snow, the avalanche conditions can change from stable to dangerous without any new snow. Watch for blowing snow on high ridges and beware the leeward sides and wind-loaded pockets at the top of faces and chutes. It seems so obvious, but this sign is the sneakiest red flag of all. The new pockets of wind-blown snow can be hard to identify and avoid, as they aren't necessarily consistent. These wind slabs may be isolated and relatively small, but they can start at the top of exposed lines or break off, run, and set off much larger slides below. If it blows like crazy and scours one side, loading the other, it is pretty obvious there is a wind slab. It's the subtle slabs formed from less noticeable ridge-top winds that can catch you off guard.

Terrain Selection

This brings up the sixth (bonus) red flag, which backcountry riders often debate over including. Terrain selection means choosing where the line takes you, and calculating how exposed you are if you fall or an avy sets off. Are you taken into a deep gully, flushed off a cliff, pushed through rocks, into trees, or into a crevasse? It's not usually included as a classic red flag, because terrain is not snow related. But remember, clean terrain can erase bad decisions. Dirty terrain can magnify simple mistakes. It's not by simple luck that I didn't die or get hurt in the slides I've experienced. Having the snow break apart and getting ripped off your feet on the side of a mountain is one of the most humbling experiences you can ever have—if you have built in the necessary margin for error.

Slab Management

Not all slabs are created equal. The depth and shape of the crown line are critical when deciding what slopes can be mitigated with slope cuts, islands of safety, etc. Beware of slabs that shoot up hill and across different aspects.

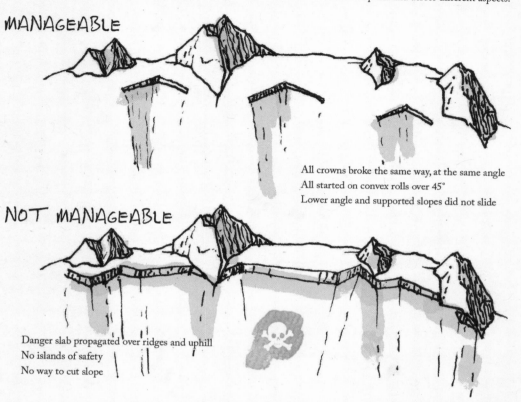

MANAGEABLE

All crowns broke the same way, at the same angle
All started on convex rolls over 45°
Lower angle and supported slopes did not slide

NOT MANAGEABLE

Danger slab propagated over ridges and uphill
No islands of safety
No way to cut slope

MANAGEABLE

	CROWN LINE	
LESS THAN 40 CM	SLAB DEPTH	MORE THAN 40 CM
40° PLUS	SLOPE ANGLE	LESS THAN 40°
TOP OF SLOPE CONVEX ROLLS	STARTING ZONES	APRONS, MID-SLOPE SUPPORTED SLOPES TREE AREAS
NO	PROPAGATION	YES

Defending the Line: Lessons from IPRW

Jim Conway was the perfect person to keep me, my brothers, and the Teton Gravity Research (TGR) crew in check and add structure and seriousness to our work. Under Jim's guidance we established a consistent protocol for mountain travel, and he established a TGR training seminar called the International Pro Riders Workshop (IPRW). Every year we get together to practice rescue scenarios, do first-aid training, and learn the latest science from the avy community. The highlight for me during IPRW is always the "defend your line." We review any mistakes or close calls we've had that year in the mountains. It can be really heavy and intense at times, but studying close calls and having the humility to talk about mistakes is critical to learning. After the debrief we always discuss whether we need to adjust our protocols.

If you do not provide room for error, even a small slide can have fatal consequences. When moving through terrain, you must be absolutely certain that the risk of an avalanche is as close to zero as possible. Especially if you are hiking up the slope.

Slabs and buried deep layers. Choosing manageable terrain while dealing with deep instability in the snowpack, such as a persistent weak layer buried down deep, is critical. In these scenarios, the Five Red Flags won't help you, as they're only signs of how new snow is bonding to the existing snowpack or changing. And not all slabs are created equal. We see the top layers, created by wind from a storm, and we have others, not so apparent, lurking below. Think of yourself as a slab detective. Slab avalanches are what kill most people in the mountains. On a bad avy cycle, slabs are like having a serial killer on the loose. Studying previous crime scenes is critical for stopping future crimes from happening. We need to know everything we can about slabs. When I know there's a buried bad layer, I spend much more time on the avy center's website to learn as much as possible about the potential killer.

I look for photos. If people are dying, it's generally not from your classic convex roll with those nice triangular slabs breaking at the obvious spot. Deeper, large propagating slabs usually break in open terrain, and the crown line shoots horizontally, uphill, or wraps around ridges. Very large sections of mountain can release. With buried surface hoar and deep, persistent weak layers, you can have avalanches where the entire slope, top to bottom, breaks at the same time. It's like the whole mountain collapses and fails at once. I have no appetite for this type of slab. Trying to figure out a safe way to ride when deep slab conditions persist is a fool's game. The only way to navigate these conditions is avoidance. Give whatever aspect and elevation these slabs are happening on a very wide berth.

Using Avy Forecasts and Ratings

In addition to the basic red flags, use your local avy center to help make decisions about when and where to ride. Today we are fortunate to have highly skilled teams of avy scientists digging pits and reporting observations and forecasts daily. It wasn't always this way. You had to really pay attention and know what was happening day to day, storm to storm, and month to month over a season to have any clue about the snowpack's risk. Now, avy forecasters and the North American Public Avalanche Danger Scale help people understand current avalanche risk via a rating system: extreme, high, considerable, moderate, low. These categories serve as a very basic guide for the chances of causing an avalanche. The rating is one factor I use to assess where, when, and if I want to venture outside the resort or my backyard—and there's much to add to each category to help you understand them better.

Low

I like "low." Very few worries. Solid snowpack without any lurking dangers. Late afternoon, springlike wet slides are the main avalanche risk with this rating. This is the rating I prefer when stepping up for serious lines on big mountains, what I call peak-bagging conditions. If you are new to the backcountry, this is a good time to start exploring. Most likely it will be springtime or after a big high-pressure system.

"Spooky Moderate"

I hate the "moderate" rating. You won't find a "spooky" category in any avy report, but despite seeming "normal," a moderate rating can actually be the most dangerous rating if there's a stubborn, persistent weak layer hidden in the snowpack. When you're dealing with a bad layer or slab, "spooky moderate" means it's unlikely to slide, but if it does, the slide could be very significant. The key to reading the moderate rating is to understand the difference between "likelihood of triggering" and "size." A true moderate rating means the likelihood of triggering a slide is fairly low and the size, small. There is definitely some risk, but nothing too serious unless you get taken into a terrain trap (such as in trees or over a cliff). However, if the size is large or historic, it may be massive, even if "moderate."

This rating often kills experts (Craig Kelly and Steve Romeo, for example). I treat "spooky moderate" as "considerable" or even "high," unless the weak layer is not that deep, and I'm not worried about large propagating slides. If there's a persistent weak layer lurking, I expect all convex rolls and anything that's 35 to 45 degrees to slide; however, it will probably take a cornice falling on the slope or a rider hitting the perfect spot in the heat of the day to trigger. Unlikely, but catastrophic if it happens.

Chances are the range will be pretty firm, making ice your biggest hazard. With the right timing, you can ride sun-softened corn snow.

Moderate

A "moderate" rating indicates no buried weak layers. The hazard usually sits only in the top 1 to 2 feet. These are movie-making conditions, where there's powder and it's relatively predictable. There may be smaller avalanches, but they're typically upper snowpack, discrete wind slab pockets, or point-release scenarios: obvious convex rolls, weak storm bonding and top layer, or big warm-up with sun and UV glare. Sounds pretty perfect, but this is the rating that kills the most experts, so don't drop your guard just because the danger is "moderate."

Considerable

"Considerable" is serious. People most often die when the rating is "considerable." If you choose to ride, be very cautious and hyperaware. Choose low-angle terrain without terrain traps that can be navigated easily without exposure to large slopes above. I tread very lightly in this rating. If a slab is deeper than 2 feet or if there are large propagating slabs, those factors usually automatically change this rating to "high" for me. When the forecast is "considerable," planning a safe ascent route is essential, as you're often climbing through the same terrain you'll ride down. On the descent, I look for slopes with lots of islands of safety, meaning if an area does slide, I can reach a safe area, out of the slide path. I stay away from big bowls and faces. I expect everything over 35 degrees to slide.

If the weak layer is not very deep (less than a foot), and the slabs react on steep rollovers and are triangle-shaped and not propagating, then with the right terrain selection I may still ride. In this scenario, I look for steep, short terrain that is easy

North American Public Avalanche Danger Scale
Avalanche danger is determined by the likelihood, size and distribution of avalanches.

Danger Level		Travel Advice
5 Extreme	4 5	Avoid all avalanche terrain.
4 High	4 5	Very dangerous avalanche conditions. Travel in avalanche terrain not recommended.
3 Considerable	3	Dangerous avalanche conditions. Careful snowpack evaluation, cautious route-finding and conservative decision-making essential.
2 Moderate	2	Heightened avalanche conditions on specific terrain features. Evaluate snow and terrain carefully; identify features of concern.
1 Low	1	Generally safe avalanche conditions. Watch for unstable snow on isolated terrain features.
No Rating		Watch for signs of unstable snow such as recent avalanches, cracking in the snow, and audible collapsing. Avoid traveling on or under similar slopes.

Safe backcountry travel requires training and experience. You control your own risk by choosing where, when and how you travel.

Going Big

Success favors the best prepared, and the biggest projects usually get ticked during the spring. Spend the winter season skiing and climbing as much as you can day after day; those distant peaks come into play in spring. Add in more daylight, a simpler snowpack, and strength, and it is no surprise that the tail end of the season is when the big lines get ridden. My risk tolerance is much lower in early winter because my main goal every year is to be healthy and fit for the spring "sending season."

to cut, has good islands of safety, and, most important, offers really clear outruns. Having good "step-in" zones where you can start small and work your way up to bigger terrain is key in these conditions.

High or Extreme

With a "high" or "extreme" rating, I'm not worried, because I'm most likely pow surfing my neighborhood hill or riding at the resort. I might sometimes tour in low-angle backcountry terrain that is unexposed to any avalanche slopes and that I know very well. "High" avy day tours are more like going cross-country skiing than snowboarding, which is why I usually stick with no-risk terrain on those days.

Rating Bumps

The snowpack is always guilty until proven innocent. Picking clean lines and avoiding terrain traps and secondary exposure is always the name of the game, no matter what the report says. In general, a few things increase a rating for me: persistent weak layers, depth of slab, and terrain traps.

Persistent weak layers. A major red flag on an avy report. There is a layer deep within the pack that is not bonding with the snow above or below. It's like a collection of ball bearings, and everything on top can slide on it. In some cases, this bad layer never completely goes away. Or it may lie dormant for weeks at a time, but,

An Unstable Snowpack
Spiderwebs around Me

ALASKA'S FAIRWEATHER RANGE, APRIL 2009

Twenty days into a camping mission in Alaska's Fairweather Range, I gained serious respect for the strong winds red flag. We were a few days into high pressure and had gained confidence in the snowpack. So much so, I was hiking a face above camp with my Petran, a binding-less board from Turkey that they have been riding for 450 years. The slope Ryland Bell and I were riding was on a similar aspect we'd been on for days without any movement. We had absolutely no reason to think this stability had changed. Camping below your lines allows you to feel every breath of wind and see every change. Maybe it was the large snow walls surrounding our tents from the absurd amounts of snow that had fallen on us that kept us from hearing it, or that we were somehow sheltered from it, but walking out of camp that morning there was no sign of wind texture on the snow or flagging on the ridges.

Three-quarters of the way up the slope, as I was approaching a convex roll, I felt a slight density change in the snow. The perfect silky pow became a little stiffer, but not so much that I didn't think I could ride it on my binding-less board. Maybe it was because I was on a slope I'd climbed multiple times before, but this slight change in snow did not set off any alarms. There was no loud crack or settlement as the slope spiderwebbed around me, swept me off my feet, and flushed me down the entire slope in an instant. As the slide slowed to a stop, and it was clear I would be on top, my focus shifted to Ryland, who was below me when the slide started. When the dust settled, he was 100 feet below me, also on top of the snow.

I'll never know if fifteen years later I would have picked up that density change. We did see slight signs of wind on the higher peaks but only through binoculars. Wind on high ridges is pretty common. Big wind events, where you see huge flagging snow flying off the ridges, forming a flag or mo-

hawk above the peaks, are an obvious sign things have changed in the snowpack and you need to go back to ground zero in your evaluation. But you also have to watch out for more subtle situations where you're in the middle of a high-pressure system, gradually progressing your way into more serious terrain as you gain confidence in the snowpack, only to have some wind blow for a few hours while you are sleeping and form small wind slabs, changing the snow from stable to dangerous. This exemplifies the complexity of the game we're playing. These subtle wind events freak me out. Twice I've been flushed off a mountain due to this scenario. These were small slides that, when I was riding, were easy to navigate out of, with planned, clean outruns. But they're serious if you are climbing the face and it breaks under you.

if triggered in the perfect spot, it can result in a massive avalanche. There's no way to game the system and ride in these conditions safely, unless you stay very low-angle.

Depth of slab. Avy danger ratings are based on the likelihood of an avalanche happening, but you must also take into account the depth of a slab. There's a huge difference between a 6-inch-thick slab and a 3-foot-thick slab. The difference in the amount of snow is astronomical. A very small avalanche, half a basketball court, is very serious when it is a 3-foot slab or deeper. When the size of the slab is deeper than 1 foot, I generally bump the rating up a notch. High = extreme, considerable = high, moderate = considerable. "Low" always stays low, unless the entire range is a sheet of ice and temps stay very cold. Then your risk is sliding on ice, not avalanches.

Terrain traps. Before you drop in, it's vital to assess the terrain below. What will happen if you set off an avalanche, even a small slide? Will you hit trees? Go over a cliff? Slide into a narrow ravine and have all the snow bury you? Fall into a lake or creek? It doesn't take a very large slide to have huge consequences. Many of my friends have triggered very small slides that took them into rocky cliffs or off big drops, resulting in serious injuries and changing their lives forever.

Snowpits: A Form of Witchcraft or Bomber Science?

The French scoff at them, the Canadians are obsessed with them, and in the United States it is somewhere in between, depending on the person and their home range. There are times I've staked my life on snowpits, and there are many times when I've

Steve's Slide

CHUGACH MOUNTAINS, EARLY MAY, 1998

It was not supposed to be clear that morning. Rounding up the crew was a fire drill. Or more of a search to find which hotel room people had fallen into in the wee hours of the morning. It was early May, and we were waiting out a solid storm in hopes of late-season high pressure so we could ride the high north-facing lines in the Chugach Mountains that only get light this time of year. Most heli ops had closed for the season, so we were flying with a new operation, a new guide and pilot, and out of a new location.

Before flying out, we were concerned with the recent snow. It had dumped 2 feet overnight, and conditions were scary. We always have a good, safe step-in line close to the heli pad for testing, but we were relying on the new guide. When we asked about riding the test line, the guide said, "It's an easy slope to cut and has a clean outrun." I was in the middle of the heli and never saw the face when we landed. Stepping off, we plunged up to our waist. It took some effort to bootpack and reach the top of the face. When I saw the line, I immediately thought this is exactly the type of step-in run we normally do not look for. We like really steep, short faces with clean outruns. This slope started short and steep, but below, it continued on a long, rolling descent. We had very little discussion at the top, but I thought the terrain was too large, and the slope the guide dropped into to ski cut seemed certain to slide. He had a decent island of safety up and away, so if it slid, I was not super concerned. He cut the slope, but too high up, clearly missing the sweet spot.

"Ski across three feet below my track," the guide yelled over to my brother Steve. Steve dropped in, cut it exactly in the sweet spot, and sure enough, the world erupted around him. The crown line was well above him and shot uphill, grabbing any and all snow. Steve struggled to get out and stay on top. He went below the surface as the snow flushed him out of sight. The avy pulled the guide down as well. The other two riders were still putting on their gear. I was the only one strapped in and ready to drop.

I took off as soon as the slide slowed enough, with the reality that my brother was buried and I was the sole rescuer. Laser-focused on the task at hand, I tried to download everything I knew about beacons. I put the transceiver into receive mode, made it down to the last-seen point, and started searching. As I came over the roll, I saw that the slope actually doglegged hard to the left. Looking down at the slide path, I saw a ski pole tip and rode right to it. Steve was attached. As the slide slowed, he had pushed his pole toward the surface as hard as he could. His head was facing downhill like a rag doll. Somehow he had a small airway, even though his head was well below the surface, and we could talk.

"Watch out for hang fire," I said, "and tell those guys not to move." I radioed back to the crew, then started digging. It wasn't until I'd dug him out and calmed my shaking that I truly took in the magnitude of the avalanche. Steve had fought with all his might to get out of the slide, and he almost made it. His effort somehow kept him out of the main slide path. The slide was the biggest I had ever seen, and it triggered multiple secondary slopes, running all the way to the valley floor. By the time we flew back to base, word of multiple avy burials had trickled in. Fortunately, no one died that morning.

The night before, it had been snowing hard when I went to bed around midnight. We'd been the first crew out that morning. It would've been a great day to forget my boots. By slowing down that morning, we could have monitored the radio and known very quickly there was something seriously wrong with the snowpack. The traditional islands of safety weren't safe. Large propagating slides were happening on most aspects, elevations, and slope angles. This would be the last time we'd make the mistake of rushing in so soon after a storm. With foot-powered snowboarding, there isn't quite the pressure to go as fast and as early as possible. When the storm does break, you use the day to fix camp, dry everything out, and sit back and watch avalanches.

All I can say is practice, practice, practice. If you spend enough time in the mountains, there's a decent chance a friend or family member is going to be under the snow and you will be called on to rescue them.

Stability Tests

The column test and extended column test are stability tests that gauge how likely a section of snow is to fracture and propagate on a weak layer. They help us raise questions about the snowpack: Did anything fracture? How easily? Where? How big? Or if nothing happened, what does that mean? This is the most common test we do when we are moving fast in the mountains but have a concern about a particular layer. It can be done in under ten minutes. Beware of clean shearing slabs.

risked my life without ever considering digging a snowpit. Snow science is still primarily based around digging a hole in the snow and tapping on a shovel to see if it slides, how easily, and on what layer—and then taking this small data point and using it to predict if the entire slope on a huge mountain face will act the same as the pit. Surprisingly, the technique is quite accurate, but it's amazing that this rudimentary science has hardly changed in the past fifty years.

In the modern era of avy forecasting, the popular ranges have forecasters analyzing snowpits every day and shooting videos of the details. This is critical info for their forecast and something I review. Snowpits are very valuable, especially if you're out digging multiple pits every day so that you have a strong understanding/baseline of what's changing. However, too many times I see people digging pits and using them to talk themselves into riding a slope. Making a go/no-go decision based on reading a snowpit is a very advanced skill that, unless you consistently dig pits, I don't recommend. Even the experts don't rely solely upon them.

I rarely dig traditional snowpits. I cannot remember the last time I dug a proper pit in my home range. However, I consistently dig hasty pits, especially when I'm hiking a steep chute or face and I feel a density change in the snow, to identify weakness in the top of the snowpack like a wind slab. I use my hand or a pole to isolate a column similar to a traditional pit, and then use my hand

Probing for a Weak Layer

We are avalanche investigators in the mountains. As we home in on a weak layer we become hyperfocused, wanting to identify where this layer is as fast as possible. Certain weak layers can be felt by gently probing the snowpack—a double black belt move used when we know what we are looking for and know *exactly* how it feels under the pressure of the probe. This allows us to identify the layer very quickly.

to pry the column toward me. If I see a clean shear pull or an easy break, I become concerned. These take less than a minute, and on a serious line I might do three or four on the way up. When I'm on an expedition into a new range with no previous data, the first thing we do is dig extensive snowpits on multiple aspects and elevations to try to understand the snowpack's history.

Hand Pits

I use hand pits many times over the course of a tour. The first time I ever saw someone use them was in the early 1990s in Alaska's Chugach Mountains. It was late in the heli season, and I was filming with my brothers and cutting-edge pro freeskier Kent Kreitler for TGR's second movie, *Harvest*, when we finally found the golden window of good weather, stability, and snow—what we lived and saved all of our money for. The rest of the range was largely cooked out, most everyone had gone home, but the due north–facing lines were getting the first rays of light after a long winter of hibernating in the dark. Hitting the window for dropping into a high, glaciated line

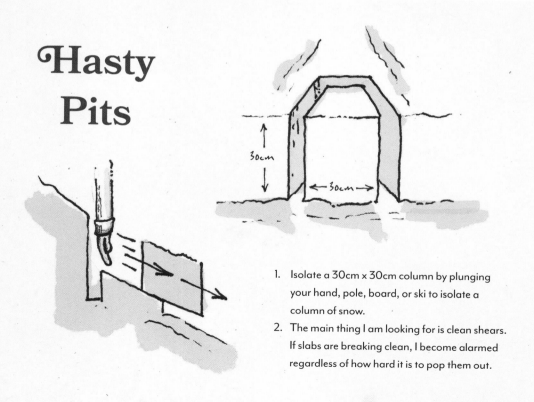

Hasty Pits

30cm

← 30cm →

1. Isolate a 30cm x 30cm column by plunging your hand, pole, board, or ski to isolate a column of snow.
2. The main thing I am looking for is clean shears. If slabs are breaking clean, I become alarmed regardless of how hard it is to pop them out.

Snowpits in Real-World
Scenarios: A Survey

Andrew McLean. Steep-skiing pioneer, guide, inventor, and author. Home range: Wasatch, Utah.

How often do you dig pits?

Aside from teaching avalanche classes, shooting a video, or going out with forecasters, almost never. I know, this makes me a bad person, but what I am really looking for is black or white, whereas pits give endless shades of gray. If you get an ECT [extended column test] result of 15, is it safe? Probably not, but what about a 10 or a 5? It depends on your risk acceptance.

Instead, I start observing snow conditions the moment I start driving or get out of the tent. Did it freeze last night? Any naturals? Roofalanches? Wind? New snow? Any signs of cracking or *whumphing*? I'll do a lot of mini test cuts along the skin track and maybe ski a smaller, safer similar line before moving up. For really big, exposed lines, I'll wait for bulletproof conditions like spring corn snow or hard, carveable foam. Conversely, now I probably wouldn't center-punch a huge line in deep snow regardless of what a pit said, although I will admit to doing so in the past before I knew better.

Chris Davenport. Extreme Skiing World Champ, the first to ski all of Colorado's 14ers in a year. Home range: Elk Mountains, Colorado.

What are you looking for in a snowpit?

Basically weak layers and how and why they are doing what they are doing. I want to see how the pack reacts to various tests. Sometimes you see something really cool or at least interesting. I like when my assessment of conditions is confirmed by any number of tests in the pit, but I also like seeing surprises, like a failure that is much worse than you might have suspected. Any time there's a bunch of energy in the pack, it's the sleeping dragon, and when you kick that thing in the right spot it'll be bad.

How many years did it take you to gain enough confidence in your pit to stake your life on it?

I'm still learning a lot, every season, but I would say a good ten years of backcountry decision-making was maybe when I began to feel like I truly was understanding all the fundamentals and ready to guide others. I'm sure I *thought* I knew a bunch of stuff earlier on, but I didn't have the experience.

Zahan Billimoria. Master and innovator of the dark arts of skiing serious Teton lines in deep winter snow, guide, instructor, and owner of Samsara Experience. Home range: Tetons, Wyoming.

How do you feel about snowpits?

It's not science, because there are too many variables; there's so much unknown in the "experiment." If it's not science, what is it? It's simply interpretation of the natural world. It's educated and informed guessing—and snowpits can be a big part of that. One of the troubles with decision-making around snow is that we are trying to interpret something that we cannot see. It is all happening below the surface of the snow, between the layers of snow. The texture of the surface can tell us something, but we have to guess at what's happening below the slab. As skiers we see one dimension—the surface—but as travelers in avalanche terrain we need to see two dimensions. For that we have to dig, we have to be curious about what's happening below. The snowpit in my mind isn't about numbers and taps, it's about what you can learn by looking at snow in two dimensions. We can try to quantify it, it's a good idea, but ultimately it's about being a good naturalist, a good interpreter.

When conditions are dynamic—for example, after a storm—I look a lot, maybe a few times in a day. But when conditions are more static, I don't look much at all. I may go weeks without one. If I'm in a new place, a new snowpack, I try to look a lot, but if I'm home, I look less. The more I can see the weather build the snowpack, the less I feel I need to dig.

Christina Lusti. Retired World Cup ski racer turned world-class Shralpinist. Home range: Selkirks, Canada.

Do you stake your life on what a snowpit reveals?
No, it's just one tool in the box. The best thing about backcountry skiing is the complexity of the mountains. You can never be certain with one thing or the other, one day is never like the next. You have to use every tool you have to put it all together.

Jon Krakauer. Climber, author, snowboarder. Home range: Rocky Mountain National Park, Colorado.

What is your approach to pits throughout the season?
I don't dig pits as often as I used to. I'll dig a real pit most often early in the season, and/or when I'm riding terrain I haven't ridden recently. But for a while now I've been relying much more on hasty pits, hand pits, and especially pole pits for judging the safety of the snowpack. Any single pit you dig is apt to give you a false sense of security, because conditions can vary so much depending on aspect, elevation, slope angle, etc. So when I'm skinning up the track, I'm continually flipping a pole and jamming the handle end as deep as it will go, feeling for the different layers, giving me a more comprehensive understanding of the pack as I travel across it. If I feel a weird layer down there, I might dig a hasty pit or even a real pit to examine the weirdness, but over time I've developed a pretty reliable sense for what I'm feeling with my pole. I'm looking for hidden instability and other lurking hazards. I'm looking for reasons not to ride the line.

What result excites you and gives you confidence?
A homogeneous snowpack without layers of crust or facets.

What result scares you?
When I see signs of wind-loading on lee slopes, it always scares the shit out of me. I also get really scared when I find deep instability in the lower layers of the pack. Finding depth hoar—a layer of facets or sugar snow down toward the ground—fucking terrifies me. And I see that a lot here in Colorado.

How confident are you with your snowpit results?
I am almost always skeptical of my snowpit results.

Time of year is important.
By spring the snowpack settles faster after storms. The
optimal scenario is when the
mountains become locked up
with prolonged high pressure.
A spring shrink-wrap. It then
snows one to three feet on
top, and all we are concerned
with is how the new snow bonds
with the old. We can check
this simply and often with our
hands.

as it's receiving the first rays of the year is surreal and challenging, especially if you are on foot. Ten minutes late and
the face is dark and featureless and the light too flat to ride.

The mountains start thinning out around this time, and
natural selection means the few people who are still around
are those with the appetite for the sharp end. This is how I
got to know Jerry Hance. A staple in the early Valdez days
before guiding, Jerry was quiet and didn't really socialize, but
he loved the gnar. He never talks about it, but my money is
on Jerry as the person who opened up the most lines in the
Valdez area. Naturally, when Doug Coombs started the first
guide operations in Alaska, he tapped Jerry as one of his orig-
inal guides. When the perfect window presented itself late in
the season, and I met Jerry, we hit it off right away. Our eyes
focused on the biggest lines in the range: Tusk and Pontoon.

The first time the two of us ventured into steep terrain, I watched as he eased
onto the face. His hands and poles were all over the slope. He quickly dug at multiple
points and aspects on the slope. I thought, *What the hell is he doing?* He looked crazy,
like he had lost a wedding ring.

The Snowpit Call of All Snowpit Calls

GRAND TETON'S OTTER BODY ROUTE, 2013

Zahan Billimoria and Brendan O'Neill settled in to examine the snowpit. Bryan Iguchi and I crowded around a little rock outcropping, staring down a massive hanging snowfield, trying to cling to something solid. The tension was thick. The results of this snowpit would determine if I took the plunge into one of the most serious lines of my life, the Grand Teton's Otter Body. You see the beautiful, most direct east-facing route from everywhere in Jackson, including Bryan's living room. The main snowfield looks like a hanging otter and starts off the top, with so much exposure that even though I'd looked at it thousands of times, I'd never really given the line much thought. The combination of conditions needed to do it safely are so rare, it really requires an immense amount of good fortune, experience in the range, and patience.

One of my all-time heroes, Doug Coombs, inspired by talks with Steve Shea, first skied the Otter Body route with Mark Newcomb in June 1996. They rode the line in spring conditions, which simplified the avalanche hazard due to the frozen snow but brought in the risk of losing an edge. It was Coombs's second attempt. He and Andrew McLean were turned around by avy danger on the first try that February. Timing was everything for the descent. They needed soft enough snow to hold an edge, but if they waited too long, they would run the risk of getting taken out by a wet slide or rockfall during the bottom rappels. The route took them over 1,000-foot cliffs, and they had very firm conditions, preventing them from skiing the entire route safely; instead they'd downclimbed a small bottom section above the rappel with axes and crampons. But they had put it together, ticking off one of the most coveted and aesthetic lines around.

The film "Otter Body Experience" depicts how technical and gnarly a feat the descent is, so well that the line had seen only a few successful attempts between Coombs's and our groups. When filming my first foot-powered film, "Deeper," four years earlier, I made multiple attempts to document a big line in Grand Teton National Park. We focused on Mount Moran, with its 6,000-foot direct fall line making it one of the best descents in the world for those who like to fly down steep, clean mountains with speed. On our second attempt we got the line in full pow, but a spring squall made it a love-of-sport lap—we put the cameras away to embrace the whiteout and just ride.

Photographer and filmmaker Jimmy Chin planted the seed for riding the Grand Teton in winter when I was working on the film "Further," but that window closed when Jimmy was caught in a major avalanche while we were building up to the Grand. The Grand again floated around as a possibility, but it was really Zahan who pushed the issue. "The Tetons are starting to shape up" was all I needed to hear to drop everything and head toward the Tetons for a closer look. Getting lines as complex as the Otter Body in good form is not something you can necessarily plan around. Success takes work, but it also needs to fall into your lap. For ten days Bryan, Zahan, and I enjoyed some easy touring in the park and gathered snow info. We worked through our climbing and rappelling systems. Zahan has an appetite for closeout lines, where the most dangerous part involves reaching the anchors and rapping off. You are the most vulnerable at this stage, so being able to build an anchor quickly, and clip in and out of it fast, is critical. Know your systems and practice them. A few minutes wasted here could cost you your life.

My main concern, however, was not the rap, despite exposure to sluffs and rockfall. Nor was crawling out of my tent on the Upper Saddle predawn or the rock climbing to the summit with our boards strapped to our packs. My main concern was focusing properly to make the right call based on the snowpit Zahan was analyzing. The Grand towers above the rest of the range, and there was no way to check and confirm snow stability. Due to the limited weather window and the fact that it's the highest line in the range, my usual "build up" approach didn't apply: we couldn't terrain progress our way into a line.

This meant I would be putting my life on the line based on snowpit results. I view pits as one tool of many to evaluate snow. That day on the Grand, however, it was our primary tool, and even a small slide would mean certain death. This dynamic was nothing new to Zahan. He and other Teton chargers use remote weather sites to help formulate their own avy forecasting in the high peaks of the Tetons. This has resulted in a major shift in thinking. In the Coombs era the big lines went down in the spring, where they worked around melt-freeze cycles. But this approach brings the possibilities of ice and taking fatal falls into the equation. As people have gotten a better handle on avy forecasting, the trend has been toward riding the serious lines with proper pow conditions. Not only is it more fun to be riding them in soft snow, it takes away the risk of falling on ice or getting caught in a wet slide.

Superchargers like Greg Collins and Brendan O'Neill progressing winter descents in the Tetons and playfully sessioning the range like it's sidecountry at the resort is precisely what the range looks like these days after prolonged midwinter high pressure. Literally hundreds of tracks on all the prominent peaks and lines make it difficult to ride a clean line a few days after a storm. The "new norm" of people riding huge, exposed lines so consistently in a complex midwinter snowpack is something I've only seen in Chamonix and La Grave.

It's a fickle game we play. The more critical the line, the longer the list of ingredients needed to make it safe. Lines like the Otter Body need to knock on your door. Ideally you are on the doorstep when they do, with the door already open. This is why I leave my schedule as open as possible for the second half of winter. It drives my wife, Tiffany, crazy, but the mountains adhere to their own calendar.

Riders need to be strong-willed and able to make the tough decision to turn their back on a perfect line because the hazard is too high. You do not get to Zahan's level without having that skill set. However, at the time, Zahan had very little experience with film crews. For the Grand the plan was to put two cameras on opposing ridges, which would require a huge effort to get them in place. We also planned to shoot the line with a gyro-stabilized camera attached to a helicopter.

I pulled Zahan aside a few days before our attempt and told him, "We need to block out all the cameras. There is going to be a lot of pressure put on the results of the snowpit. It's just us and the mountain. Block out all the effort being put toward the moviemaking." There were twelve people involved and a lot of money hanging over our heads, but it was essential to step away if the snow wasn't right, despite all of the effort.

Zahan brought Brendan as a fourth. He is the most badass ski mountaineer you've never heard of. I'll never know how many new lines Brendan has pioneered because he never talks about them. He was the perfect addition because he couldn't care less about the camera (in fact, I'd bet he has never watched a ski or snowboard movie in his life).

"His great desire was for the spirit of man to exercise itself as freely and fearlessly and joyously as a climber on a hill."
—Cottie Sanders on George Mallory

After a few tough climbing moves and some summit high-fives, we shifted our focus to the descent. Before Zahan and Brendan started down the main face, I pulled Zahan aside again and looked him in the eye: "You've got six kids and three wives in the pit with you."

Thankfully it was a screaming yes. One after the other we dropped into no-man's-land, making big, open powder turns on the enormous, exposed face down to the first rappel. The snow was perfect, nothing moved. We moved down the rest of the line efficiently but struggled to find the anchors for the final set of rappels. Precious time slipped by. The mountain started talking to us with some small sluffs raining down on us as we finished the final rappel. We celebrated with a long and glorious party run down into the exit canyon. Clouds began to show themselves, and by the time we reached camp, the next front had arrived, a day earlier than expected. Window closed.

Jerry has his own approach that has evolved over the years. I've gotten into some of the most serious lines of my life with him. His comfort on big, exposed faces covered in pow is unique. He rarely digs snowpits, but his hands are always in the snow. He feels his way up the mountain, assessing what is happening as we move. The hand pit—also called the mitt pit or the hasty pit—really stuck with me and is something I've embraced.

I caught up with Jerry in the spring of 2020 after not seeing him for many years. Incredibly fit and still addicted to the steeps, Jerry was getting ready to harvest seaweed in Prince William Sound. "I could never understand the whole snowpit thing," he told me. "It is one speck of data from one spot on a mountain. There is valuable information, but in the same time it takes to dig that pit, I could be getting multiple data points with hand pits." Jerry recognizes there's a proper time and place for in-depth snowpits, but he digs a hundred hand pits for every full pit. A hand pit won't tell you what is going on 5 feet below the surface, but it will give you a sense of how the top of the snowpack is bonding. If I'm worried about a layer much farther down, I am not in serious terrain. For assessing avalanche potential in the top few feet of the snowpack, hand pits can be very effective.

The key to getting good information from hand pits is to do them the same way every time so you build a consistent baseline. When digging these pits, I already have a pretty good understanding of the snowpack. I am looking for a specific weak layer already identified or trying to find recently formed wind slabs. As in a traditional compression test, I isolate a small column, cutting with my fingers and an upside-down pole. I pull on the back of the block to see if the snow collapses and

Going for the Ride: Surviving Avalanches

I asked two veteran riders, Xavier De Le Rue and Jimmy Chin, about their real-world experiences surviving avalanches.

Xavier De Le Rue

"In a more pragmatic way, [being in an avalanche] has been the best lesson I could ever get. Looking back, it has given me the chance to completely reevaluate the power of the mountains and our fragility as little human beings when being up there. By doing so, I have the feeling that it has made the decisions to drop or turn around from a line a lot easier. When I would hesitate at the top of a shred because the conditions would feel weird or because of not being in the right state of mind, remembering that avalanche has always made it easy to turn back from a line and pick and choose the days that I would hit big things, when all the stars would be aligned."

Jimmy Chin

"The power of the avalanche was magnitudes bigger than any force I've ever felt. At points, it felt like I was going to be ripped apart. It was completely overwhelming and I felt completely helpless. In the moment, I was 100 percent sure I was going to die. It felt like death was happening. I vividly remember having an out-of-body conversation with myself: 'I always wondered how I was going to die, and now I know.'

"I've felt a sense of invincibility for much of my career. I've had a few close calls but came out of all of them unscathed. I have been really lucky. I always thought it wouldn't happen to me. I was too smart, too calculated to have anything like this happen to me. Boy, was I wrong. I was damn lucky I didn't die that day. The avalanche changed that attitude for sure. It shook me to the core and made me question everything I had been doing with my life and why I had been doing it."

If I see the words "Deep Slab Instability" or "Persistent Weak Layer" in the avy report, I consider the danger to be "High."

how easily. If a clean slab breaks, I become concerned. This could then lead me to do a proper pit. Even just plunging your hand straight into the snowpack can identify a slab or weak layer. If you consistently dig hand pits, you'll begin to understand what a weak layer feels like. I don't use the hand pit to green-light a run, but to red-light it.

CHAPTER 7

Health and Fitness

**Health is the currency with which we pay the entry fee for a life
of adventure. No health, no play. I am not sure if it is where I
grew up, or if it was a generational thing, but the conventional
wisdom was that, as you got older, you had to stop serious sports.
For some reason, my dad's fortieth birthday sticks in my head.
He wasn't given a lounge chair, but he might as well have been.
The birthday cards read like a funeral for his athletic life. Jokes
about knee and back stiffness, hobbling around, and worse. He
had entered a new phase: "Hope you enjoyed it, it's all downhill
from here."**

The snowboard industry is even more critical of aging. Right around twenty-eight,
I thought I was on my last contract. Just watch the X Games, where "legend status"
is thrown around at age twenty-five or twenty-six. There is a lot of truth to this,
however. To be successful requires going all out. And if you're riding to your max
level, you will eventually get hurt—most likely a lot. The question is, do you have the
discipline to wait the necessary time to properly heal? That's a lot to ask of a twenty-
something-year-old whose income is based on getting the shot. The moment when
I thought *I am not sure my body can do this anymore* came at the ripe old age of thirty.

Injuries

Between the ages of eighteen and twenty-four, I rode about 230 days each year. I
never took days off, which drove my coach nuts. Days I wasn't training were spent
freeriding and hitting whatever zone I had scoped while training. If I was somewhere

with really good freeriding, I would switch to my soft boots as soon as the race was over and ride the rest of the day nonstop. Every so often we would get a few days off, and we would pull all-night drives to reach the Jackson Tram line at dawn. As soon as race season ended, I flew to Alaska. I was running myself ragged—not resting, living on fast food, sleeping in cars, in closets, on couches. Something had to give, and that something was my back. At first it was a steady pain that I could block out, but by twenty-three I had to accept the pain would not go away. I spent the summer before the 1998 Olympics largely flat on my back, trying to heal bulged discs on my lower spine.

This was a pivotal time for me. I came to terms with the fact that I was not invincible, and if I wanted to keep riding, I needed to take my health more seriously. My legs were superstrong, but I realized that health is not just about strength. By no means did I become a health nut, but I started observing athletes who were pain free and much healthier and stronger than I. Much like in the mountains, I found smarter, experienced teachers. When I hung up my hard boots at twenty-four, the fact I was no longer pulling the g's on a race course helped. I sought out people with their own back issues to learn from. The problem is no two back issues are the same. My time on the mountain did not decrease, though. I was riding bell to bell every day, whether it was bulletproof and bumpy or soft and smooth. I had not yet embraced the importance of rest and recovery.

On a scale of 1 (negligible) to 10 (extreme), my back pain fluctuated between 2 and 6, which was fine by me. It wasn't until I was twenty-seven or twenty-eight that my back started going out. When this happened, the pain hit 9 or 10. I was immobile. I couldn't stand up straight; I was hunched over like a ninety-year-old. This was a dark time for me. I decided to really get serious about treatment: yoga, physical therapy, massage, and acupuncture. I needed to get better and I would do whatever it took. For the first time in my life, I questioned whether my snowboarding days were over. But keeping my back problems quiet was critical. Word gets out that you have chronic knee or back issues, especially in your late twenties, and sponsors are likely to think your days of high-end snowboarding are coming to an end. By the time you're twenty-seven or twenty-eight, sponsors start questioning your age in any case. Throw in a back injury, and your career is most likely over.

I never had a plan B. Never had an answer to "What are you going to do after snowboarding?" With nothing to lose, I drove down to northern Baja to see a Polish doctor who was practicing a form of prolotherapy—an injection of irritant fluid into dead scar tissue to stimulate blood flow. He was banned from practicing in Europe and the United States and had set up shop in a house outside Ensenada, Mexico.

Clare Gallagher: Ultrarunner

Clare Gallagher is an endurance athlete and environmental advocate based in Boulder, Colorado. She holds the fastest known time (FKT) records on the Zion Traverse and Joshua Tree Traverse and has won many major races, including the Leadville 100, Western States (2019), and 101K CCC (2017). I spoke to Clare about suffering, pushing through the pain, and when to listen to your body.

Can you explain the different phases of suffering?
In the context of running, there are many phases. First, there's fast road running suffering: it's a deep pain in your body and mind, but it never lasts long, say, even from a 5K to a marathon, you're not running more than three hours if you're fast. It's a fitness type of suffering: the more fit you are, the less you'll suffer. But in trail and ultrarunning, there isn't that same pain since the races are usually so much longer and therefore your body isn't running that fast. The "suffering" is more body + mind. For the body, you'll feel the terrain in your bones. Whether a lot of uphill, technical rocks, or rolling singletrack, you'll feel the corresponding bodily fatigue. There's also the post-30-mile pain, a slow burn that you have to learn to settle into. Then past 60 miles (like in a 100-mile race), that's when the crying phase is most likely to happen. *What the fuck am I doing to my body? Why am I racing one hundred miles? Why do my feet hurt so badly? Why can't I stop crying?* It's a phase you cannot indulge in because it's energy intensive! Get your cry out, but settle back into the body fatigue and keep moving. So much of the long races require intense mental focus and the ability to block out distractions or indulgences like thinking about how you actually feel.

How do you know when to push through the pain and keep going, or listen to the pain and stop?
Experience helps teach me what is an injury vs. just the natural pain of ultrarunning. I've DNFed [did not finish] a 100-miler with a knee injury at mile 93. It fucking sucked. But I was crawling and sobbing and couldn't bend my leg. I knew I was injured, so I called it. I ask myself, *Will I be able to run a month from now if I push through this?*

When did you learn there was more in the tank?
The 2019 Western States, I was winning at mile 90. Though I had a comfortable lead, it was just getting dark and I couldn't see a headlamp creeping up on me. At mile 93 Brittany Peterson caught me. This is very rare in ultras. We stayed together for a mile and then I dropped all my excess weight [food and sunglasses] and I never looked back. I ran the fastest end split in the history of the women's race. My competitive drive taught me I had more in the tank, because I won by ten minutes. We are more capable than we ever imagined.

Have you pushed it too far?
I'm pretty conservative. My biggest fear is getting too cold. There've been some runs and skis that I've

pushed my limits, failing to keep my extremities warm. That's why I cannot fathom what you snow people do! I don't overtrain. I run max 70 miles a week. I just try to play most runs safe. I love running too much to risk anything too crazy, in a race or in training. I just want to be able to run. For ultras over 50 miles, half of the work is mental. I always perform well when I'm a little undertrained but over rested, when my mind is calm. Then the race is just a gift, a privilege to get to run all day.

What have been the biggest changes you have made to improve your fitness and racing?
I rest more. I take my running less seriously than I used to. I just feel grateful to get out on the trails with friends. It's a selfish sport, so bringing the community love into my running as much as possible has honestly made me faster. It's in the conversations with others, those more and less experienced than me, especially with my crew in Boulder, that I learn ways to improve.

At this point in my life I was surrounded by great healers, but they thought I was crazy to let someone stick a huge needle millimeters from my spinal cord. Walking into his makeshift waiting room filled with other desperate people, some with IVs hanging from the ceiling, was surreal and terrifying. Over a few months I would get twelve injections. They did exactly what he said they would. It was not a fix-all, but combined with everything else I was doing, as well as embracing more foot-powered snowboarding, my pain slowly subsided.

By thirty, my back was going out more frequently, and each time it happened, the severity of the pain increased. The problem was, it didn't go out just when doing serious riding. Simple things like putting on a sock could flare the back pain again. Midwinter, I generally took time off to heal. But April was playoff season for me, the only time I would ride seriously hurt, the only time I would take high levels of ibuprofen. I rode some of the most serious lines of my life while in serious pain—a triple blind roll spine line that required multiple airs and precision routefinding in spines so steep that there was no way to stop after dropping in. I ended up naming this line Dr. Seuss, because it was closer to a fictional cartoon than real life. *If I can strap in,* I told myself, *I will be fine.* I was so self-conscious, trying to hide my back pain from my riding partners for fear of word getting back to my sponsors. This experience of living in constant pain was the darkest period of my life and has given me great empathy for people living with long-term injuries and chronic conditions.

Never Waste an Injury
It's not a question of *if* but *when* with injuries. Embrace them, own them, and find peace with them. Injuries force downtime; see it as an opportunity to work on both your physical and mental health. Focus on what you can do, not on what you can't do.

"You can walk on flat pavement for two miles," one physical therapist told me after three weeks of primarily being on my back. I was so excited, I immediately started searching out the best 2-mile section of flat, paved bike path.

The injuries that develop over time are the trickiest ones to heal. For me it has been my back, for others it's usually knees, ankles, or shoulders. These injuries need to become part of your life. Slow your approach way down. Become an expert on how to warm up and cool down. How to strengthen without hurting. Find other people with similar injuries and ask a lot of questions, but recognize no two injuries are the same. I am an expert on my back, but some things that work great for me may end up hurting someone else. With all injuries, embrace water. Swimming or exercising in water uses a third of the gravity, so you can use your muscles with a third of the impact.

Time Heals

As I was healing my back, I became a regular at Ladd Williams PT in Truckee, my hometown. The go-to spot for serious athletes, Ladd heals 150 knee injuries a year. It is here I met Michelle Parker, C. R. Johnson, J. T. Holmes, and Kirsten Clark. I actually knew Kirsten from high school, at Carrabassett Valley Academy. Kirsten was considered the best. A natural, Kirsten competed in the World Cup for thirteen years. She did a great job staying healthy, but she had a sore knee that made her a regular at PT along with me. She eventually retired to have kids, which coincided with when I had kids. Now I was seeing her at the ballet classes and swing sets. One day I asked Kirsten how her knee was.

"It's better," she said. "It basically fixed itself once I gave it a break." Life has a strange way of working itself out. Looking back, I see my back injury as a blessing, not a curse. My bad back made me write off flat landings at a young age, which certainly saved my knees and forced me to take my health more seriously. A loose shoulder should also be taken with extreme care. You need to be able to fall. A loose shoulder can come out with the simplest of falls. This type of injury paused Bryan Iguchi's career for four years. He lost all his sponsors and became a sushi chef. He never lost his love for boarding, though, and battled through multiple surgeries. He finally fixed that shoulder, and today he is ten years into his second career as a pro snowboarder and jumping like a thirty-year-old.

Transitioning to Foot-Powered Snowboarding

I started to feel the confines of heli, sled, and sidecountry riding around the time I rode the Dr. Seuss line. I always knew there would be a time when I would shift my focus to getting more into splitboarding, but it came faster than expected for a few reasons. First, I loved it! Second, I couldn't push my riding any closer to the edge with a heli, which meant it was getting really hard to continue to progress my snowboarding. I always viewed my seat in the heli as a privilege, knowing that every snowboarder in

Ruedi Beglinger: Mountain Guide

Ruedi is in his sixties and climbs and rides more than anyone else I know. He manifested his own destiny through hard work and commitment, creating Selkirk Mountain Experience, a multi-hut touring mecca in a remote section of the Selkirk Mountains. I spoke to him about fitness and balance.

"I think there is this balance: If I don't push myself, I won't be fit. But if I push myself, then I pile myself up. So where is that balance that I don't get hurt, or if I get hurt, not too bad, so I don't feel the devil of arthritis and all the crazy stuff? Count on luck a little bit, so you don't have to have hip replacements and this and that. I was very lucky. I try to stay flexible. I do lots of stretching, and, in the summer, I go climbing—climbing is a healthy sport. I just stay active. Recognize that when you're sixty, you can still do it. Maybe not everything, or maybe not as aggressive.

"To me, the biggest gift is that I can still be that strong and that flexible and ski that well, snowboard that well, climb that well. I can literally do what I want."

the world wanted that seat, and feeling that it was my duty to push myself and my snowboarding to new levels every time I rode. Third, I grew more aware of the impact helis have on the planet. It bothered me that my snowboarding was causing so much harm.

Get fit, get educated, and get going!

Health was also a factor in my transition to 100 percent foot-powered snowboarding. With splitboarding, I would start at the trailhead in pain, but slowly the low-impact, full-body movement of skinning would warm up my body, and within an hour I would be feeling great. It became very clear that if I wanted to achieve my foot-powered goals, I needed to be as strong as possible. The best way to do that was to hike as often as possible. This simple, symmetrical movement done hundreds of thousands of times has realigned my body and is why I remain healthy.

Going all in on foot-powered snowboarding meant I needed mentors. The world I had become so engrossed in, that I had helped shape—fellow riders, heli pilots, guides, filmmakers—all went away. I found myself hanging out with unsponsored, underground chargers. The snowmobile trailheads, like the helipads, were overflowing with film crews and local pros. Switching to the foot-powered zones, I was once again the young kid in the lot. Legends like Jim Zellers and Glen Poulsen became new mentors. The best part was they had ten to fifteen years on me and were kicking my ass on the uphill, making it hard for me to keep up. These guys were fit and motivated and still progressing. Contrast this to the riders of a similar age I was seeing in the lift lines and at the helipads who were hanging onto the past and dealing with chronic injuries. I knew I had found my fountain of youth.

Not only were Glen and Jim leaving me in the dust, but before long I was sharing the skin track with *their* teachers, Otto and Wolfy Schaefer, who were in their sixties and seventies. A few years later, I was waiting out weather for a plane drop in the Wrangell Mountains when I met Ruedi Homberger. He was trying to climb and ski a major peak in the Saint Elias Range. He was hoping to do the 7,000-foot climb in a single push at age seventy-five, which he ended up doing.

"What's the trick?" I asked him.

"Eat light, easy-to-digest foods, especially at dinner."

"Eat mostly plant-based food."

"Keep going, don't stop."

Finding Fitness Role Models

It is good to see what works best for a variety of people. For example, Mark Twight's book *Extreme Alpinism* was very helpful for me, even though I do not plan on doing forty-six-hour single pushes up 8,000-meter peaks. Mark showed me what

High Sierra Strong

MAMMOTH, SPRING TRAINING, 1994

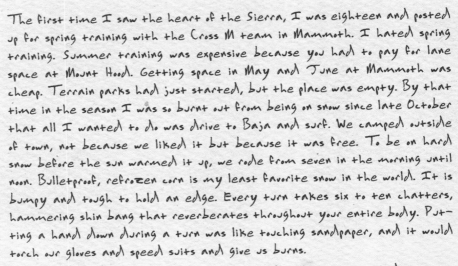

The first time I saw the heart of the Sierra, I was eighteen and posted up for spring training with the Cross M team in Mammoth. I hated spring training. Summer training was expensive because you had to pay for lane space at Mount Hood. Getting space in May and June at Mammoth was cheap. Terrain parks had just started, but the place was empty. By that time in the season I was so burnt out from being on snow since late October that all I wanted to do was drive to Baja and surf. We camped outside of town, not because we liked it but because it was free. To be on hard snow before the sun warmed it up, we rode from seven in the morning until noon. Bulletproof, refrozen corn is my least favorite snow in the world. It is bumpy and tough to hold an edge. Every turn takes six to ten chatters, hammering shin bang that reverberates throughout your entire body. Putting a hand down during a turn was like touching sandpaper, and it would torch our gloves and speed suits and give us burns.

Spring training was the only time in my life I was not excited to train, but I could not deny the beauty or the grandeur of the High Sierra. On the drives down from Tahoe, I would mind-surf the mountains. From the lift I couldn't stop staring at the 3,000-foot Bloody Couloir, the Minarets, Ritter, and Banner, and imagined what lay beyond. But as beautiful as they were, I looked at them with disappointment and thought, "What a shame nobody rides them." I couldn't use a heli or snowmobile to access those beautiful lines. At the time I considered them overprotected by regulations and too hard to get to. Two decades later, I fully understood the vastness of the range and was grateful for those who fought to protect it from engines, chain saws, and bulldozers. In doing so, they created a dreamscape for foot-powered Shralpinism, one that includes more than a dozen easy-access drainages stacked with hundreds of snow-covered, granite-laden peaks over 11,000 feet.

In my ignorance, what I didn't know then was that people like Bonnie and Jim Zellers and a handful of locals from Tahoe to Bishop were enjoying the range largely to themselves. Ski equipment had improved enough to work on the steeps, and Jim figured out that if he got started early enough, he could cover a ton of springtime ground in tennis shoes with his boots and board on his back. Over time, stories of 3,000-foot couloirs lined with tall granite walls for as far as the eye could see came across my radar. The few sections of the range that allowed snowmobiles had become crowded, I had ridden all the major lines in these zones, and I was merely riding the foothills.

When I switched to foot-powered snowboarding, I aspired to riding lines not covered by the guidebooks. My hopes were crushed when I struggled to hike the lines I could see right off the road. An average day in the High Sierra starts at dawn, walking in the dirt to snowline; eight hours and 6,000 feet of climbing later, you're finally at your objective. A few hours more and you are stumbling in the dirt back to the car.

Getting High Sierra strong is humbling. Basically I go out and hike, climb, and skin until I reach a point where I am struggling to get back to the car because I am so tired. Much of my focus since 2006 has been on getting a layer back in the bigger ranges. To be able to function deep into protected ranges for long periods of time and snowboard at a high level is a huge logistical and physical challenge that requires a master's degree in fitness, frugality, and winter camping skills. Riding unknown peaks deep in the heavily protected areas of the western United States has been a far greater challenge than riding huge Alaskan lines via plane-established base camps.

the human body is capable of, if you train properly and work hard enough. The three people I've studied the most are Laird Hamilton, Tom Brady, and Jim Zellers—all for different reasons. They represent very different paths, but each one has the same goal: to play his sport forever. Cherry-picking techniques from their regimens helps me to know what *great* looks like. The trick with studying the great ones is to grab achievable nuggets you can bring into your own life.

Laird Hamilton

Laird is a superfreak. He has taken his own approach to staying fit, with the clear goal of charging the biggest waves the ocean has to offer. His book *Force of Nature* is one of the most accessible fitness books I've read. I had the opportunity to spend a week in Alaska with Laird in 2007. No surprise, he can ride a snowboard at an elite level. What surprised me was how much energy he has. We rode all day, and back at home he would just keep going: splitting wood, cutting the perfect hole for cold plunges through 3 feet of ice, and snow kiting on a lake.

Like me, Laird is allergic to the gym. One day we hiked through deep snow to get to a line, and he asked, "Do you ever run in powder?" I can honestly say I'd never thought of going for a run in powder. "I am always looking for the deepest sand to run in," he told me, "but powder is a whole new level." What keeps him going? "My upbringing helped with not being satisfied with the status quo," he said, "not being satisfied with *this is how we do it; this is what we do; this is the way we do it; that's how we've always done it.*"

"Slow and smooth is fast," he explained. "When everything's slow and deliberate, that task process is a good distraction for you to not get into your own head, to not let that fear part of your brain start, where it's saying, *Hey, you don't wanna do that* or *What if this happens?* That little voice that's really not you, it's this other piece of you—a narrative that feeds the thing that ultimately keeps us from doing dumb stuff. It's why it's there, but if you listen to it, it ends up being your own worst enemy. Having that real ritualistic process gives you a real direction."

Tom Brady

Yes, I am a football fan. And yes, I am a Patriots fan and have been my whole life. Which means I've watched them lose a lot more than I've watched them win. In 2001 there was a lot to be optimistic about. We had our best quarterback in franchise history, Drew Bledsoe. He could sling a ball like never before, he was a skier, and we were well on our way to making a run deep into the playoffs, when in true Patriots fashion, Bledsoe got hurt. Out walked a kid we had never heard of. He looked like he was fifteen and his name was Tom Brady. No one imagined Brady would win a Super Bowl that season and that the Patriots would become the winningest team in football history. When you are that good, the haters come out—and come out they have.

Zahan Billimoria: Mountain Training

What's your approach to training?

The biggest mistake athletes make is to grind. To allow "training" to be about hardship and pain. About beating your will into submission. That's a terrible idea. Training is just the process by which you become the physical specimen you want to be. That should not suck, it should not be a grind. It's an awesome process—you gain control of your life and your body. It's a lifelong process of shaping your own physical destiny. Train in a way that contributes to your life, that makes life better. Training serves life—not the other way around.

What is the best way to get in shape to climb mountains?

Step 1 for mountain athletes is to build endurance. Humans are endowed with remarkable capacity for endurance. It's how we have survived and evolved as a species. We are not terribly fast, and we aren't terribly strong, but we are built to go forever. In modern life we can lose that capacity. What we don't use, our biology will discard. It's simple, but not easy. My four rules of endurance are: (1) go long, (2) go slow, (3) avoid rests, and (4) train fasted when possible.

1. **Go long.** This is relative to each athlete, but to build endurance, you have to give your body something to endure.

2. **Go slow.** Endurance is about the ability to keep going, to be highly efficient in terms of energy, to rely on our most energy-efficient pathway, the oxidative system.

3. **Avoid rests.** In order to stimulate the changes you need to succeed in the mountains, you have to maintain the effort consistently. Going nonstop for forty-five minutes is more effective than being out for hours with frequent rests.

4. **Train fasted.** The body has three different engines and virtually unlimited fat stores but very little glycogen (carb) stores. So if you want to climb big mountains, you need to use a plentiful fuel—fat. A simple way to get better endurance is to do some of your training (as much as is safe and possible) with low glycogen. That will teach your body to burn fat and will favor your oxidative energy system. In short, fasted training will make endurance training much more effective.

If you have one hour a day, choose which and how many days to dedicate to movement training, strength training, and endurance training. The right answer will depend on your goals, your own body's natural strengths, and what you have the most passion for. Doing fewer than four days of endurance work per week will prevent much improvement. Strength and movement work can be combined because we want to learn to produce strength in the patterns of human movement, so they should be trained in tandem with each other. For a lot of athletes short on time, two days of strength and movement work will be a great start.

How has your training evolved over the years?
My training used to be all about the engine, all about improving endurance and increasing strength. I've realized that I'm missing a huge piece of the puzzle—movement, or "Athlete IQ." The best athletes don't just have the bigger engine or more strength, they move better. Movement quality has long been a mystery in science. We know that the brain governs movement, timing, precision, but how does the body execute it? Can it be trained? What do elite athletes have that ordinary ones don't?

The answer lies in fascia, the most ubiquitous tissue in the human body, that wraps every organ, nerve, muscle, tendon, and bone—a continuous web of elastic tissue that translates the brain's intention into an action. We cannot understand human movement, and how to train it, without studying the science of fascia.

Early on, I was drawn to Tom's work ethic and stick-to-itiveness. He was one of the last picks in the draft (the draft doesn't even go that deep anymore). His predraft videos have become a thing of legend due to how unathletic he was. Up until Bledsoe got hurt and Tom Brady took over at twenty-four and won a Super Bowl, he had never had a secure starting job. He had been working for this opportunity his whole life. Tom was more fit and healthier at forty-four than he was at twenty-four, and he did it with innovative and unorthodox methods. Traditional sports trainers have equated his methods to those of a snake-oil salesman. His critics have become fewer and fewer, though, as he has rewritten what is possible in sports.

Tom threw a grenade on traditional sports fitness by forgoing heavy weights for stretch bands. He focused on long, pliable muscles instead of big, stiff muscles. In his book *The TB12 Method*, he dives deep into muscle pliability. I had never heard of this. Breaking down scar tissue before and after working out helps soften the tissue in his muscles. Tom moves through his muscle groups, contracting and releasing each muscle in two- to five-second bursts. This process wakes up the muscle and connects the brain to the muscle. These two things are critical. When I use this technique, my injured areas fire slower, like I've forgotten about them.

Jim Zellers

I'm playing the long game. I do not enjoy working out for working out's sake. My goal is simple: I want to snowboard, surf, climb, and bike my whole life. No one personifies this lifestyle better than Jim Zellers. He is a high-ranking member of the Church of the Seven Day Recreationalists. I've been trying to keep up with him riding the resort, on the skin track, and single track, and following him up granite splitter cracks. Jim is not a health nut; I am pretty sure he has never been in a gym or ever even stretched. He is ten years my elder and recreates daily. Every time I call him to bike, climb, or snowboard, the answer is always yes, which makes him one of my key adventure partners.

Considering I've spent more time with Jim than anyone else in the mountains, I should have more insight into how he stays fit, but he downplays his fitness. Unlike most athletes, who love talking about how they train or what they eat, Jim has no interest in the subject. To him it is simple: Just do it every day. Keep going. When I was thirty and he was forty, I couldn't hang with him. *I will get him when I am forty*, I thought. That has not happened—I think I have a chance at fifty, but I'll have to stay in great shape.

I've talked to Jim a lot about taking risks. He and his wife, Bonnie, along with big mountain legend Tom Burt, have pioneered groundbreaking big mountain descents in the most serious mountains around the world. When Jim was thirty, he had kids and made a decision to back away from pro snowboarding. *Walking away* from getting paid to snowboard is something I've rarely seen in the world of professional skiing or snowboarding. Most people are *forced* out. To do it on your own terms is rare. Jim and Bonnie walked away from the media side of the sport but went all in on pioneering splitboarding in the High Sierra. Mammoth became the epicenter of pro snowboarding when the snowboard park exploded. While hundreds of pros descended on Mammoth, Jim and Bonnie were quietly ticking off first descent after first descent in the same range.

Home ranges are the great teachers. The masters.

Jim spends so much time out there that he knows when the steeps open up. The ease with which Jim walks away from lines that have consequences is impressive. There is no discussion about it. "I'm going around," or "I like this shoulder over here." No ego, no FOMO. This may be the best health lesson I've ever learned from Jim: that balance of charging and the carefree ease of avoiding high-consequence situations. Jim's acute understanding of his abilities on a bike or board or while rock climbing puts him in a master class of his own. His vibe and approach may come off as mellow, but Jim is performing at an elite level. Watching him climb is probably the best example. His trad climb leading is bold but steady. Jim makes it look easy, but he is often one step below his limit the whole time.

I was out touring with Jim recently, at a well-known trailhead that he'd been to hundreds of times over the past twenty-five years. Dropping off the back to access the next range behind, Jim weaved through a bony south face and put us on a perfectly spaced treed glade that had just enough northern tilt for cold winter snow. "I can't remember the last time I improved," Jim said to me later in the day as we topped out in a spot on a ridge that would complete the perfect three-run tour through two drainages and put us back at the car without hardly crossing a track, even though it had not snowed in two weeks.

"Bullshit," I said. "That was a masterful tour. You're moving through the mountains with more efficiency and are more effective than ever before." Jim didn't argue the statement. I benefit from his linking of drainages and lines, and I struggle to keep up, especially with changeovers. This is a great example of the beautiful and never-ending learning process. As kids, we can learn a new trick every day, hit bigger cliffs, reach new speeds. As we age, however, evolution takes longer, but there's still great satisfaction in moving through terrain with masterful efficiency and discovering new lines.

Compounding Returns vs. Diminishing Returns

The renowned investor Warren Buffett talks about the power of compounding returns. It's the same in health and life. Following a steady routine focused on developing the mind and body does not seem like it does much at first. Do it every day, though, and over time the benefits are significant. Life can get hectic; control the morning by waking your body and mind, and put your best foot forward.

Morning Routines

I heard a TED Talk from skateboard pioneer Rodney Mullen, who used a screwdriver to break up scar tissue in his hip so he could skate again. *I refuse to go quietly into*

the night, I thought, and decided I needed to up my health game. I got the inversion table I'd always talked about and committed to a morning routine. The key to this is to set the bar low. If it is too hard, it won't last—unless you are a Navy SEAL or Ironman, but that is not me. I am just a snowboarder who wants to ride his whole life. Most of my injuries occur in the morning. I am a diesel engine that needs a proper warm-up to get going. If I warm up properly, I feel great.

Jimmy Chin: Squeezing in Fitness

"My mantra has always been: 'It's not about getting into shape; it's about never getting out of shape.' It is a constant battle for me to stay fit. Over the course of the year my fitness climbs and dips, but I am always training and finding ways to get something in every day: going to the climbing gym, strength training in the hotel gym for an hour, a ten-minute core crusher routine or yoga in the hotel room, push-ups, pull-ups, a twenty-minute Thera-Band workout, a run . . . anything I can squeeze in."

Over the past twenty years of trying everything under the sun and seeing dozens of experts, I know what works well for me: the "if you only do one thing, do this" exercises and stretches I've learned from a variety of trainers. Depending on timing, I have a five-minute version or a twenty-minute version. Every body is different. We all have seemingly unfixable injuries that can become chronic. Find what works for *you*. Become an expert on you. Nobody knows your body better than you or has more invested in it. Every day, before I get out of bed, I spend a minute or two firing my glutes and lower back. When I am camping, I spend even more time doing this. It is a way to warm up my body and sleeping bag. I focus on ten slow, full breaths. Being present for ten complete breaths often requires multiple attempts, so I go back to the start every time I lose my focus. Breathe in through the nose, exhale slowly through the mouth.

Mind Awakenings and Morning Pages

Just like properly waking my body up, I do the same with my mind. I always have a morning book around, like *The Daily Stoic*, *Rules for a Knight*, or *The California Field Atlas*. What I call heavy or thick reading, but taken a few pages at a time, it is digestible. Starting my day with ten to twenty minutes of writing is another practice. What I write about is not important—it is the *act* of writing that matters. A way to dump some thoughts and clear the mind. Between the exercises, reading, and writing, my routine varies between thirty and sixty minutes, depending on how early I wake up.

Morning Routine: The Minimum and the Maximum

For me, the daily bare minimum is the following:

» Use the inversion table one or two minutes, incorporating spine-lengthening principles learned from yoga.
» Roll out my legs on a foam roller.
» Do a deep lunge stretch. I spent a long time with an ex–football player yogi who understood stiff hips better than any other instructor I've found. Over the course of three one-hour private lessons, he taught me how to do four poses perfectly. The lunge is easy to do on the skin track or while waiting in line or on the phone. But you have to learn how to pull into it.
» Do a plank and go through my body, firing major muscle groups.
» Do five to ten one-legged bridge squats, while focusing on firing the glutes.

But if I have more time:

» Spend more time on the above exercises.
» Release the psoas. Learning how to do this is critical. It is hard and there are different techniques. Find a teacher. I lie on a grapefruit-sized ball and am able to get a serious release in a minute or two. If you have a bad back, your psoas is probably tight and making your hips off balance.
» Do an active hamstring stretch.
» Do ten push-ups with your hips on the ground. Most of us are naturally hunched over when doing our sports. This exercise keeps you from being hunchbacked when you're older.

Gym Allergy

Being allergic to the gym, I use different sports to balance out and build strength and fitness: slacklining for the small balance muscles; tennis or pickleball for explosive cutting; surfing to give my legs a break and to build my core and upper-body strength. Climbing is my power yoga, and mountain biking helps condition my quads, hamstrings, and knees, and maintain my overall fitness. It also keeps my downhill reactions tuned up. When I am really busy or traveling, I will run. It is simple and fast. In the fall, work can get really busy, so I make sure to wear running shoes to my office so I can run the 3 miles home. The only time I formally work out is in the fall. I circuit train in my yard or at the beach, which I try to visit right before winter arrives. High-intensive core training, mixed with explosive lunges and hops, with balance work on a PT ball makes a difference for early season. As winter rolls in, I ease my way into riding, slowly increasing time and intensity on snow. I walk and ride myself into shape. I am very conservative with my early riding season. The snowpack is usually complex, the base thin. Just like the snowpack, I'm focused on building my base—no need to rush it.

"Ride for tomorrow, tomorrow is a good day too." —Tommen

Rest Days

The only bit of fitness knowledge I've managed to pull out of Jim Zellers is the vital importance of rest days. These are rare and infrequent, but Jim takes them very seriously. "A rest day is not a work day," he says. "Couch, kitchen, some computer, reading, TV, bed. No socializing, no cleaning, just rest. Rebuild. Rejuvenate." I have a different definition. My rest days are spent in front of a computer battling my inbox or on the phone. But learning to take even these days "off" has been an important adjustment. If there's snow on the trees, I have a really hard time resting. I will do active rest days. Go for what I call a "lactic acid flush." Usually on a tour, moving slowly and not breaking a sweat. By switching days between lift service and touring, I get a break from one or the other while not missing a day of riding. Come spring the missions are bigger, and the objectives more serious. When a good window hits, it is common for me to go dark to dark for a few days and push it to a point where I can't walk anymore. During these periods I'll take three to five days off in between missions.

"A rest day is not a work day. Couch, kitchen, some computer, reading, TV, bed. No socializing, no cleaning, just rest. Rebuild. Rejuvenate." —Jim Zellers

The oldest snowboarder I know lives in northern Norway. His name is Tommen, he is seventy-five and looks like Santa Claus, and he may very well be. What is his trick? "Ride for tomorrow, tomorrow is a good day too." This is a far contrast to the "go big or go home" mentality, but it sits in the front of my brain, especially through the dark months of winter. This is why when riding with the hard chargers, I let them go first so I do not get overamped and do something that will jeopardize the spring sending season.

Performance-Driven Nourishment

A nutritionist once made me do a saliva test to learn what foods I should eat for better performance. I've done a blood test for allergies too. If you start spending a lot of time on longer treks outdoors, you'll find out what types of food you run best on. Knowing which foods you digest easily and which foods make you bonk is critical. It primarily comes down to balancing carbs and fats, understanding the role simple sugars play, and deciding how much you want to eat while on the go.

I try to avoid talking about diet. Like all aspects of my life, my diet is always evolving. Understanding where my food comes from, what impact it has on the planet, and how I feel during, after, and the next day is the basis on which I make my food decisions. I avoid putting labels around diets like vegan, vegetarian, keto, paleo, and so on. Personally, I embrace a plant-based diet. If I had to put a label on the way I eat, it would be "cheating vegan." I ultimately came to a plant-based diet because I realized my body could digest plants much more easily than anything else.

Ode to the Weekend Warrior

You work all week, you drive all night, you fight through the weekend crowds, and you have heard "Should have been here yesterday" a thousand more times than "Today might be the best day of the year." Forty-eight hours later you're driving through traffic and another storm, knowing Monday will be firing. I lived this life throughout my childhood. Five hours each way. Before the ubiquity of cell phones and other technology and in the back of a sedan wedged between my two brothers. You may question your sanity, but it is worth every second.

To take advantage of your opportunities, you need to be in shape for whenever they arise. Two of my closest friends, both elite skiers, are two examples of right and wrong: One rides his bike forty minutes to work every day and is as fit as I am. When the weekend hits, he is ready to crush mountains. The other does his best to stay fit, but he doesn't do any activity—even something little, every day—and is twenty pounds overweight and full of aches and pains. The key is to focus on regular, short high-intensity workouts that fit into the daily schedule. When I am on prolonged promo and sales tours in the fall, I sneak out to a local park for midday runs in my street clothes and do a few explosive hop sets and dynamic stretching. I always sprint the stairs and do five- to fifteen-minute core workouts right before dinner in the living room. When I have a break in my schedule, I tour a city by running and walking. Just keep moving.

I found myself at restaurants thinking about how certain things would make me feel after eating. As a kid, my go-to dinner out was steak. Later this evolved to other forms of meat, but over time, given my experiences with my body in many different situations, I realized eating meat put me in a food coma—my body had to work incredibly hard to digest and store it, making for restless sleep.

As I gained more awareness of the impacts of large-scale meat and dairy agriculture on the planet, I asked myself, *Do I really need this burger?* One pound of ground beef requires roughly 1,800 gallons of water to produce, among other environmental consequences. My wife, Tiffany, realized before I did that I had slowly stopped eating meat. Pretty soon I lost the taste for beef and chicken. The biggest benefit was that I dropped three or four pounds without even trying. This change helped my back and made me feel spryer and fitter without even doing much new.

It wasn't until I watched the film *The Game Changers* that I fully quantified the benefits of going this route. The film documents the transformation of athletes who switched from a meat- to a plant-based diet. Contrary to my kids' belief, I am actually pretty casual about my diet. I love potato chips, I drink one or two beers a night, and if I show up to your grandmother's house and she is serving her famous meat lasagna, I will eat it. When it comes to travel, my dietary "rules" get significantly bent. Try spending a few weeks in a remote Austrian village where the only vegetable is iceberg lettuce. French fries and a vegetable salad work for only so long. Because of scenarios like this, I make sure I have a bite of meat every few months so my stomach doesn't reject it.

I overheard Greg Collins, Jackson underground superhero, tell his clients climbing Denali: "We have six hours of movement today. We are going to time it for the most efficient time of day to move."

Eventually I met people in their seventies, like Ruedi Homberger, still getting after it in the mountains. At seventy-five, he had just ascended and skied an unclimbed 12,000-foot peak in Alaska. "What's the trick to doing this at your age?" I asked. His answer: "Never stop doing it and eat light" and "never get seconds." As I get older, I think about how what I eat affects my joints. Extra weight is an obvious issue. If you are dealing with a nagging injury and are overweight, that places added stress on that injury and on your body all day, every day. Another major factor that a diet adjustment can drastically affect is what I call "microswelling"—a very slight swelling of joints. A few micromillimeters of swelling is often the difference between a good day and an achy day for me.

Clare Gallagher: Calories

"Eating is everything. Calories make the difference between winning and losing. When you're racing a hundred-miler fast, you're expending so much energy over so many hours. You need a constant glucose and caffeine drip. I choose Coca-Cola and Honey Stinger gels. If you don't eat, you eventually can't run. It's simple. It's math—that's why there's no excuse to not eat."

Finding What Works for You

It's nice to see plant-based diets getting more attention, but I hate the strictness of some programs. It takes time to incorporate diet adjustments into your life. Too many times, friends have made abrupt diet changes and declared themselves "vegans" or "vegetarians," only to go back to eating meat a year or two later because it was too hard. I would rather see large quantities of people scale back on eating animals than a small quantity of people become plant-based warriors.

It amazes me how much food I eat during a self-supported, foot-powered trip; I lose about a pound a day, even though I am constantly eating. There is really no way to replenish everything, and the longer the tour, the more weight I lose, even though I never let myself get hungry on a trip. Dialing in the right amount of easy-to-carry, easy-to-cook food that tastes good is an art form, especially if you're going out for more than three or four nights. When I'm really cranking, I keep my diet simple. It is 90 percent CLIF Bloks. The key is eating regularly so you don't bonk. And to refuel later with water, carbs, and protein back at camp. There are many excellent resources on the dietary front; experiment and find what works for you. Learning from endurance athletes whose entire careers are built on fitness has been helpful. Working with CLIF Bar over the years, I've had the opportunity to hang out with elite runners, cyclists, and other elite athletes. I pepper them with question after question about prerace, during, and postrace nutritional protocols.

Backcountry Meals

You want simple foods that do not eat up fuel or time—more time for riding and camp life! Palate is the trickiest thing to satisfy on huge days, because you have to eat so much. I crave salt, so I'll have a salty trail mix to complement the sugars. Nibbling on an energy bar adds substance. If you feel a bonk coming on, stop and deal with it. Eat a CLIF Blok or a gel, hydrate, and just keep walking. Below are my favorites for breakfast, lunch, and dinner as well as some ideas for quick power snacks and freeze-dried meals.

- » **Breakfast.** Enhanced oatmeal. Add protein and other nutrients. Dried goji or blueberries, acai, walnuts, hemp, and chia seeds. Coffee: super-easy-to-use microground instant coffee. I enhance it with MCT and Ashwagandha.
- » **Lunch.** I splurge on snacks of different textures and tastes at the health-food store. Camping is a cheap endeavor. This is why I buy fancy snacks that I normally avoid, such as vegan jerkies and really good chocolate. I also like a selection of different trail mixes: sweet, salty, tangy, and spicy.
- » **Dinner.** Keep it light. The key to traveling well is lightening the load. Stick with simple dinners that don't take up much space and weigh next to nothing. Enhance ramen or pasta. Add dried mushrooms, hempseed, seasoned sunflower seeds, broccoli, sun-dried tomatoes, seaweed.

The day before an endurance event, prehydrate by drinking roughly one to two gallons of water. Eat more than normal—as much as you can comfortably digest. The more worried I am about whether I am fit enough for the day, the more I rely on simple-to-digest power foods. I have one bottle just for electrolyte mixes. I eat two CLIF Bloks every sixty minutes, depending on how hard I'm working.

- » **Freeze-dried meals.** I lived on traditional freeze-dried dinners for winter camping for a few years. I hit my limit and now just thinking about them makes me sick. However, Mary Janes Farm has a good couscous. I like to add different spices and beans. For long trips, such as my ten-day Sierra crossing for the film *Ode to Muir*, we ate this every night. Bring a lot of different creative flavor enhancements.
- » **Snacks and power foods.** A variety of nuts, goji berries, mulberries, kale chips, and bars.

I am always messing with my diet and evolving my eating habits. There is a trend right now of eating less in the mountains. The key to this, which includes intermittent fasting, is to be well nourished and hydrated before heading out. The real benefit is being able to walk for long periods of time and not have to stop to drink or eat. To achieve this, you need to walk slowly, at a zone 1 heart rate. And nailing your recovery right after riding is essential, or you will wither away.

The Send Manifesto

Send while you can!

I have lost too many friends, nursed too many injuries, and toiled through too many droughts.

When the stars align and the mountains open their arms and say, "Come, come one and come all, today is your day, you can have it all."

It is not an infinite resource—health, snow, stability.

When the perfect conditions constellation fills your northern sky and your body is working, cash in those household credits, go into social debt if needed, burn that bridge (those who know, know), drop everything, and go, go, go!

It's as fickle as a Lake Tahoe swell, as complex as chemistry, and as fleeting as solar totality.

Don't pause, don't hesitate. Push away life's laws and get over your flaws.

Say your sorrys, push the chores to the side, beat the sun, and jump the day.

Grab life by the neck, wrestle every last step, go far, and touch every last star.

Hydration

Water is the key to life. The first thing I put into my body every morning is a glass of Athletic Greens, a daily supplement. Lemon in warm water with salt is also a great way to start. Adding electrolytes is something I do in the mountains. I think of it as getting more hydration out of less water weight. Leading up to a big day, I try to prehydrate a day or two beforehand, taking a cue from fitness icon Tom Brady, who drinks over 100 ounces a day. If you have trouble drinking enough water, try adding flavored electrolytes, which can help when you're really getting after it in the sun. I also like coconut water.

Recovery: Postmission Protein

It is amazing what good recovery can do for you. When conditions are firing, I give everything I have and am often stumbling back to the tent. Getting protein in your system within twenty minutes of completing a big day is critical. Pistachios are something I always have at the trailhead so I can immediately start my recovery. (I like to have a banana too.) When camping I rely on a powdered protein drink, followed by miso soup, right away. So often I think *I am cooked. There is no way I can ride tomorrow.* But I know that if I recover properly and start out slow, I can go day after day in the mountains.

Mountain Meditation

There are many forms of moving through nature: walking, hiking, biking. I do them all. But nothing is as spectacular as setting your path on the blank white winter canvas and letting your skins take you wherever you want. You are not restricted to a hiking trail and do not need to be as focused on the six feet in front of you as you do on a bike. I like to leave my options open for as long as possible. I pick a starting point, have a loose end point, but really just let the world swallow me up in all its magnificent wonder and awe.

My wife, Tiffany, looks at me like a crazy person as I leave the house to ride day after day after day. Not on those bluebird powder days—that she understands—but on those days when it has not snowed in weeks and the wind has battered the slopes and I am rushing out early anyway to beat the sun like it is the best day of the year. On these days it is often more about the up than the down. If it was all about the down, then I would just ride the resort. If it was all about riding powder, I would not be rushing out on hardpack days over and over again. Instead, it's about the simple act of walking in nature.

"In every walk with Nature one receives far more than he seeks." —John Muir

Nature Bathing

The juxtaposition of myself in nature vs. myself in the city is how I realized there was more at play with my interactions with nature. I had long acknowledged that snowboarding was no longer just a way to get huge shots of adrenaline. But it was not until I started doing a deeper dive into my mind and spirit that I began to comprehend the importance of nature therapy. Is this why even after more than thirty-five years and thousands of days of sliding on snow, the pull is still so strong? I have not learned a new trick in a decade, but my snowboard still regularly gives me new experiences in nature.

I started carrying a pocket notebook to record my thoughts when I'm in the woods and mountains. It is in these notebooks (much of which formed the basis of this book) that I work out my most pressing issues, both in life and in business. Movie concepts, board shapes, design ideas, how my kids—Mia and Cass—are doing in school, what needs to be done around the house, how Tiffany is doing while I'm on tour. Out there is where I reset my personal and professional compass.

Embracing this approach is especially true in snowy mountains with avalanche conditions, when you might not get the line you hoped for. But there's also truth in the fact that one must always be fluid in the mountains, simply take what they are giving you that day. Sometimes it is the line of the year; other times the steeps are scoured but the low-angle gullies are fast and smooth, allowing you to surf through meadows that would normally bog you down in deep snow. Looking at my ride logs from over the years shows that on average I ride up to twenty-eight days a month. Some days are only a few hours, but you can see the consistency is there regardless of the conditions. There has to be something more at work here. Jim Zellers likes to say he is a devout member of the Church of the Seven Day Recreationalists, of which I am also a proud member. "The Church matters," Jim says. And it does. Sometimes our only salve is in nature.

When I'm traveling for shows and events, campaigns to combat climate change, or tours for movies and interviews, I find myself looking on Google Maps for green sections indicating parks or woods. If possible, I try to get into a city a few hours before the event. When a local guide or friend offers to take me around the city, I say, "No, take me to the closest park!"

"You live in the mountains—don't you want to see the city?"

"Yes, if I have time, but first I need to see the trees." Sometimes I sneak past houses or climb fences at rest areas, to run into the woods and find the most powerful tree I can to soak up its energy. Sometimes I might only have twenty minutes, but it's enough. I come back to the car or hotel a new person, ready to spend the night in yet another city, present to crowds, give interviews, maybe have some hard conversations about the mountain environment. I stumble home after these travel obligations, feeling half the human I was when I set out weeks or months earlier—my time in nature has been reduced to all-time lows. Physically I am able to maintain a baseline of fitness, but it is the mental part that becomes unglued. After a few weeks of heavy nature bathing, I slowly get my mind back and I start having clear thoughts again.

Even just walking has huge benefits for the mind. Ryan Holiday, in his book *Stillness Is the Key*, sums up what I have been feeling for so long but could never put a finger on: "How does walking get us closer to stillness? Isn't the whole point of what we are talking about to reduce activity, not seek it out? Yes, we are in motion when we walk, but it is not frenzied motion or even conscious motion—it is repetitive, ritualized motion. It is deliberate. It is an exercise in peace." Holiday goes on to discuss the Buddhist concept of "walking meditation." This focuses on "movement through a beautiful setting, can unlock a different kind of stillness than traditional meditation. Indeed, forest bathing—and most natural beauty—can only be accomplished by getting out of your house or office or car and trekking out into the woods on foot."

Just imagine how this idea translates on a cold winter morning as the sun beams through the towering pines and reflects off the powder as you stride with ease through the soft bed of snow crystals! Eventually the trees thin out, the alpine reveals itself, the pitch steepens, you feel the weight of your board on your back, and your hands, feet, and knees are all working and alive as you march straight up the chute, surrounded by monolithic granite spires piercing hundreds of feet into the atmosphere above, creating a perfect hallway to take you to the top of your world, allowing you to reach the highest of heights and see all the landscape around you. Now add the way down and imagine what we do on our boards when conditions are perfect.

This is when I enter into a world so mystical and magical that it is no wonder I dedicate and shape my life around it. This is Shralpinism—a love of shredding, yes, but even more a love of the alpine, the mountains, the forests, the natural world.

CHAPTER 8

Gear and Backcountry Travel

When it comes to riding, the first order of business is finding a board that fits your abilities, style, and goals. Sometimes this might mean more than one board—say, one for hardpack steeps and groomers and another for soft snow and powder. There are lots of great boards and board companies out there, but I prefer Jones boards. Ha-ha. Seriously, the best thing to do is go to your local demo and try out different skis and boards. Get advice from an expert at a shop or from more experienced friends who can help you figure out the best board shape, style, and size for you.

Picking the Perfect Board

The one mistake I see over and over is that people think they are way better than they actually are and go for a very stiff, pro-level flex. I am guilty of this with my surfing. I wasted years and countless waves trying to surf a board more suitable for Kelly Slater than for someone who surfs only forty days a year. Companies make so many different boards because there are so many different skill levels. Some are best suited for experts, and others for intermediates and beginners. Countless times people ask to buy our stiffest, most expensive "ultra" series boards. I tell them to read the description, which could not be more clear: "This board is for pro-level freeriders who log over 100 days a year, leg press 400 pounds, and like to stomp huge cliffs and straight-run moguls." The person asking the question usually rides less than thirty days a year and is a midlevel rider. He reads the description and tells me, "Yeah, that's what I want."

Be honest with yourself. Do your research. Rent before purchasing, if possible. Learn about flex, sidecut, and rocker and why these features matter. This hands-on education is a huge reason why local shops are so important. Pick a tool that matches your level and you will have a better time. Here are the basic things to consider:

- » **If speed is your game,** you want a long sidecut with a stiff flex.
- » **If playful is your jam,** a tight sidecut and softer flex will liven up a board and make it more maneuverable.
- » **Waist width** is probably the most important measurement, especially in snowboarding. Specifically, how big are your feet? How narrow a board can you ride before getting heel and toe drag? A narrow board reduces chatter, which is critical in bumpy, firm, bulletproof conditions. Wider boards add float.
- » **Light vs. right:** board weight and boot stiffness matter, albeit more for skis than boards; they need to match one another, otherwise you'll be in

Board Choice: Optimizing for Performance, Fun, and Conditions

Board choice is really important, and you want to optimize for fun. If you're having a blast in all conditions, you're on the right equipment. If you find yourself getting bored on the mountain unless conditions are perfect, think about making an equipment change. The basic quiver:

- » **Directional freeride shape.** My do-everything daily driver. This is the board I always travel with.
- » **Surf shape wide and fat.** My go-to for powder. Brings variety to groomers and spring conditions as well. My second board in the bag.
- » **Hardpack buster.** Narrow, heavy camber, and freestyle-focused board.
- » **Big gun.** This board, for the super-deep pow days, sees the least amount of use but is clutch when needed.

Getting More Out of Less

Despite all the amazing boards out there, getting more out of less is critical to long-term health and happiness. I see it every time I'm out with people ten, twenty years older than I am, as happy as can be in simpler terrain. There is a time to shed the shackles of safety and tickle the edge of life and death, but it is not in the middle of prolonged storms with questionable stability in the snowpack.

Figure out how to be happy in low-angle terrain. Maybe it is dropping a knee? Standing sideways? Or simply a wider pair of skis or riding with your boots unbuckled so you can bring some ankle freedom to your noodling. A lot has to do with the right equipment. Near my home in Truckee, we have the perfect go-to pow lap during high-avy conditions because it is just flat enough to not slide. It is also just flat enough to barely move in pow. The right board makes it fun. The wrong board has me sniffing at steeper terrain, talking myself into it being safe.

for a wild ride. Lightweight skis, and sometimes boards, can be too light for really stiff boots and vice versa.

» **When in doubt, always optimize for fun.**

» **Build your quiver:** have your "daily driver" that handles everything. This board will be ridden most and will need replacing every few years. Adding an alternative shape that turns the mundane into magical is a nice complement. Also the big "powder gun" that seems ridiculous when it's hardpack but is gold when it really dumps. These alternate boards will not see as much time on snow and therefore could last a lifetime, so pick wisely.

Basic Upkeep

Keep your equipment well-tuned. People often think they need a new board, when in reality they just need a proper tune. When it's firm out, sharp edges are crucial. A good shop can make a beat-up board feel new. If your board is in good shape, it is easy to keep it sharp with a basic edge file. Keeping your base smooth and moist is simple and essential. You should own an iron and wax frequently. It is the difference between blasting that side hit or bogging down on the way to it. In the spring it is good to add structure to your base.

The Storm Chaser: Turning the Mundane into Magical

POULSEN'S GULLY, OLYMPIC VALLEY, 1999

My appetite for overcrowded lift lines has lessened over the years. This means in a good winter I'm riding a lot of rolling tree pow. Getting the most out of rolling tree runs led to the development of surf-shaped boards with Chris Christenson, a renowned surfboard designer. Chris's designs have been embraced by big-wave paddle-in surfers Greg Long and Ian Walsh. When surfing, how a board glides on water is everything. A fast-gliding surfboard can turbocharge a knee-high wave into a racetrack. Success or failure is based on how efficiently the board glides. A faster board means more waves, making more sections, and getting longer rides. With snow, gravity is a constant. Nobody is going out and getting skunked because their board is 5 percent slower and they cannot catch a wave or make a section.

I vividly remember riding one of my favorite gullies at Squaw (now called Palisades Tahoe) on a deep day. To find it requires keeping speed through tight, flat trees before it opens up, the pitch steepens, and you find yourself in the natural half-pipe lined with side hits. I was on my pow board, I had first tracks, and my favorite hit was calling, but as I approached I bogged down, and instead of flying forever into a bed of bottomless crystals, I barely made it off the ground because my board was bogging.

It took ten years, but I finally found a board that turns 30 degrees into 40 because there's no friction. The board is the Jones Storm Chaser. Chris and I designed it in his shaping bay using the same surf tools and curves he has been refining his whole life. The board incorporates his fastest bottom contours, which were passed down from his mentor, Skip Frye. After a few hours we eyeballed our way into what felt like something that resembled a snowboard. It was shipped off to be scanned, turned into a file, and eventually, a snowboard. My engineer looked at the specs in disbelief. "Are you sure you want me to make this? It's 147 centimeters long and 27.5 centimeters wide. We will need to develop new tools to make something like this. It will cost three times more than a normal board." At the time Jones was only two years old, so this was a huge investment for a board that I assumed would only work in powder. The specs were so far out of the box. I would have never handed over those dimensions for a board before, but I stood by what Chris and I had made. It felt right standing on it in his shaping room.

"Pull it from marketing," I told them. "This is why I started a company, to do new things." The board ended up working in a wide array of conditions, but most important: it made the mundane magical. It was a great lesson on the importance of not being shackled by preconceived notions.

Keeping Skins Happy

Skins need a lot of love. If you keep them happy, they'll take you places you never imagined. Skins can be fickle, and if not properly cared for, they can make your day or trip a nightmare. Different conditions call for different kinds of care. For instance:

- » **Midwinter.** Keeping skins sticking on multi-lap days during dark winter can be difficult. The snow is dry and often deep, and there's very little sun. When I take my skins off, I brush them against my thigh or edge to scrape off snow. I fold each skin together and often put them inside my jacket to keep them warm. Warming your base in the sun can greatly help them stay sticky.
- » **Spring.** The concern at this time of year is having the glue from the skin stick to the base. The glue is really hard to get off and will make your board really sticky on the descent. Keep the skins and your base out of the sun.
- » **Glopping.** In spring or midwinter warm-ups, skins can turn into the dreaded "Frankenboot." If your skins get wet in warm snow, and you cross into colder powder, the cold snow sticks to the wet skin and creates a huge glob that can build up, making climbing impossible. Wax your skins to help them glide better and to help prevent buildup.

Skin Failure

Having a skin fall off and not stick anymore is not only a total pain in the ass but potentially life-threatening—especially if you are in a drainage and your only way home is up and over a mountain. Recently a person died deep in the mountains because his skins fell off, the snow was too deep to hike, and he could not make it through the cold winter night.

» Stop it before it starts: monitor how your skins are sticking to the bases. If there is any question, stop and take care of them.

» Get skins working again: if they are really bad, you might have to bootpack a little with them in your jacket to warm them up.

» Create a nice flat platform to strap in and restart skinning. Skins usually come off in steep sections when they are under the max torque, so this might mean booting a steep section to get to a flat space. If you can start walking on a flatter, firm track, you can often walk your skins into sticking again.

» Overcompensate on the steeps by putting weight on your poles so you are stressing your skins less.

» You should always have ski (tension) straps

» If your skins are failing, after getting the snow off them as best as possible, wrap the straps around the skin. If you have enough, also wrap them where the skin is failing, usually right behind your binding and on the tail.

Backcountry Camping

Camping opens up opportunities for vast expanses of terrain that cannot be reached in a day. Few things are as humbling as waking up in a dark tent, covered in frost, and motivating yourself to leave the sleeping bag, put on the boots, reach outside into the vestibule to turn on a stove, and feed yourself so you can slog up a steep mountain. The question of why is never stronger than on those predawn mornings. Back in the comfort of home, maps spread out, beer in hand, buddies around the table, the why is simple. The desire to get past "I can walk there in a day," to those gray areas off the map. The chance to go where perhaps no one has been before. The opportunity to connect with nature in the purest form possible. To meet the land on its terms.

Or maybe it's the simple fact that for me—I have hit the biggest cliff I'm going to hit, have tipped the inclinometer as far as I am comfortable with, and have reached my top end speed—getting deep into the backcountry is my way to keep

If you have a chance to take a NOLS (National Outdoor Leadership School) course, do it. It changed my brothers' lives and therefore changed mine. I can spot a NOLS-level-certified camper a mile away.

progressing, learning, and evolving. Maybe it's even simpler than that. Maybe my addiction to seeing new mountains and finding out what's around the next corner is so strong that I will put myself through great hardships. More likely, it's the fact that for years, I searched the world's greatest ranges at lightning speeds with the use of helicopters, snowmobiles, and planes at a high resource cost. Now I want to have those same experiences, but where the barrier to entry is not money and resources but my own energy and commitment.

As painful as it is to carry a heavy pack all day, get out of a warm sleeping bag in the morning, and battle to cram my feet in frozen boots, once I'm moving, I always get an overwhelming feeling. *This is the coolest thing I do, and this is where I belong.* It's getting to that wonderful place on the planet at a moment in time where I think, *I need every bit of knowledge and fitness I have to be at this point in the universe right now.* That I couldn't have reached that place in life a minute earlier. To bump my personal progression time line forward has taken millions of steps, trillions of calories, and a constant tweaking of my approach.

Hiking with a Heavy Pack

"In pain in the membrane" is a twist on a lyric I often sing, because hauling a heavy pack hurts. On average, I carry about seventy-five pounds, including my board and gear. I just put my head down and walk as long as possible until the pain is unbearable, and then hike ten minutes longer. Give yourself all day to hike as far as you can hike with your heavy pack. It hurts, but it is also relaxing to walk into new country and take in the new views without the pressures of where to ride. It takes a lot of energy to haul a heavy pack on and off. When it's on, I'm walking and covering as much ground as possible. When I stop, I get the most out of my breaks. The Navy SEALs have a saying: "Never stand when you can sit, never sit when you can lie down, never stay awake when you can sleep." This is why I keep my foam pad accessible on the outside of my pack. During breaks I unroll my pad and lie down to get the most recovery.

What's in My Backpack: Expedition

Beyond the obvious—board, bindings, boots, skins—I'm also carrying:

» Transceiver, probe, shovel
» Crampons
» Ice axe
» First-aid kit
» Repair kit (bailing wire, extra screws and nuts, zip ties, tape on my poles)
» Multi-tool
» Tent, sleeping bag, pad
» Food and stove
» Clothing
» Ski (tension) straps

The Whys, the Whats, and the Hows

Curiosity and intrigue are at the heart of how I interact with, observe, and travel in the mountains. This is how you pick up the signs and start the conversation with the mountains. Some questions are obvious, while others take years to understand. Never stop asking the whys, the whats, and the hows. Why does this face get twice as much snow as the one next to it? What is the perfect temperature that allows snow to stick to steeps? Why did this northeast face slide naturally and not that one? Why did this face spine up, but the one right next to it didn't?

Where to Camp: The Perfect Spot

How do you pick a spot to camp and explore? I prefer thick sections of ranges as opposed to narrow sections. Tightly stacked peaks catch the storms and offer the best chance to find a hidden dream line. My home range is 400 miles long. Over the past fifteen years, I have been systematically prospecting the range. You only have so many steps on this planet—I want to use mine to see as much of the Sierra Nevada as possible. This is why I rarely hike the same mountain twice.

Snow level, road closures, and time of year narrow down the options. Avoiding long dirt approaches and getting to skinning on snow as fast as possible are critical. Carrying everything on your back for long distances is a brutally fatiguing way to start a trip. What elevation is holding the best snow? Often, the high peaks are wind hammered, especially earlier in the winter, so I focus on mid-elevation spots. Mid-elevation, in tightly stacked sections of the range, often hides the most rippable lines with the best snow.

Picking the trailhead is the trickiest decision. From there, I largely let my eyes do the rest. I don't spend much time pre-scoping maps, Google Earth, or other sources. These tools aren't a bad idea, but I'm always pinched for time and just trying to get to the trailhead. Plus, I like to keep things a mystery. You only get one chance to walk into fresh wilderness, and I want to keep it a mystery for as long as possible and not tarnish the experience with preconceived ideas based on Google Earth images. That's not to say I don't fall down the Google Earth rabbit hole, but it rarely pans out. The Google hero lines are often too big and gnarly in real life. Having a potential objective as a goal is nice, but a certain line often brings me to a zone, and I end up not riding the target line because I fall in love with other lines I did not know about.

> The greatest discovery is a backyard discovery. It is like finding a bonus room in your house. A hidden Christmas present.

The three most important aspects of a winter camp spot are water, elevation, and sun direction.

» **Find water.** Water is essential. You'll save hours of time and tons of fuel if you can find a water source. Sometimes this means shoveling down and breaking holes in the ice to get to water. In winter, open water is usually not an option. Dial in a snow-melting station that's going nonstop when you are in camp. Waiting for snow to melt and fill water bottles takes hours, lots of fuel, and greatly slows down getting out of camp. In spring, I put camp at the highest lake possible with easy access to water. I carry a six-liter dromedary bag in my pack in case I find water while hiking. In warmer spring weather, I create drip systems into pots and bottles to catch the water melt from the rocks. If done right, you can come back to camp to full pots of water at the end of a day in the mountains. Being water-rich as opposed to water-poor can change the whole camping experience and keep everyone hydrated, happy, and moving.

» **Consider elevation.** Camping above treeline is taxing on your body. Trees provide shelter and oxygen. Above treeline, you're generally at about 11,000 feet or higher in most ranges. The difference between 11,000 and 9,000 feet is significant. When I crossed the Sierra in 2018, I was above 11,000 feet for five nights. I didn't know how beat up I was until I descended into the trees. Being around the pines brought life back into my head and body. I spent two nights camping by a river at 9,000 feet and totally rejuvenated myself, as if the trees had doubled the oxygen level.

» **Respect the sun.** Above 10,000 feet the sun sucks the life out of you. As I write this, I'm still recovering from four days above 11,000 feet. It's been three days since I got home, and my lips and tongue are still blistered. The higher you go, the more intense the sun. On Denali, I was blessed with eleven days of clear skies and sun, which in the summer never totally sets. There I learned to time my travel with the sun. Hiding in a tent during peak sun hours can save you from frying your skin, brains, and body. But on summit days, or if you are only out for a few days, this is probably not an option.

On extended spring trips, when the days are long, I wake up early and stay out late, choosing to do my traveling and riding when the sun is not so vicious. This often allows for a midday siesta at some point, either in a tent or under the shade of a tree. Have the right hat, face protection, and sunscreen. Sunscreen the inside of your nostrils when spending a lot of time on snow. On Denali in 2013, Freeride World Tour champ turned coffee shop owner Ralph Backstrom showed up with a handmade leather face shield attached to his glasses. I laughed at first, but by the third day of sun, I would have paid a lot of money for it. For very cold, heart-of-winter camping, you want the earliest sun possible, so find an east-facing spot. The sun will start warming you right away, making it much easier to get out of the sleeping bag.

Once you locate a camp spot, flatten out your tent site with your skins on. Get everyone together to dig out a quick kitchen. A horseshoe-shaped trench is the most efficient way to create bench seating and a table. Make sure you're out of the wind and have a good view! You will spend a ton of time by the stove making water. Dial the table so you're not hunched over. "Stove back" is real!

Tent or bivy? It's a special feeling being up in the mountains as the colors of day transition slowly into night, the moon rises, stars fall, and the Milky Way floats across the sky, eventually giving way to the rising sun. There's no better way to experience this spectacle than sleeping outside without a tent. In summer, it's easy to leave the tent at home, unless some rain or high winds are in the forecast. Winter is a different story. The tent adds warmth and a nice place to lay out all your stuff. It also provides a break from the elements if you're sleeping high. Bottom line: Go with a tent if you're sleeping above treeline, camping for more than four nights, or serious weather is forecast and the temps will be below 15 degrees F. If you're sleeping at or below the snowline, at lower elevation, and in well-protected areas without any rain or snow, bivy all the way!

Boots. My feet are always cold. Be proactive about keeping your feet warm (or, rather, not frozen). Swing your feet to get blood back into them. Take your boot off and rub your toes to get some warmth back. Taking proper care of your boots helps too. Dry your boots and liners any chance you get. Sun's out—boots out! I sleep with my liners wrapped in a shirt or thin shell. Remove the insoles too. When winter camping and riding hard all day, however, your boots are never going to really dry out. An extra pair of dry socks is nice, but the difference between wet socks and dry socks is about twenty minutes. Keep your laces dry. In the past, my laces would get wet, freeze, and become useless. Dropping into the Wall of Walls after sleeping on top of the line, I couldn't get my laces tightened because they were so frigid they wouldn't flex. I often had to ride a serious line with frozen, unlaced boots—not ideal (or safe), but that was the norm when I first started hiking big lines in Alaska. Thanks to lace covers, this is no longer an issue.

"It's still extremely hard to get good technical gear in small sizes. Companies still make female ski boots much softer than men's. And the high-end men's boots often don't go small enough. I haven't had a ski pack that fits me in three years." —Christina Lusti

Sleeping bag and pad. I skimp on clothes, layers, and other stuff, *but never my sleeping bag.* A warm and good night's sleep is critical to recovery and getting moving first thing. While I'm freezing as I eat dinner, it's nice to know I'll be warm as soon as I get in my bag. Whatever the low temp forecasted, I subtract 15 to 20 degrees to get the bag rating I want. Low of 15 degrees F = 0-degree bag. My 0-degree bag is what I use 90 percent of the time. In Alaska, sleeping on a glacier, it's common to have single-digit temps. I have a −10-degree bag for these conditions. Splurge on the best bag you can afford, take good care of it, and it'll last for decades.

On really cold nights, I take my midlayer puffy and put it over my feet and knees while sleeping—a game changer. I'm a big fan of using a closed-cell foam pad and a lightweight Therm-a-Rest on top. When I'm hanging out, I always have my foam pad to sit or stand on. Even when standing around in camp, it's better to stand on an insulating pad to prevent heat loss. Some people go with the lighter sleeping bag but bring puffy pants. Do your own research. Check out what the alpinists or speed

Fill a Nalgene bottle with hot water. Sleep with it by your toes or chest. Make sure you do not sweat, though, because the water will eventually cool down, leaving you chilled.

What's in My Backpack: Day Tour

» Multi-tool
» Transceiver, shovel, probe
» GPS or emergency location device
» First-aid kit
» Repair kit
» Sunscreen
» Small battery charger for big days
» Headlamp (having a light could be the difference between making it back to the car or having to spend the night out; I have a light headlamp that lives in my pack)
» Puffy jacket (essential if there's an injury or you have a forced night out)
» Ski (tension) straps
» Zipties
» Para cord
» Extra screws
» CLIF SHOT Double Expresso energy gel (emergency use if I'm too tired to make it back to the trailhead)

hikers are doing. Experiment to figure out the system that works best to keep you warm.

Stoves. "What happens if the stove doesn't work?" Chris Edmands asked Tom Burt as he was prepping for drop-off 75 miles from town for our first foot-powered Alaska trip. "You die," said Tom. Sounds dramatic, but he was right. Melting snow is how you get your water in the backcountry. No stove, no water. No water, no life. Making sure your stove works is critical. With current lightweight stoves, it's easy and important to pack a backup when on a longer trip. Also critical: make sure you have enough fuel. The length of your stay is more often about how much fuel you have, rather than how much food. Most people, myself included, bring too much food. Extra supplies aren't necessarily bad: they're good to have in case something happens, and they also give you the option to stay an extra day if your dream line needs more time.

Nailing the fuel isn't an exact science. But follow the guidelines below and add 30 percent. For midwinter camping, it's nice to have one stove for every two people. Otherwise, making water becomes a lengthy burden. Know how to fix and repair your stove. Carry the parts you might need in the field.

» **Butane canisters.** The canister/reactor/Jetboil stove has gained in popularity for good reason. It's simple and boils fast. However, cold kills canisters. With spring camping, cold is not a big deal, but with proper, dead-of-winter camping, butane does not perform nearly as well as white gas. Some people sleep with the butane canisters to help keep them warm. If boiling fuel for water, you'll need *a lot* of canisters, which adds *a lot* of weight, and they're not that comfortable to sleep with.

» **Traditional camp stove.** The traditional MSR WhisperLite white gas stove is one of the greatest inventions in the modern camping era.

This timeless workhorse has withstood the test of time. Boiling water takes longer, but you can use much bigger pots, which is a huge plus. Cold isn't a big deal. For longer trips I like to have at least one WhisperLite stove on hand.

Tools of the Trade

Most riders know they need a shovel, probe, and beacon for the backcountry, but these items are useless if you don't know how to properly use them. Practice and check your gear regularly. Make sure your beacon's batteries are above 60 percent, otherwise change them out. Only use alkaline batteries. Check your probe to make sure it unfolds easily and locks into shape solidly, and don't keep it in its stuff sack. Another critical factor is where the gear sits in your pack. When your friend is buried under the snow and you need to dig them out, timing is critical. Knowing exactly where your gear is and getting to it fast is an easy tailwind during a rescue.

Beacon Checks

When you wear an avy beacon, make sure it is turned on! I can't overstate the importance of beacon checks. As I've increased the frequency of beacon checks, I'm amazed at how many times someone has not turned it on, left it in the car, or simply forgotten it. Among experienced riders, someone forgets to have it on nearly 10–20 percent of the time. These riders may be the most vulnerable to complacency. Not wearing a beacon in the backcountry is a massive problem. Wearing a beacon but

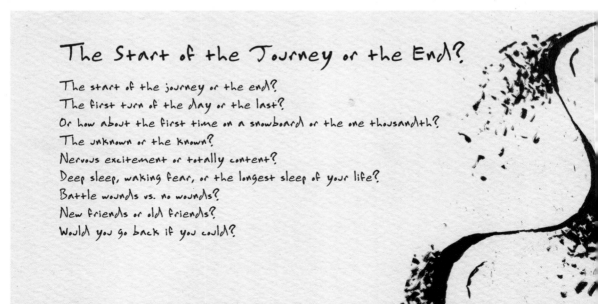

The Start of the Journey or the End?

The start of the journey or the end?
The first turn of the day or the last?
Or how about the first time on a snowboard or the one thousandth?
The unknown or the known?
Nervous excitement or totally content?
Deep sleep, waking fear, or the longest sleep of your life?
Battle wounds vs. no wounds?
New friends or old friends?
Would you go back if you could?

GPS Emergency Device

After spending a lot of time in the backcountry, I can say that people usually do not carry the proper equipment for moving someone who's hurt and cannot walk. A simple injury can require a rescue if it happens more than a few miles from a trailhead. If you've ever tried to evac a friend who cannot ski or ride out under their own power, you understand how important outside medical help is. This is why my emergency GPS lives in my pack. Cell service is usually spotty at best in the mountains and never reliable. A GPS device that can send texts and mark your location is vital. Communication can make the difference between life and death. I prefer the Somewear device, because it's so light and holds a charge for weeks on end.

not having it turned on is an even bigger issue. Without a beacon signal, it's virtually impossible to find your friend.

Over the years, I've forgotten my beacon a half-dozen times. When I do, I let my partners know, and we discuss whether everyone is okay with me continuing into the backcountry with them. This is an interesting exercise in backcountry travel. Going into avalanche terrain without a beacon changes my risk tolerance, but, as with an airbag, should it? Studies show that 35 percent of people caught in serious avalanches die of trauma, and 40 percent die if they are buried more than five feet down.

Why do we take more risks just because we wear a beacon? My decisions the few times I went into the backcountry on a suspect day without a beacon were hyperfocused. I was totally engaged at all times and had heightened awareness on routefinding and terrain selection, careful to stay out of avy terrain. These issues all point back to the most important question: *What if it slides?* Protocols, training, and working beacons keep you alive.

To Airbag or Not to Airbag?

Airbags work. If given the option to choose between us all having airbags or having a beacon, shovel, and probe, I would choose airbags. Thankfully, I don't need to choose. If there's any question in the snowpack, and I'm still riding, I wear my airbag. As the cycle progresses after a storm, and I learn more about stability and am comfortable with the hazards, I pull my airbag canister out of my pack to save weight. This is a personal decision. As pro-airbag as I am, it may come as a surprise that I rarely wear it in my home range. I'm not looking to outsmart the avy danger. Our snowpack is predictable most of the time. It snows a bunch and then is dangerous. High pressure fills in, the sun comes out, and a day or two later the snow is usually stable. I've seen it go from high avy danger to low in twelve hours. Knowing our snowpack settles so quickly, I just give it the needed twenty-four to forty-eight hours after a storm before starting to prospect steeper terrain.

The High Sierra is a different beast. The snowpack, especially in winter, can have much more complexity, and the terrain is much larger in scale. If word gets around there's instability in the range, I typically avoid the danger altogether. A small day in the High Sierra involves 6,000 feet of climbing and often starts way before dawn, hiking a dirt trail. Having as light a backcountry kit as possible proves essential for success on big days, and the added weight of the airbag can really drag me down. When camping on a glacier in Alaska, lines are usually 1,000 to 2,000 vertical feet, and 90 percent of the time I wear my airbag. The routes

> I thought about my decision to not pull my airbag. It was a stupid call. There was a moment in the slide where I was deep enough to get buried.

up present a lot of complexities and decision-making, which takes time. In Alaska, I rarely climb 6,000 vertical feet in a day. Having an airbag in this situation isn't a big deal. Europe is similar. Touring is mostly lift assisted, and the snowpack is often complex, so I wear an avy bag.

The lingering question remains: Do you take bigger risks with an airbag? It's important to ask this question every time you wear one. Does it change my outlook on stability or terrain? Would I ride the line without an airbag? There shouldn't be a difference, but there seems to be.

Helmets

Helmets are a personal decision, although I recommend one (hitting my head on rock is not an option). Helmets also keep my goggles in place when I cartwheel. My head seems to end up in the snow a lot. It's not uncommon for me to cartwheel once or twice, time my rotation, find my feet, and ride out. Without a helmet, odds are I'd lose my goggles and waste time searching for them. I feel helmets are mandatory equipment during low-tide conditions and when riding lower water content snowpacks that have rocks lingering below (places such as Utah, Wyoming, Montana, Colorado, and Europe). One accident report involving a famous snowboarder brings this point home. As he was riding slowly down a flat ridge, roughly 10 miles per hour, the tip of his board hit a rock just below the surface, he fell forward, hit his head on a rock, and died. There were no other injuries. A sobering example of how a simple impact to the head can be deadly serious.

I Should've Pulled

TORDRILLO MOUNTAINS, ALASKA, 2015

The only time I've been in a slide with my airbag, I did not pull the bag. I should have. I was riding in on a solid, stable snowpack. The avy danger had been rated low, prior to a brief "dusting" of snow by Alaska standards, 3-6 inches and up to 8-10 inches in the deepest spots. There had been clear signs of avalanche activity with this new snow on obvious slopes with steep convex rolls. I chose a line that had a clear pocket, about the size of a basketball court, that I assumed would slide. It hung above a chute and had defined ridges on either side.

Dropping in, I expected the slope to slide. My plan was to ride really fast, release the slope, and straight run through the chute and ride out in front of the sluff. The outrun was clean, no rocks below, and no terrain traps. Just the classic flat Alaskan glacier that allows the debris to fan out, so I wasn't worried about getting buried. I assumed the slope would slide lower down where it rolled and got steeper, but when I entered the snowfield above the chute, the entire thing buckled and cracked all at once. I could have potentially cut out, but that would have put me over a cliff. They were not that big, 20 to 30 feet, but they weren't something I wanted to cartwheel over. Sticking to my plan, I pointed straight toward the chute between the two cliffs and I was going fast, maybe 50 miles per hour, in hopes of beating the slide.

As I approached the chute opening, the slide engulfed me. It didn't hit me hard, it was more like a big sluff with a powder cloud that blinded my view. I kept it pointing

dead center and took a little air in the middle of the chute, but I couldn't land it due to the speed and the fact that I couldn't see. I cartwheeled once, righted myself, and felt the weight of the avalanche push down on me. It was like a wave hitting, and it pinned me down for a second or two. As the avalanche fanned out on the big lower apron below, I quickly came to the top, upright and on my feet as the slide slowed down. My worst-case scenario had happened and I was able to free myself from the debris with my hands.

Prior to dropping in, I had made myself commit: "Whatever happens, aim for the chute, the outrun is clean and the avalanche will not be deep." I didn't even consider pulling the airbag on my back. I'm not proud of the line and although the shot was dramatic, and would've had the audience amped, we decided not to put it in the film. (My younger self wouldn't have cut it, but I've really shied away from showing avalanches unless we break down the exact situation in the film.) I rode through the day and I couldn't get anything else to budge. Lying in my tent that night, I thought about my decision to not pull my airbag. It was a stupid call. There was a moment in the slide where I was deep enough to get buried. Dropping in, I had a plan, but it didn't include pulling my airbag—it should have.

Sharp Stuff

While helmets are a personal option, you'll definitely need crampons on some routes, and an ice axe—and knowing how to wield it—can save your life.

Picking the right crampons and axe. In steep snow, I go as light as possible, which means aluminum crampons and an aluminum axe, 60–70 cm. Go longer depending on your height. For technical climbing and riding, in steep snow with water and glacier ice, I use a "techgnar" setup, which includes two aluminum axes with steel tips and steel crampons. It's rare for me to use this setup—it's heavy but holds. As I've become more comfortable with crampons and hiking steep faces, I rarely bring an axe.

Using poles as axes. If you're hiking and fall, slide your hand down the pole all the way to the basket. This turns the part of the pole under the basket into a sharp point that'll help arrest you even in firm snow. This is a critical move if you fall while skinning. When I'm climbing steeper terrain and concerned about falling, I drop both hands down to the baskets and use the poles like two axes. If I'm concerned

Probe Strike

The one and only time I've heard of a successful recovery with a probe strike happened with Teton Gravity Research. Skier Nick McNutt was skiing out of the bottom of his line when his sluff triggered a pillow that sideswiped him through some trees, fully burying him in the process. The wreck caused his beacon to switch off (this model has since been criticized by the industry; while the transceiver has not been recalled, the brand did voluntarily make an aftermarket carrying case available). His partners quickly realized there was a problem with his beacon, even though they'd done a beacon check first thing. They had started spot probing when Ben Dann arrived on the scene—he was the drone pilot and had best eyes on where Nick was last seen. Ben hit a successful probe strike right away. The rest of the group was ready to shovel immediately, and they dug Nick out in under six minutes. He was five feet down and his only injury was a broken arm. This example shows the importance of "eyes on." Post someone to watch the rider through the entire line, so that if something goes bad, they can mark the last-seen spot and scan the slide path for any signs of gear. This technique greatly reduces the amount of time needed to reach the actual search zone.

This is an incredible story. Out of all the training I have done, I have never had an experience like this. I am not sure there's another instance of someone being found alive five feet down with a probe strike. The fact that they abandoned the beacon search so fast even though they had done a beacon check a few hours earlier is impressive.

about hitting firm snow on a descent and don't have an axe, I use one pole like an axe. Done right, this can catch a fall if you lose an edge.

Putting on crampons midface in firm snow or ice. If your crampons are coming off repeatedly, it's usually due to too much torque. This often means the only things holding you to the mountain are your ice axe and the frontpoints of your crampons. Losing a crampon here is really dangerous, so if your crampon is coming loose, take immediate steps to fix the problem. First, use your ice axe to make a ledge where you can safely stand without wearing a crampon. Next, secure yourself in place with an ice screw or axe. Now settle in to make the optimal work space: create a space for your pack as well as a spot to sit down comfortably; this is critical because you need to be able to get that crampon to stay on perfectly. Once you can safely place both feet on the ledge, place one crampon on the ledge. Step in and fasten it, locking

Small wins give me confidence. Finding my entrance on a cornice-covered ridge, front-point traversing white ice over exposure, successfully crossing a bergschrund, or negotiating a glacier crossing.

the strap, then repeat with the other foot and crampon. Stay away from crampons that are low in the heel. Petzl, Grivel, and C.A.M.P. all make great crampons.

Don't be surprised if your crampons still slip: on one ice traverse that still haunts me, my crampon came off nine times.

Ice Axe Moves and Self-Arrest

Training how to stop a fall with an axe is critical. It's a basic safety requirement of any intro mountaineering course, and a vital skill to possess so you don't fall to your death on firm snow or ice, even when the slope isn't very steep. A POV shot of Chamonix rider Xavier De Le Rue is burned into my head. He's enjoying nice powder on a steep face when, in an instant, his board hits glacier ice under the snow. His edge caroms off the ice and out of the snow. As he starts to accelerate, Xavier falls on his

Tricks of the Trade

Over my decades of being in the mountains, these are some of the lessons I've learned:

» Ride to live another day.

» Read the avy report every day.

» No matter how tired you are, you can always keep walking.

» Dry your skins and boots every chance you get, especially when camping.

» Respect exposure and move through it as fast as possible.

» Limit "you fall, you die" scenarios.

» Ego is not your amigo.

» Give yourself extra time; you can always slow down in the mountains, but speeding up takes energy.

» Sleeping with a warm water bottle adds 10 degrees to your sleeping bag.

» Know your outrun.

» Keep your base waxed and out of the sun.

» Have at least two good anchors for your tent.

» Celebrate turning around.

» Mountains speak; wise people listen.

» Speak up if you have funny feelings.

» Never approach the edge of a corniced ridge blindly.

» Make the switch from skinning to cramponing sooner rather than later.

» Don't travel to a snowpack with deep slab instabilities.

» Be bold, start out cold.

» Send while you can.

» Sleep in when the avy danger is high.

» Don't get hurt in December.

» Don't boot the skin track.

» Slow and steady wins the race.

» With rescues, slow is fast.

» Expect slopes to slide.

» Don't pee in the skin track or at the change-over spot.

» Don't tailgate on the skin track.

» Don't post locations on social media.

» Pick up hitchhikers who have skis or boards.

» Be a part of the community.

» Consume as much food and drink as possible on the way to the trailhead.

» Have snacks and beverages in your car for the end of the day.

» An upside-down ski pole makes a great probe for finding crevasses.

» A switchback while skinning is a good spot for a stability test.

» Cracking snow between your tips while skinning is a serious red flag.

» A buried stuff sack filled with snow makes a good anchor for your tent or tarp.

» Melting snow for water is a full-time job; start as soon as you get to camp.

» Crossing bergschrunds is often the crux of the climb.

» Start with the bottom of the line.

» Carpool if you can.

» When possible, put in a track to the base of the climb the day before an alpine start.

» Skins need to be kept warm when it is very cold; ride with them in your jacket.

» A thousand vertical feet takes roughly an hour to climb.

- » When you put your beacon on, turn it on.
- » Do a beacon check every time.
- » Turn off your beacon at the end of the day.
- » Check others by going into search mode.
- » Have proper avy gear (shovel and probe) and know how to use it.
- » Practice avy rescue every year with your partners.

- » Avoid wind if you can.
- » Climb the safest way up, especially if there is avy danger.
- » Look before you leap.
- » Know your landing.
- » Beware of the expert halo effect.
- » Don't sluff your exit.

axe, driving the pick in, stopping the fall. If he had delayed for even a millisecond, I'm not sure he could have stopped the fall, and he might not be alive today.

Learning proper self-arrest technique requires practice. Start by just riding with an axe and getting used to having it in your hand. It is a powerful tool that can seriously hurt you if you plunge it into your leg or fall on it. Next is learning how to fluidly place the axe with each turn, because the best way to stop a fall is to catch it before it starts. On a steep face where it's easy to hold an edge, make hop turns while placing your axe at the end of each turn. As your new edge is landing on the snow, so is the tip of your axe. The heel turn is the most critical. Not only is it harder to do this, but the reality is that if you are going to be caught off guard and slide off a mountain, it is probably on a heel turn. You need to have the axe in your front hand and lead with it. This move should be instinctual, so you can react in an instant.

Riding Your Axe

Off the summit ridge in Nepal's Shangri-La in 2013, my riding partner Chris Figenshau placed me on a loose belay as I dropped into the 2,000-foot fluted face. I felt out the snow with cautious hop turns. My board punched into a thin suncrust, and then denser snow, holding a good edge. When I reached the end of the short rope, I unclipped, no thought of hiking back up the 50- to 60-degree face. The snow was not optimal, but I felt I could get down the line in good form. I assumed the suncrust would soften as I dropped down the line and the temps warmed.

Unfortunately, the snow became firmer once I was off the rope, and I ended up in a battle for my life while negotiating the most technical spine wall I'd ever ridden. Thankfully it

My axe is my third edge. My safety net to the world. Occasionally I test myself with a turn. It is rehearsed over and over. Every body movement. Especially my axe placement.

Anticipate you're going to lose your edge and be ready to stop the fall immediately, because stopping a fall on hard snow once you pick up speed is almost impossible.

wasn't ice. At 40 degrees, it probably would have ridden fine. But it was 50+, and I struggled to hold on to the mountain. I largely had to ride my axe, a very effective way of getting down firm snow. The basic technique is to get on your toes, reach down toward your feet, and place your axe in the snow. You slide your board down the hill as your axe pick stays in the snow until it aligns with your waist or chest, depending on your confidence. Making sure your snowboard edge is holding, release the axe and place it back down toward your feet. If you start sliding, you can quickly stop, because the axe is already in self-arrest position. You'd be amazed what you can stick to. I used this technique on belay down the ice waterfall on the Tour Ronde. Xavier De Le Rue had me on belay, and I descended, riding my axe, without weighting the rope. I was still very happy to have the rope! But I learned a lot about what the limits are.

I didn't spend five weeks trying to ride Shangri-La just to sideslip the whole thing. With all I could muster, I picked my spots and made some turns down the

The Last Ski Bum

"He chose to be rich by making his wants few, and supplying them himself."
—Ralph Waldo Emerson

It is a simple life.

You can find him at the tram before it opens. After that you will not see him.

The wind, sun, and snow guide his movements. A few degrees off this rock, a left at the dead tree, a slight fade to the north to get the most out of the evening's wind.

A ski cut here, a fade there, an upweight over a convex roll or a purposeful push to clean out a future slab before it gets too big.

The layers in the snowpack are his friends, the trees and rocks his family.

People move in and out of his life like the season's snowpack.

Some didn't make it home while others found one.

His compass set long ago. Unchanged.

line. Doing hop turns at 20,000 feet is similar to doing box jumps. Each turn left me doubled over like a two-wave hold-down. Twice I had to stop a fall on my heel edge. The heel edge self-arrest is snowboarding's version of a 5.14 climbing move and took me years to learn.

One fall happened the instant I landed on my heel edge. I quickly got swept, but thankfully I had good axe placement. The fall was so fast and sudden, I felt like my shoulder was going to be ripped off my body. Watching the video, you can barely see it, because I stop the fall so instantly. For years I'd practiced this move in low-consequence places, which saved my life multiple times on this one descent. Getting to the heels is easy, but you have to plant your axe instantly or you will get swept off the face. To execute this technique, hold your axe in your front hand and have your front hand lead the turn. Place your axe toward the snow in anticipation that you're going to fall.

PART THREE

Art

What is art? Painting, photography, sculpture, music? My dad is an artist who paints every day, not for money but because of how the process makes him feel. "Get on the other side of your brain and let it take you for a ride," he likes to say. Art and writing have always been a part of my life—not for the end result but for the process, for the exercise sketching and writing give my mind, for how they complement my physical life in the mountains. To light up the creative side of my brain.

The benefits are unquantifiable, but I make my finest art with a snowboard on a blank white canvas, a life of glide. Like art, there's no right or wrong way to put the track on a mountain. Art is the stuff that happens once all of the observations, data, science, and experience play out. Art is simple, dynamic, endless possibility. Art is becoming flow ready and embracing your superpowers. Art is raising shredders, finding inspiration in nature, and working to protect our winters. Art is the creativity that comes when you lose yourself to what you've been dreaming about and living for.

CHAPTER 9

Life of Glide

I don't know exactly when snowboarding went from sport to art for me. From the start, there was always something more than just gliding down the mountain, learning tricks, and getting adrenaline buzzes. Early on, there's so much obvious progression sitting right in front of your face, there's no time or reason to question the why. Overcoming fear, unlocking new levels, getting so close to the edge you can taste the adrenaline in your mouth: what kid doesn't love that? However, what happens when you get hurt and you have to pull back on the reins? If it was all about new tricks and you couldn't do that anymore, wouldn't you move on to something else? That's exactly what many high-level riders and pros have done. There's nothing wrong with that. But it was obvious to me who those riders were, and I kept my distance. Why is it that I'm waking up earlier to ride now, enduring harsher conditions, and starting seasons earlier and ending them later than I have in twenty years?

Transitioning to Freeriding

My first pro competition brought me to California for the first time in 1992. Much to my surprise, I placed third in the gate race and fortieth in the half-pipe. I lost $150 in the pipe comp and made $900 in the race. I was officially a full-time racer. I kept making just enough money to stay on the road with the help of Mark Fawcett

> The backcountry sank its teeth into me at a young age, and the grasp has only tightened with time. At our worst the down can be a wrestling match with the mountain. At our best this is where sport transforms into art.

and his van, which we called home. Racing would be my passport to the world over the next six years. I could hang at the North America comps, winning a few and consistently making the top ten. Racing in Europe was a different story. I fought to stay in the top thirty.

By my mid-twenties I'd raced my last race and had transitioned to freeriding. My brothers' film company, Teton Gravity Research, had found some stability, and all my attention was focused on being ready to film in March and April. I settled into a yearly cycle of training and getting really strong in the Tetons and Tahoe by riding lifts and hiking sidecountry. I'd film a little bit if the stability and sun lined up, but my main goal was to ride sixty to eighty days before stepping in front of a camera. I treated film days like contest days. You don't get in front of a camera unless you are ready to send. The sponsors wanted good footage that'd make the cut, and so did I. My job was to create a few four- to five-minute high-action segments.

Unlocking the Unknown

The unknown comes with a knotted stomach, shallow breath, and uncertainty. The difference between the first person and the second is significant. Walking in uncluttered territories carries weight.

What's on the other side? Is this a bad idea? Is it possible? Is there black ice? Crevasses? How will the sluff run? Is the landing flat? Is the bergschrund a catcher's mitt? What's that ridge like to climb? How steep is it? Where is the entrance? What's that texture going to ride like? Is it going to slide? Any new step is taken seriously. Once the line is in, it is like the opening of a zone. Follow the track, it's safe. The unknown is gone, the edge is off. First descents matter. I used to think otherwise, but over the last few years I have really understood their significance. New ground is hard to achieve. It takes commitment. It is a measure of progression. Riding an old face but in a new way is also progression. I enjoy both, but the unknown stuff stimulates me the most.

A good edit required a dozen or so shots of tickling the edge of life and death. Each year needed to be better and more aggro than the last. To get a movie-worthy shot was pretty much a mini miracle. The location had to be perfect. The riding flawless. The lighting perfect. Each face had a ten- to thirty-minute window of optimal light. A three-minute roll of film cost $200. Getting the right camera angle required a ton of work as well. And then we didn't know if we'd gotten the shot until a few months later when the film was developed. To make a name for yourself, the reality was you needed to take a sledgehammer to the door and announce yourself. The trick was to not kill yourself or get too injured along the way. I treated every opportunity I had in front of a camera like a World Cup race day.

Simple, Dynamic

By 1995, competitive snowboarding had reached a fever pitch. A win meant keys to a new car and a five-figure check. Craig Kelly's last US Open was my first of eight. The fact that the sport had gotten this big, this fast had a lot to do with Craig. He brought the perfect amount of fun and professionalism to the sport, along with an engineer's mind to help craft the tour and product we used.

Only So Many Steps

Dark moments lead to white moments.
Stay in your comfort zone or dance on the edge?
Sounds nice, but are you willing to pay the price?
Take up space or find a new place?
Follow the trend or follow your heart?
Only so many steps to spend.
Place them wisely to ensure peace in the end.

Sunrise Salutations with Craig Kelly

COAST MOUNTAINS, BRITISH COLUMBIA, 1998

When I was twenty-three, I had the incredible opportunity to spend a week with hero Craig Kelly at a new heli op in British Columbia. Conditions were stable and sunny, and I had one of the best weeks of my life following Craig around. What amazed me was how committed he was to getting the shot. It was all smiles and stoke, but he'd hit a cliff, do a perfect method, stomp the landing, and then run back up to do it again because he thought he could hold the grab longer. This was when Craig was on top of the snowboarding world and had nothing to prove. His passion for riding and the mountains shone through on this trip. He was obsessed with seeing the sunrise from the top of peaks. Every morning, he pushed the crew to get in the heli and go. The heli operation had a take off curfew, but he pushed it. "We could be flying right now," he would say. Every morning, we took off fifteen minutes earlier. On the fourth day, we landed in morning alpenglow. I assumed Craig wanted to get a sunrise shot, but he had us all pause and watch the sunrise in silence. This love of sport is critical. Passion outperforms hard work every time.

This passion component became crystal clear when I tried to qualify for the 1998 Olympics. I worked really hard, but my heart was not in it. No matter what I did, I could not get over the training grind. It just wore me down. When I didn't qualify—missed it by one spot, which my cousin Adam Hostetter got!—I was relieved, not sad. It reminded me of the weight that lifted when I graduated high school. I was free to do what I wanted again, and what I wanted was to take the energy I was putting into racing and focus on freeriding. As I'd done when racing, I developed clear goals and broke it down into steps to get there. I had real purpose, and I was literally jumping up before my alarm to get out there. I realized the power of following passion. It's here that we do our best work. Sounds cliché, but it's true. It didn't feel like work, and I had way more drive to evolve my freeriding than I did to bash gates at the Olympics.

The only reason I ended up on the heli trip with Craig was because I did not qualify for the Olympics. I was actually riding with Craig during the Olympic snowboard races and never saw the event. Craig clearly had that drive, which led him to three world titles. On our trip, at that stage of his career, he was a legend and probably had more photos published in magazines than anyone else in the world. There was no pressure for him to get the shot. The drive he had was more based on his love for the sport, for getting the most out of each day. Craig was ahead of his time, always evolving. When things reached a state of cruise control, he would crank the wheel, air off easy street, and create his own path through the sagebrush.

> If humankind eliminates all risk from our lives and we live in padded rooms until we are one hundred, what is the point of life?

When I heard Craig was retiring from competition to pursue "freeriding," I didn't really know what that meant, because no such thing existed. Sure, there were some movies being made, and people like Jim and Bonnie Zellers and Tom Burt were paying rent checks with money earned taking photos, but if you wanted to be a top pro, you still needed to compete. When Craig shifted to freeriding full-time, his career—along with the sport—boomed. He created imagery and an atmosphere that captured the imaginations of the masses and drove the sport into a golden era. I'm not sure if it was calculated, or if he just liked Greg Stump, but Craig started appearing in the world's biggest ski movies, putting on clinics about how to flow down a mountain.

One such shot in the film *P-tex, Lies, & Duct Tape* had such an impact on my path that I highlighted it in my film *Life of Glide*. Craig dropped down a steep face, making beautiful, surf-inspired turns, launched a perfect method, hit a few more cliffs, kicked off a small avalanche, and straight-lined it to safety. He displayed simple, dynamic, and timeless snowboarding. In the film, Stump asks Craig how he picks a line; Craig responds, "I think, *What if I dropped a basketball down the mountain right now, and where would it go?* That's what I try and emulate."

Defanging Blind Rolls

Standing on top of a big face that rolls away into the abyss is hands down the most terrifying and tricky scenario to charge in. Do everything you can to see more of the face. This could mean climbing up or down rocks, or going on belay and hiking down the side of the line. It can be a ton of effort to see a few extra feet, but it can make a huge difference. Having a photo is critical here. Ideally you see a tip of a tree, or match a cornice on the ridge or some rocks, so that you understand where you are on the mountain. Start building a mental map from there. This could take thirty minutes or more. Having someone across the way with a radio is really helpful. By throwing snowballs you can build the map.

Being able to charge blind rolls and even use them as airs is superhero stuff.

"That image transfer in your head of watching a face from across the way and then recognizing it when you're in it is a very specific exercise that has taken years and years for me to master. The more comfortable you are on your feet, the more you can concentrate on finding your way."
—Xavier De Le Rue

Endless Possibilities

With the new millennium, an obsession with terrain parks and freestyle took over the media, and the message was clear: "If you're not learning a new trick, get out of the sport." Around this time, I had a prominent magazine editor tell me I should spend all winter learning tricks. It wasn't bad advice. If you wanted to get in the mags, you weren't freeriding. However, for a small crew of dedicated, stubborn freeriders, things were actually moving very fast. By my count, four pro snowboarders filmed in Alaska in spring of 2003. It was my second year in Haines, and I had one of the best sessions of my life with Johan Olofsson, a big mountain freestyle pioneer. Johan shattered what we thought was possible on a snowboard on his first trip to Alaska to film with Standard Films. His *TB5* video part from that trip is still considered the single best segment of the film even more than twenty years later. For the next few years, he would become my main Alaskan riding partner. His riding was so far outside the box that I stopped trying to guess what his line would be. I was hanging on by a thread trying to keep up with his level, which certainly upped my riding and opened my mind. We'd finally cracked the code on spine riding. It was probably my single biggest year of progression, largely because we had found a spine paradise outside Haines and were forced to figure out how to ride it. This steep progression had its price; by the end of the trip, many of us were hurt from getting sluffed off the fluted faces. But the possibilities now seemed endless.

Johan and I were the only healthy riders left, and we went on a nine-run first-descent binge. Johan put on the single best day of snowboarding I've ever seen. We'd

Contents of Contentment

Big storms
Warm fires
Mountain
Sunrises
Old trees
Soft snow
The perfect board
Protection from the elements
Warm tea on a cold day
The perfect moment—a few seconds in time but
    stays with you forever. Content. But always
    focused on more.
A peaceful quest with no destination.

never been so amped about our trip and the filming and photos that went down. It was the highlight of my career up to that point. I couldn't wait to keep pushing my riding. During this time I held true to the lesson I'd learned from watching Craig flow down years before. I ended up following my passion and kept after it as hard as possible.

CHAPTER 10

Alaska and the Birth of TGR

Late at night, during my twenty-fourth birthday party, my brother Todd suddenly became very serious, grabbed me by the shirt, and said, "Twenty-four is gnarly, don't die." I was living in Jackson, and we'd just come off a good run of weather, riding nonstop, sending without a thought about tomorrow. He said it with both vigor and seriousness. "Make it past twenty-four!"

There was nothing more to say. I got it. But I thought, *It won't happen to me.* I was riding almost all year long, had avy classes under my belt, knew how to work a beacon, a harness, ropes, axes, and could fire lines in my sleep. In short, I had just enough knowledge, or rope, to hang myself. Cutting slopes and releasing avalanches down serious terrain was fun. Exposure, what's the big deal? I wasn't disrespectful. Not a loose cannon like some of the punk rock, fearless riders who didn't even ride with a backpack, but I had an air of invincibility about me.

Collective Progression, Early Filming Forays, and Doug Coombs

It was a collective progression going on, but for my brothers and me, Doug Coombs was the guy we watched and listened to the most. Not only was he leading the charge, but he was approachable and an amazing teacher. He saw something in my brothers, because when he eventually started the first ski-guiding operation in 1994, he tapped them as guides. We would be stuck on Thompson Pass outside of Valdez for days

Andrew McLean:
Enjoying the Process

"It's a fine line between bravery and stupidity. To climb and ski big lines takes mental confidence and fortitude, but it is very important to know when to hit the brakes. Be willing to chalk attempts off as 'recon missions' and come back with new knowledge and in safer conditions. Learn to enjoy the process as much as the goal."

with cliff-swallowing storms, and when it did clear, Doug's was the first group out. His goal was to get on lines as fast as possible. I watched his approach evolve in front of my eyes—he held court in the dirt lot at the end of the day.

"Have a starting slope," he'd tell us. "Something short and steep with a clean outrun, so if it slides you will be fine. Build from there. Step up to bigger lines as you gain confidence. Find slopes you can ski cut or drop a small cornice onto. Ski fast and light."

There were virtually no snowpits dug at the time. Terrain progression was our basis for decision-making. The longer the high-pressure system went on, the more serious the lines got. The real serious lines would go down at the end of April or beginning of May. An extended high pressure this time of year helped progression the most. The higher sun made the snowpack settle faster. Most aspects cooked, and we focused on the north faces getting sun for the first time that year. This was when the monumental lines went down. Super Spines, Tusk, Pontoon—all first ridden at this time of year.

Sluff Management

I'm not sure if Doug Coombs coined the term "sluff management," but I heard it from him first. Start left, end right, and never sluff your exit. A simple concept, although it wasn't at the time. Before the Valdez era, which helped people realize that skiing and riding steep powder lines didn't have to mean suicide, I took my first avalanche class in 1998, in Jackson Hole, put on by the legendary Rod Newcomb. The course was taught by older guys and scientists who looked at riding anything over 30 degrees as a death wish. Rod's son Mark gave a talk about riding in Valdez. At the time he was guiding for Coombs and breaking boundaries in Alaska and in Grand Teton National Park. Like his dad, Mark is incredibly smart, soft-spoken, and methodical about his approach in the mountains. He's a humble scientist with an appetite for the bold.

As Mark broke down his approach to riding big lines in Alaska, in powder, the old-timers weren't having it. "Do you guys use explosives?" (Mark: "No, we consider it dangerous using dynamite with a heli.") "Ha-ha! You think that is dangerous compared to dropping those lines in powder?" (Mark: "We have an approach we've been refining for years based around terrain progression, and it's really working.") "May work if you are at an elite level, but you can't guide people on slopes like those." (Mark: "Actually, we do. We make them use fat skis and teach them sluff management. With the right approach and equipment, people perform great.")

Around this time Mark started exploring Grand Teton National Park with a small group of other visionaries, riding big lines in cold winter snow. These days, hundreds ride in the national park every day in winter. Back then it was crazy and ground-breaking. I'm not sure what role Alaska played in this progression, but it was the same people from Jackson Hole I saw in those Alaska parking lots who led the charge in the Tetons.

My brothers Todd and Steve started guiding for Coombs at the same time the Hatchett Brothers and Standard Films made Valdez the focal point of their movies. They were the biggest filmmakers in snowboarding, featuring the world's best riders at a time when marketing budgets in snowboarding were ten times what they are today, and the cost of a heli ride was ten times less. Todd and Steve had a front-row seat to the best snowboarding in the world, with the best film crew in the world, with special appearances by the best skier in the world, Coombs. My brothers decided to form their own filming company, Teton Gravity Research, in 1996. Coombs was the star, and the films were anchored around top-to-bottom skiing, shot from opposing peaks—the style the Hatchett Brothers had perfected. .

Finding the End of the Rainbow

Haines, Alaska, is a place my brothers speak of in magical verse: "Nantucket with gigantic spine walls." They'd first passed through Haines years before while

Becoming Flow-Ready

In turns out that becoming flow-ready requires much of what you're already doing in the mountains. Movement, being curious, challenging yourself, and getting out of your comfort zone are keys to finding the flow. There are a lot of things out of your control in the mountains, but the one thing you can control is your mind. Give everything you have to being present and aware.

Focus on one step and one section. Linking steps leads to linking sections. Linking sections leads to summits. Be present to what is: you and the mountain, you and the group, you and the snowpack, you and the line.

Sluff
Management

FUNDAMENTALS

 1 HAVE A PLAN

 2 LEAVE YOUR EXIT CLEAN

 3 KNOW WHERE YOUR ISLANDS OF SAFETY ARE TO PULL OUT IF SLUFF IS TOO BIG

SPINES

SLUFF AND EXPOSURE

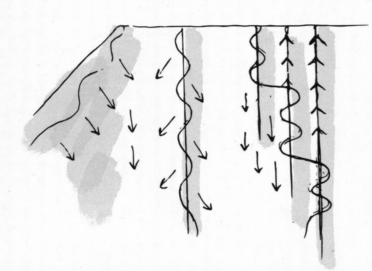

CROSSING SLUFF

- Same concept as crossing a river in a kayak
- Momentum is key
- Accept that the sluff will take you a bit

LOCAL RIPPER

TWO OPTIONS
- Beat your sluff to choke
- Ride over exposure leaving choke sluff-free

SLUFF RACER
- Only way to avoid it is to beat it
- Check sluff before crossing
- Bail out spot if sluff is too big and too fast to cross

PHD
SPIT OUT OF TUBE

- Chutes are often concave, which creates a fast narrow river in the middle of the chute
- Stay on double fall line walls
- Slow and steady
- Up high in chute you can often cross the sluff funnel

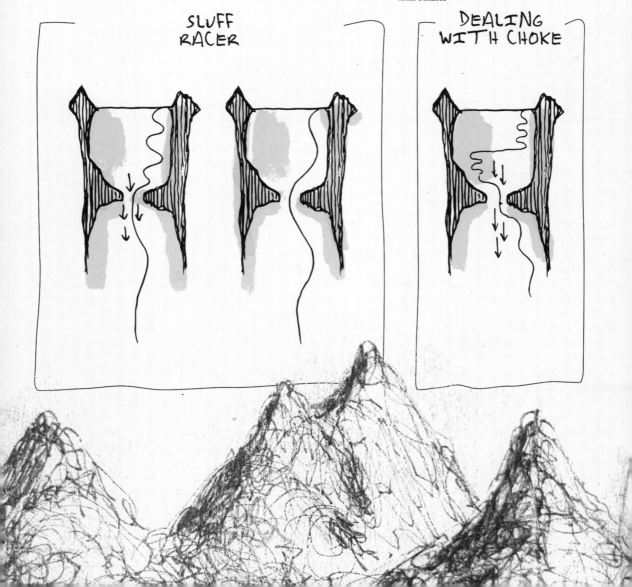

SLUFF RACER

DEALING WITH CHOKE

The Oven Effect

SKAGWAY, SOUTHEASTERN ALASKA, 1999

By 2008, there were three or four heli-guide operations in Valdez, the ski bums priced out or turned into guides, and the seemingly endless terrain was being regulated and fought over. My brothers and I did the unthinkable—we turned our backs on Valdez and focused on Southeastern Alaska. Heli-skiing and -boarding had been going on outside of Juneau for years, but horror stories of three-week storms and wet snow kept us away. To leave Valdez, the mecca, was really difficult. Our life was built around the town, and Thompson Pass and the Chugach were an anomaly. The perfect convergence of terrain, glaciers, mountain pass, proximity to the ocean, and size of the mountains made for a place so unique, it couldn't be matched anywhere else.

Our first foray was Skagway. We shared resources with Standard Films, convinced the winter ghost town to open a hotel and restaurant early, and put all our chips in the Skagway pot. As we stepped off the ferry, a brisk wind scoured and grabbed anything it could carry. Our hotel had been built during the gold rush and soon the funny ghost stories were not so funny, as people retreated from the far reaches of the hotel and started sharing rooms due to otherworldly encounters.

The trip was a complete disaster. Our worst ever. The crew and I were first pinned down by a fifteen-day storm. When it finally cleared, low clouds and fog clung to the mountains for an entire day, while sun heated them from above. This was my first experience with the "oven effect." The next day, we flew at first light. A new world, coated with feet upon feet of fresh snow. Options and potential everywhere. There are few things as exciting as unexplored terrain, and we were the only ones out there. It was go time, the forecast was perfect, and we were set to make movie magic. I'd never been so pumped. We landed, jumped out of the heli to get ready to ride. Immediately, our exuberance gave way to disbelief. A solid two-inch crust capped three feet of powder.

Usually, suncrust or windboard is aspect specific. The north side might be crusted but the south perfect. However, with the oven effect, the sun beats down on the low-hanging clouds and fog and heats the entire range equally. The moisture sticks to the mountain and new snow, creating a death crust after the nightly freeze, on every aspect and elevation. We spent the day sighting and checking every aspect and elevation that might have been spared. Toward the end of the day, as we trended west and were dropped off on a high point, we saw a line of unfamiliar peaks across the horizon. Unlike

> The mountains don't know your calendar, don't care about your schedule. Time and again, that door creaks open the day after the trip is supposed to end.

the Skagway Mountains, which were jagged and rock-laden, the far peaks shone white and glowed in the evening light. Skagway had defeated us. Our greatest failure. The crew was pale, haggard, and some were legitimately haunted. Bags were packed, and plans changed, but we could not get those snow-covered mountains out of our heads. We pulled out a map and realized the range was 25 miles north of Haines.

commercial fishing. Back then, after spending all their money riding Valdez during the spring, my brothers made the pilgrimage to get work on a boat. They hitched from Valdez to Haines, a multiday endeavor. At one junction there was a makeshift bench with "two days" or "four days" carved into it for hitchhikers waiting for rides. They got on the ferry to Juneau and walked the docks looking for work. This migration actually led to the birth of TGR. The fishing money was so good that after their second season my brothers decided to pool it and invest in a movie camera.

The day after our defeat at Skagway, we hired a plane and set out west to see if there was gold at the end of the rainbow. As we approached the interior, out of a sprawling sea of white rose a tall peak with a steep, clean flank. The pilot landed us on a flat shoulder. Our excitement fogged the windows until we got out and found—crust! The face was every bit on the scale of a Valdez classic. Something we had yet to see in our three weeks in Skagway. It was clean, steep, and spined. I snapped some photos, and we struggled down a long, low-angle run, negotiating a wicked crust to the valley floor. This range had not survived the wrath of death crust. We pulled the plug and started our long journey home.

> What I am realizing is that when you find a really special line, then why not spend the time to ride it? Set up camp, build up to it by riding the surrounding terrain, wait for the right conditions, like it, and ride it.

Later that summer, when I finally got my photos back, there was one that stuck out. The photo showed what we hadn't grasped—a trophy line that provided reason for yet more exploration. A few months later, we were planning our Alaska spring trips. TGR connected the dots, and eleven months after taking that photo, we posted up again in Haines. As we started targeting specific areas, it was clear we had discovered a spine paradise. Two years prior, legends Noah Salasnek and Doug Coombs had ridden Super Spines, and that accomplishment changed our perception of a dream line. Their success led to our spine obsession. The number of possible lines overwhelmed us, and we spent every moment charging new walls. We became so preoccupied that we didn't make it to the trophy peak for another year.

Breathing: Unlocking a Superpower

Getting fired up has never been an issue for me. My mind and body are usually turned up to eleven. I first learned this lesson when I was fifteen. When it came to racing, I was virtually unbeatable. I had the perfect January birthday and was the oldest kid in my age group. I won something like thirty-five races in a row, and I was putting down times that would get me into the top-15 of the regional pro division. This is when I met the devil, also known as ego. The kids around me were getting faster. I started looking more at the pro times and started taking chances. The first time I blew out, I was fine with it. I was riding well and made a simple mistake, no big deal. However, things started getting weird. Pulling out of the gate, my mind was in chaos. Stupid crashes were followed by fear of taking risks and now I was getting beat riding at 80 percent. For a kid whose entire life was focused on winning, it was a catastrophe.

I'm not sure how I figured it out, maybe someone told me; I was getting advice from a lot of people at the time. It was like unlocking a superpower. I worked on my breathing. Conscious breathing. So simple, so effective. It silenced my mind, while making me laser-focused on the two or three key sections of the course.

> The beauty of breath work is simple. Close your eyes. Big inhale, big exhale. Repeat. Slow down and feel your presence. Focus on the breath and nothing else.

A year later, at sixteen, I competed in my first pro race and took third. The lessons I learned during that slump I still use to this day. The more serious the line, the earlier I go into awareness-breathing mode. My mind becomes clear and empty, except for one or two key points. My ego got the best of me one day, on Tomahawk Peak. Breathing went out the window. We'd been on a spine bender, and I let my guard down. Crashes and mistakes happen—learn from them and let it go. Getting knocked down a peg or two in the mountains is a good thing, if you leave room for error. I've done my best riding after blowing a line. Breathing returns as part of the plan, allowing you to focus on your target.

Kicking the Habit

There was a time it definitely wasn't art. I was consuming adrenaline at unhealthy levels. My body was beat up. I was trading infinite amounts of future powder days, pushing through the pain to get one more shot so I could get one more contract. Late in the season, I would take a lot of ibuprofen. I assumed my pro days were numbered, and I'd be a beach bum by age thirty-five. My attitude as I approached heli-boarding season was: "If I'm not progressing, I'm an asshole for taking someone else's spot and using so many resources and spending so much money." If I wasn't fit or riding well, exploring new terrain, then I wanted out.

My move away from helicopters to foot-powered snowboarding happened for a multitude of reasons, but as much as reporters tried to pull it out of me, environmental concerns were low on the list. At the top was the simple fact that I realized I was getting more out of the backcountry, using my legs to climb what I rode. This

Tomahawk Peak: An Origin Story

The mountain was every bit as beautiful as I remembered. Just a perfect peak. A steep rollover from the top into a long, clean face with a handful of broad spines to add some excitement. My internal fuse was about to blow as I dropped in. I let gravity take me for a few seconds before easing into my first gigantic turn. The scale was enormous: 200-foot turn after 200-foot turn. My face inches from the snow, arm, hip, and body working to keep it all together. Halfway down, I center-punched the only cliff on the mountain, an 8-foot rock with a perfect takeoff. I had no anxiety leaving the lip but soon realized my "small" air was not going to end any time soon. My landing zone passed well below my feet halfway through the air. My landing gear failed, and the cartwheels started. Six, eight, ten tomahawks later, I found my feet and somehow managed to ride the rest of the line. The next two riders after me met a similar fate, which is why the peak was named Tomahawk.

became crystal clear on a May morning after a heli season where I had filmed five segments in eight weeks.

Starting in the dark from a trailhead an hour from my house, I set out to climb a line I'd never seen before with my friend Chris Edmands, who was in the middle of making the first foot-powered snowboard film ever made. On the approach to the line I was taken aback by the beauty of the sun transforming the landscape from lifeless and gray to a slow transition through every tone of purple, pink, and orange, and finally settling on yellow. At the base of the chute I switched to crampons and an axe. Climbing the rock-walled chute, I became ultra-focused, present, and connected to the mountain in a way I had never been before. The higher off the deck, the more alive I became. Hiking through the steep crux, clinging to the planet with just the tips of crampon points and my ice axe, I didn't want the climb to end.

> This line here is one of a thousand that lie in the range. It did not require flying to the other side of the world or a lot of money to ride.

Dropping into a blind roll at the top, I made some controlled hop turns through the exposed crux. The snow was suncupped and challenging to start. The chute doglegged, widened, and my turns grew wider and wider as the snow improved. The chute went on forever, walled by towering cliffs. Coming out the bottom, I was at top speed, and I made a series of huge turns before coming to a stop at a frozen lake 2,000 feet below. First came the screams, then weeping. I didn't really understand the emotion at first. I had just spent two months heli-boarding in the most remote, most badass mountains in Alaska, in the best possible powder conditions, and it was here in this sun-cooked, boot-top pow in my backyard that I achieved a rare "white moment." I had created something, with my own two feet!

With a setting sun and two more lines under my belt, I followed our morning skin track back to the car. Exhausted, alone with my thoughts, a rising moon, and the first star above, I mulled over my season. By all accounts, my most successful ever. Movie parts equal contracts and, with five in the can, I was confident my key sponsors would renew. I was thirty, though, and because pro snowboarding years are much like dog years, I was considered very old, and these contracts could be the last. My goal that season wasn't making as many movie parts as I could. I wanted to actually embrace foot-powered snowboarding more, and eventually set up an Alaska camping and riding trip outside the heli zone. The sponsors and movie companies entertained the initial idea with "That could be cool, but I'm not sure how we'd film it," or "Sounds interesting, but no one's doing that."

That night at home, after riding the line with Chris and walking back to the car, I knew it was time to change direction. Of the five films I'd done, the one I was most proud of was a low-budget, foot-powered DIY film, *My Own Two Feet*, shot by Chris in the California Sierra. On the other end of the spectrum was the mega-budget Travis Rice film *That's It, That's All*, which I'd filmed with a broken arm strapped to my torso. It might possibly be the most successful snowboard movie of all time, winning every award that year. Driving home that night, it hit me: I needed to make my own foot-powered film. Producing and directing a snowboard film was something I'd never wanted to do. I saw up close how much work it took. Just sitting in the editing bay overseeing a four-minute segment was painful enough. To achieve my new goals, however, this was the only way. I was sick of getting the runaround from the film companies I was working with, hearing that we couldn't keep lenses from fogging or batteries charged on long camping missions. Chris was the key to it all. He figured it out on a smaller scale. We could next ramp it up to Alaska and beyond.

Filming Foot-Powered Movies

Chris Edmands proved that filming foot-powered movies was possible and worthwhile. My time working on *My Own Two Feet* was super exciting. Even though the riding was nowhere near the level of the traditional TGR/Absinthe films, I enjoyed it more, and it really made me proud. The multiday winter camping splitboarding trips required for *My Own Two Feet* were where I felt most out of my comfort zone; I was pushing my boundaries, challenging myself, and learning a ton of new things. Most important, I was getting my biggest highs. I'd experienced a lot of success over the years, but nothing matched the pure backcountry foot-powered experience. A big trip back then was two or three nights. Every day was a great day. Even if it hurt.

I was connecting with nature on a level I had never reached before. With the help of my splitboard, I could eventually travel large chunks of terrain. I realized that by sleeping in a tent and hiking all day, everything was now in play in the Tahoe region. Previously, most of my riding in Tahoe was either at the resort or filming using snowmobiles. The snowmobile trailhead was now very crowded, and I'd already hit all the prominent lines. I had reached the boundary, not only in Tahoe but also in the heli zones in Alaska and the sidecountry in Jackson. But there were massive areas that I hadn't even seen, with an unimaginable number of peaks and objectives, all off-limits to machines. A map confirmed this—90 to 95 percent of the mountains in western North America were off-limits to everything but my two feet.

To break new ground with a heli or a snowmobile required taking enormous risks. When it came to the remote backcountry, foot-powered zones, I was a cheap drunk. I was riding and seeing new lines in my backyard every time I went out. My connection to nature and the mountains was way more intimate. This is not to say it was easy. The suffering I endured starting out was like nothing I'd experienced. I often stumbled back to the car in the dark with no headlamp, out of food and water, wondering if I'd even make it. I knew the mountains well, but the whole foot-powered approach was new. I went headfirst into it, with full commitment, and made every mistake you could make.

"Complexity is the enemy of execution."
—Tony Robbins

Winter camping was mysterious and scary. I remember looking out the window from the comforts of my house the night before a January mission and thinking, *Am I really going to sleep out there?* The other huge learning was hiking the lines. No longer was I dropping in from the top and on the slope for only minutes as I raged down the mountain, kicking off small slides and racing sluffs. Hiking the lines meant I was on the face for hours, which greatly increased the risk because a small avalanche or sluff could knock me off my feet. This upped the complexity of a line tenfold, and I loved it. I was finally meeting the mountains on their terms, one-on-one. To achieve success, I would need to nail all facets of my approach: from weathering multiday storms to staying nourished so I could hike from dark to dark for days on end to nailing my approaches and climbs. And this was all just to get to the top of the line on the heavy, clunky splitboards we used in the early days.

You only walk into new terrain for the first time once . . . it is a gift. Slow down and acknowledge how fortunate you are to have the opportunity.

Simultaneously, we were having to relearn how to film. By the end of most trips we were down to one lens that was not fogged, only a few minutes of battery power, and nearly out of memory. One line in particular stands out for the fact that we pulled it off by the skin of our teeth. Ryland Bell and I climbed a 3,000-foot couloir in the early evening, reaching the top at twilight. We dug into the side of a cliff to bivy on top of the line. Throwing our camping gear down the couloir, we climbed and dropped into the biggest spine wall of my life with boots so frozen I could not lace them up. We were barely able to document the descent, but it worked. It was a very emotional moment for Ryland and me.

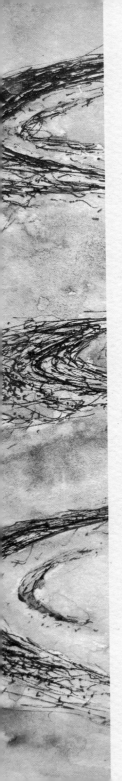

Blind Rolls: Pontoon

CHUGACH MOUNTAINS, ALASKA, 2019

Dropping in, I always want a clear plan. I want to know where and if I can change that plan, to know my exits, and to know when the only option requires total commitment. The hardest lines offer very few options: total commitment, because hesitation means losing valuable time while racing sluff. This is fine when you can see the entire line, but add a blind roll to the equation, and I start getting the dry heaves up top. To have the guts to point a blind roll, totally committed, especially if there are fatal consequences, is one of the hardest and most dangerous decisions to make. To take the teeth out of these situations, I do everything I can to see even a couple more feet down the route. I scale rock faces, hike opposing ridges, get onto a rope—anything it takes. The Chugach Mountains in Alaska are the land of the never-ending blind rolls, and Pontoon Peak and Meteorite Mountain are the masters in this land.

Standing on the top of Pontoon, I wondered if I still had the appetite for the sluff-racing, cliff-jumping center punch of the northwest face. The younger me dry heaved my way through my fears and did just that. With twenty years of experience and scars, I deferred to my heart for guidance. I let gravity take me uninhibited over the blind roll but gave it a short leash as I slowly faded my way right to left, tickling the void of the northwest face but not delving into it. Almost the entire line is blind except for 20 feet in front, but with no pressure to race my sluff, I enjoyed some mid-radius turns down the never-ending flank. The lower half became the crux, due to the snow heating up, and I moved fast and took extra precautions, stopping at really safe spots to assess. Out in the flats, I finally let my guard down. My decision to take the mellower line was the right one. Hiking and riding a line as serious as Pontoon is dangerous enough. Adding a sluff-racing, cliff-jumping line to the equation would've been selfish and stupid.

The small plane that shuttled us back to town arrived a half hour later, and the pilot surprised Cody Townsend and me with a few beers. We basked by the wing in the fading sun, looking at one of the most beautiful peaks in the world. Smoked physically and mentally, we toasted another Alaska season. Flying back to town, I asked the pilot to fly by the Tusk. The peak glowed in all its glory, shining with the last rays of the day. A familiar devil reared its head as if to say: "Stay and climb it. It's in perfect shape, you're so close, when will you get another chance like this?" A younger me might have listened, but temps were getting warm, and I felt good about climbing and riding Pontoon and Meteorite. Time to pull my chips off the table. Plus, one line down the Tusk was plenty. Just looking at it made me shiver.

When I walked away from helicopters, my previous crews thought I was crazy. That I was taking my environmental actions too far. Saying things like "How's the hippie movie going?" They didn't realize that I felt limited by the boundaries of where you could take a snowmobile or helicopter because of land restrictions. The other barrier was how far you could hike in a day. It was clear to me that if I could live for long periods of time beyond the areas you could hike to in a day or, in places like Alaska, beyond a plane-assisted base camp, then my playground would virtually be endless and untouched. However, it wasn't until Ryland's and my descent on the "Wall of Walls" two years into this mission that I could say without doubt that I had ridden the best line of my life—and had done it on foot. I was way out of my comfort zone, but I always knew I was just scratching the surface of what was possible, because I had immersed myself in cutting-edge alpinist literature. Reading about Steve House's Nanga Parbat mega-push and other climbs like it, I understood my suffering was at a kindergarten level.

> The energy harnessed from being out of my comfort zone has been so positive on my brain. The brain needs stimulation or it grows stale. Challenge your brain and you will see the benefits in all facets of life.

The Times of Our Lives

Chris and I were having the best times of our lives. Everything was new: the terrain, the approach, and the experience. We named one remote Tahoe face "Hippy Cove," even though it was the most serious line I'd ever hit in Tahoe. Switching to foot-powered expeditions rekindled my spark for snowboarding, much like transitioning from racing to freeriding had in 1998.

I hadn't realized how much that spark had dwindled, but going all in on foot power exploded my internal flame, which I'm still fueled by today. Without that

The reality is, until we get up and on the face, there is little use in worrying. That is where the good decisions need to be made. It's either in my ability or not. The snow is right or not. All we can do is give it our best, have a clear head, not get caught up in the moment, and do what feels right.

creativity, stoke, and energy, it would never have worked. If I was out there thinking, *Man, I wish I had a heli right now, but it's bad for the environment,* I'd never have had the motivation to climb out of a warm sleeping bag in the predawn hours, put on frozen boots, and hike the heaviest lines.

Going Deeper

Chris and I made every mistake possible. Our budget the first year was $10,000 vs. $150,000 to $800,000 for a traditional film. Working on a shoestring budget to get production started, I had to front money for Alaska, our only non-Sierra trip during this first year. I worked harder than I ever had before. There were times of extreme frustration. We missed some of the best shots, but I didn't really care. My body felt great, and I was in awe of the mountains and wilderness. I was having such a great time with new friends exploring at a much

different pace than before. That hunger and excitement and wonder is all that has ever mattered to me, and here it was, seemingly limitless.

That summer I left my longtime sponsor, Rossignol, after nineteen years to start my own snowboard company. Just as making my own movie was something I'd never wanted to do before, I'd also never expected to be starting a company. But Rossignol had no interest in making splitboards. Like everyone at the time, I cut solid snowboards down the middle and made them into splitboards, which really softened them. I set out to find a sponsor who would help make a better splitboard, but the response was always the same: "We have no interest in splitboarding or the backcountry." The idea to start making my own boards came in May of 2009, and by June, I'd gone all in on what I would eventually call Jones Snowboards. Six months later, I attended my first trade show, where my one and only splitboard prototype was stolen from the booth. Other than Voile and Venture, Jones was the only company with a splitboard in the lineup.

That fall, I premiered my first film, *Deeper*, at the 1,200-person outdoor amphitheater in my hometown of Truckee. An hour before the show, I was ready to throw up. I just hoped at least a hundred people would show, but the parking lot was almost empty. As I was signing posters at the new Jones Snowboards tent, a friend explained the holdup: "Dude, traffic is backed up to the other side of town." An hour later, as I introduced the film, I looked out at a completely packed venue. Watching the film from the back of the amphitheater, I thought, *This is the perfect ending to your career. What more do you want? Call it.*

My mother apparently had the same thought. "I'm so proud of you," she told me, "but I hope this is the last one."

> Soon we will launch. A loose plan. Eight days of food on our backs, and an open mind.

> What is clear is that I am onto something good. Something that will last. Something that has no limit.

CHAPTER 11

Raising Shredders

A tear welled in my eye as my daughter, Mia, took her final step to the Mount Shasta summit. She was fourteen and had just climbed the 14,180-foot peak with a smile on her face the whole time. It was a breathless, beautiful day that started in the early morning darkness 7,200 vertical feet below, after a short sleep in the dirt. The pace and the approach were no different than if I'd been hiking with my friends. "I'm so proud of you," I said, giving Mia a long hug. I thought back to her birth, how I could barely talk when I called my mother to tell her the baby was a girl. The story goes that my mother also cried the day I was born, but hers were tears of sadness that I was the third boy. She was so sure she was having a girl, she didn't have any boys' names ready. "Jeremy is a nice name," said the doctor.

My mother and I can now laugh at that moment. Although we may have had a rocky start, our relationship is so close and full of love. Having a daughter has opened me up to a whole new universe of princesses, pink, and ballet classes. Shane McConkey and I had daughters at the same time, and we really bonded at the ballet classes. Often, we'd be the only dads at the class sitting on the sidelines, encouraging our daughters to pirouette across the floor. Those tiny dancers were so foreign, so distant from our mountain worlds, that they left us in awe then (as they still do today).

After a long summit picnic, Mia and I made our way off the peak and toward our intended descent, the Trinity chutes. To access it required more hiking. I gave Mia the option to take a closer, more direct line, but she didn't hesitate. "That line looked awesome, I'm fine with hiking some more." I helped her spot her turns, explained she was in a no-fall zone, told her to stay out of the gut so she wouldn't get caught by her sluff, and pointed out a safe stopping point for her to wait. Before Mia dropped in, I gave her one last piece of advice: "If you're feeling it and the snow holds, don't be afraid to take it to the bottom." She slowly dropped in, gained confidence after testing the snow, and executed perfect, beautifully rounded turns. She gave a sluff lookback before crossing the gut, blew by her island of safety, and continued to rail big turns all the way to the bottom.

For a dad, it doesn't get any better than this moment. Sharing a day with my daughter on one of my favorite mountains in the world. A mountain that up until I filmed *Deeper*, *Further*, and *Higher*, I'd thought of as too hard and too big to climb. A mountain where I've seen many a seasoned rider run out of steam and have to turn around. I can't help but wonder about the impact of such experiences on Mia. How will they shape her? She has the nature gene. This will help her through life. She will be happy because nature is free. Nature is simple. You just need to go. And she will go.

Don't Push

My biggest fear as a parent was pushing my kids too hard in the sports I wanted to do with them, burning them out to the point they wouldn't want to participate. This fear led me to slow-play activities. To never force anything on them. To help motivate and inspire, yes, but never force. With surfing, Tiff and I brought the soft-top board to the beach, but Mia and Cass had to take it out or ask us to go. For years, I bit my tongue as they played in the shore pound and bodyboarded. Both kids started in a ski program at three-and-a-half. It was at a small resort, Tahoe Donner, above Truckee. We started snowboarding without bindings in the backyard whenever they wanted. At age six, both kids wanted to snowboard instead of ski. I made them finish the ski programs, but on the side taught them how to snowboard at the resort. Going back to the magic carpet was tough, but they learned quickly.

Cass was a natural skier, and for a while he did both skiing and snowboarding, which I totally supported. We had one rule going to the mountain: you had to do at least three runs. If you did three runs, you got a cookie, which for them was a big deal. Early on, three runs was usually their max. I didn't push them any harder. My kids learned that the mountain is a sacred place and that complaining about anything was not allowed. However, I assure you it was not all unicorns and rainbows. I often wondered if the effort was really worth it and definitely spent many Saturdays building snowmen in the backyard because I didn't want to deal with the hassles of resort riding with my kids. My end goal has never been to create pro riders. I want them to enjoy the mountains. Ideally, I want to spend the rest of my life enjoying this mountain life with them, sharing the common bond with the places that have shaped me and given me so much.

This is why I was so excited spending that day on Shasta with my daughter. Mia has many interests, which I totally support, and her identity isn't based around being a boarder. She jumped at the opportunity to come to Shasta with me. When I connected with her lower down the mountain, her usual quiet demeanor could not mask her excitement. For the next 3,000 vertical feet we hooted and slashed our way down rolling flanks of perfect corn. Our father-daughter relationship put on hold, we were just two snowboarders who'd climbed a big peak together and shared some turns. It was a coming-of-age moment for both us. For me, it confirmed I wasn't pushing too hard as a dad, and that there was a good chance we would have many more summits in our future. For Mia, the impact will probably not be clear for some time. Our day clocked in at 7,919 feet of climbing over an eleven-hour period. Numbers like that will put you on top of most mountains in the world, meaning that day should give her confidence that she can look to any summit and know she has the fitness to stand on its peak.

> It was not until I started spending time in the mountains with my kids that I fully understood the mountains' full power and value. Out there, our relationship changes from parent/kid to just riding partners helping each other put in the boot pack, line up airs, and charge lines.

Driving home that night, we were tired from the day and the few hours of sleep we'd had in the parking lot. We made our way through the night to get Mia home for school the next morning. I told her she could sleep, but she was too amped, so

Hilaree Nelson: Ski Mountaineer

Hilaree is incredibly comfortable in exposed situations and has an ability to endure like few I have ever seen. She has many firsts to her name, including the first ski descent of Lhotse, the fourth-tallest mountain in the world. She's been featured in films, recognized as one of the "most adventurous women of the last twenty-five years" by *Men's Journal*, and is the mother of two wild boys. I spoke to her about risk, suffering, aging, and sexism in our sport.

Telluride and the San Juans have some of the most serious mountains in the world, coupled with one of the most dangerous snowpacks. How is it that you have ridden so many big and exposed lines in powder there?
I have lived in Telluride for twenty years and, yes, the mountains are very serious and the snowpack can be terrifying. I have not made it through my time here completely unscathed—I personally have not been in an avalanche, but I have had some very close calls and have friends and loved ones impacted by the dangers in these mountains. I do my best to charge hard while mitigating risk as best as possible. That involves reading the local avalanche report every day. I also talk to the folks that are out in the snow or have skied something similar to what I am wanting to ski. I spend a lot of time scoping different lines from afar and try to be out in the snowpack as much as possible to stay in touch with the subtle changes that can make or break a day in the mountains.

When was the last time something in the mountains caught you off guard and the snow behaved in a manner you did not anticipate?
This last winter we had one of the scariest snowpacks I have ever seen in twenty years in Telluride. Early in December I went out of one of the resort's high backcountry access gates with my partner. We skied the absolute lowest-angle route possible We knew the snowpack was very touchy. We had skins in case we needed to go back up to get out. What we saw was fracturing and settling whumpfs on very low-angle terrain. We triggered several avalanches remotely and noticed some avalanche activity on every elevation and every aspect. Needless to say, we didn't go out there again until March.

We are both parents. Have your goals and approach to the mountains changed since having kids?
Yes, my approach has changed. Part of that is kids and part of it is just that I am getting older and with each year I gain more knowledge and expertise within my backyard. I listen to my "gut instinct" much more now. If I don't like something, I am able to communicate it much better to my ski partners. I am not afraid to try something, not like it, and turn around.

You clearly are as dedicated as ever when it comes to stepping up to bigger and more serious lines. Does it surprise you that you are still so committed? Is it harder to get motivated? Is the hunger the same as it was ten and twenty years ago?
It does surprise me, but I also think it's logical to be in this position at my age. Ski mountaineering is a very niche sport that combines a lot of skill sets. I am still learning and as I learn I consistently want to test that knowledge and use the full range of my skill set. Now I just need my body to keep up with my mind.

It is harder to get motivated. The hunger is not the same. My objectives are not the same though either. I no longer say yes to everything that comes my way. I am very focused on specific goals that I have either tried before and want to try again or that are incredibly focused expeditions that I have been working toward for twenty years.

From talking to mutual friends who have been at altitude, you seem to excel the higher up a mountain you get. Is this a mindset thing? Due to better training? DNA?
I think being successful and strong at high altitude to some extent is simple genetics—either you are built for altitude or you are not. Once I found out I was good at altitude, I wanted to really lean into that and be as good as I possibly could. That's when the mental component comes in: once I have the confidence my body can adjust, the mental side pushes it to go farther and faster.

How do you train for high altitude?
It's hard to train for high altitude. It's not the same as training for skiing or a marathon. I make sure I am well fed and well rested. I try to spend long days in the mountains. Telluride is fortunately quite high for the Lower 48, so I can spend long days climbing, running, and skiing at or above 12,000 feet.

You are one of the most composed people I have been with over exposure. How have you become so comfortable in the no-fall zone?
Hah! That is very flattering! I'm not sure what's going on inside is always what you see on the outside. I get scared with exposure, but one thing I learned over the years is that being scared, panicking, losing focus absolutely does not help the situation. To deal with it, I have learned some tricks: breathing slow and controlled, I train myself to focus in on what immediately

needs to be tackled and don't get overwhelmed by looking at too much. The easiest way to explain this, and it sounds overly simplistic, is I don't look at the exposure. I look right in front of my feet or my skis, I look at my hands and the knot I'm tying, I focus on my partners and keep my vision reeled in to what is immediately in front of me. One step at a time . . .

You have a knack for suffering. How do you keep going when your whole body is screaming to stop?
Good question . . . Similar somewhat to the answer above. It's about focus for me. I know that suffering is a whole-body experience, but mentally I can focus on individual pains and within physical distress those pains always shift as I keep moving. This keeps my mind active and the feedback loop tells me that no pain is constant; it's shifting and changing and therefore I can keep going because suffering is fluid. Plus I always want to see what I can handle and every day is different so why not keep going and burst through the ceiling.

When you were making a name for yourself, do you think people treated you differently because you are a woman? Is this still an issue?
Yes, I was treated differently early on in my career because I was a woman. I was given a lot of opportunities to be the "token female" on expeditions that, at the time, probably punched above my pay grade. More often than not, this was a good thing, but there were occasions when it made for bad team dynamics. Early on I chose to do a lot of all-female expeditions so as to avoid those dynamics and also because I learned way more in a team of women than a team where I was the only female. This dynamic is different today. My expertise level is much higher; I create my own expeditions instead of being the token female on someone else's expeditions.

Note: *Tragically, Hilaree was lost descending Manaslu just before this book was published. Her life and spirit continue to shine for me. RIP Hilaree.*

we listened to music and talked the whole way home. I was fourteen when I first left home, and I never went back for more than a few months at a time. My hope is that snowboarding and surfing give us anchor points to commune around for years to come.

Osmosis and Realism

My son is a different beast. By eight, like any kid who has grown up going to the mountains, Cass was riding most everything. Around this time, we were hitting the upper mountain. One day, Cass complained most of the morning and said he wanted to go down. He wouldn't let up, and I reluctantly left good riding on a quiet, sunny day. The drive home was silent, but I couldn't hold my anger anymore when I stepped into the house. It took all I could to not explode on him, and I sternly but calmly said something along the lines of "Snowboarding is really special to me, and it breaks my heart to see you disrespect it like you did today. I don't care if you ever ride again, but if you decide to go riding, I expect you to bring a good attitude. I don't ever want to go through what we did today. Please stay home if you're going to act like that."

My wife, Tiff, thinks this hit a nerve, because after this talk, Cass became much more focused and grateful to ride. The past few years his snowboarding has developed into a mini version of mine. I even have photos of him that resemble my exact style and hand positioning. My daughter is not far off. This form comes from years of following on my tails, hitting every hit, slash, or chute that I ride. I call it osmosis learning.

This past winter I had the opportunity to follow one of my favorite snowboarders in the world, Gigi Rüf, and his kid. It was a surreal experience, because it crystalized my osmosis theory. Jump after jump, turn after turn, kid followed dad, tracing the lines exactly. I guess I shouldn't have been surprised when my son showed up to his first contests and proceeded to win. Now the trick is keeping his ego down while still being excited for him. Like all his friends, and like probably many boys Cass's age, he wants to be a pro snowboarder. Growing up in Tahoe, that's actually a viable career path. Just look at the X Games or the Olympics—dozens of Tahoe athletes compete.

Even with this success, I'm amazed at how seriously kids, or rather their parents, take these sports. My kids' classmates have been pulled from school at lunch or have missed whole days or more since first grade for training and competitions.

Now that Cass is in sixth grade, he's one of the only serious riders still in school on a Friday afternoon. Skills are important, but only one small part of the equation. I'll take immense hunger, drive, and commitment over a spoiled and lazy kid with talent. Spending four years at a ski academy showed me the dangers of skiing and riding every day.

To reach the next level requires a ridiculous amount of time on snow. The burnout rate is immense. My guess is 80 percent of the kids I went to school with now put ski or snowboard boots on fewer than ten days a year. It's hard to say who has it and who doesn't at a young age, but by fifteen, you get a pretty good idea. What does a kid do then? Raise their hand and say, "I don't have it, I'm sick of going to the mountain, I want to go to school on Fridays instead of going to the mountain"? Maybe in some cases, but it is rare. The more common path is "I'm bored with riding, let's smoke weed and just cruise."

Jumping Cliffs

By keeping Cass off the mountain midweek while his friends ride, I've potentially created a monster. My slow-play tactics have started a fire in him that is now a raging inferno. He rides the mountain with purpose and urgency. As COVID-19 hit, shutting down the resorts, Cass took to splitboarding out of necessity. He's not there for hippy turns. He wants to tag lines and hit cliffs, which puts me in the unique spot of having to try to reel him in for fear of his getting hurt. I've always viewed the backcountry as a no-mistake arena, because I've seen how serious a simple sprain can be when you're just 2 miles from the trailhead. One day, a particular air caught Cass's attention as we skinned up a ridge above Donner Lake. It had a small and supported cornice takeoff that would put him above a sloping cliff band and into a really steep pocket to land. To

The Serious Business
of Sending Cliffs

CHUGACH MOUNTAINS, ALASKA, 1994

Sending even the mellowest cliff can be serious. When I first went to Alaska, toward the end of my trip I was asked to fill a seat in the helicopter by "Transworld Snowboarding" staff photographer Eric Berger. This opportunity was a big deal and led to getting my first two-page spread in the biggest snowboard mag in the world, along with a handful of other photos. Back then pages in the mags were coveted. More pages meant more money.

My memory escapes me on the rest of the riders except for one, Myles Burgett. Myles grew up in Valdez, Alaska, and was the same age as me. The biggest freeride comp in the world was the King of the Hill, and Myles exploded onto the scene, charging harder than anyone had ever seen. He treated the intimidating Chugach Mountains like a small-town resort, which for him was all he knew. When he dropped in, everyone stared, because we had no idea where he was going but knew it would be radical. The first time I saw Myles ride was during the comp. I was standing on a ridge down from the start. He dropped in, hardly turning, and rolled out of view into complex terrain going really fast. Ten or twenty seconds later the valley below filled with a huge cloud of snow from a slide or a sluff. As was always the case watching Myles, you held your breath. The tension broke when he emerged out of the cloud, going as fast as possible. If you were competing that day, you immediately knew you were riding for second place.

A few days later, I strapped in next to Myles on a knife-edge ridge feeling really intimidated by him and the "Transworld" photographer. As much as I wanted to prove myself, I knew better than to try to step up to his level. Run after run, I watched Myles do things I didn't know could be done on a snowboard. He'd soon be sponsored by Burton, filming for the biggest movies, and making real money. Then tragedy struck. Myles was riding for a movie when he hit basic air, something he'd probably done a thousand times, very small by his standards, and he missed his landing by a few feet, landing in a field of rocks. He hit his head, entered a coma, and, while he recovered to some extent, his life was certainly never the same. It's a story I tell often, especially to my kids and their friends. Jumping any cliff is serious business, especially if you are trying to land in a tight pocket.

execute it properly would require riding down the ridge and turning off at the right spot and with the right angle and the right speed to clear the cliff and land in the proper place.

Cass and I did a test run on the face down some simpler terrain near the air. He pulled up midslope while Tiff, Mia, and I took it to the flats below. "Dad," he radioed me, "I really want to hit the air. I can do it safely." We've spent so much time together that we have built some serious trust around risk-taking. My son is not a loose cannon on his snowboard. To be clear, this was not daredevil stuff. It was a good learning cliff but still warranted caution. I trusted Cass and didn't have to tell him how to line up an air safely, because it was ingrained day after day.

Jumping cliffs is usually a blind move. To make sure you line up right, draw a directional arrow in the snow that points to your landing. Speed is the other critical element. Too fast and you overjump the landing. Too slow and you land on rock. Doing mock inruns to test the speed helps find the cadence. Often you cannot get to the edge of the cliff. Throwing snowballs into the landing with the help of a spotter works well. Some cliffs need to be popped, while others require you to suck up the lip, then launch. When approaching the lip, you want a solid stance, hands outstretched over the tip and tail, not making any quick moves. It can be hard to do nothing when reaching the lip, but this is key. Ride more forward than you think you need to. Once in the air, you bring your feet toward your chest and remain aware not to roll down the windows. This is a common mistake. Flapping is not great style. Jumping off ledges into water during summertime helps with staying calm and tight in the air. It's also a simple way to get in a lot of reps coming over the lip and hitting the spot you set out to hit. Missing spots is a dangerous mistake that'll catch up with you. Landing

The adventure is still flowing thick in my veins. The call of the wild is as loud as it has ever been. It is just that my objectives are not quite as "teethy." My edge not as sharp. I am not bothered by this. I embrace it. To be able to howl at the moon, touch the stars, and taste life on more mundane terrain is possibly my greatest accomplishment as a snowboarder.

where you plan to land is the first rule in cliff jumping—something my son had been consistently doing all winter.

Backslapping or butt checking is the most common mistake skiers and snowboarders make when hitting cliffs. Watching the Freeride World Tour will show you how much harder it is to stomp cliffs on a snowboard. Skiers make it look easy, while snowboarders struggle to not butt check. A simple way to not butt check is to focus on making a toe turn right after your air. Cass's track showed exactly this: he was starting a toe turn. He came over the lip, brought his board to his hand, held a grab until the last second, and landed perfectly in the pocket. He compressed deeply, almost held on, but sprang out of his landing into a front flip.

> Where to put my steps is really the only part that takes thought. However, when done right, it can and should be effortless. Flowing through the landscape, listening, looking, and following my nose.

It was a proud effort. The fall showed me how committed he was to stomping the air. First, he landed on the center of his board. I would way rather see him land centered and get pitched forward than butt checking and riding out. He was so close to stomping one of the biggest cliffs of his life. He wanted a redo, but his bomb hole was so perfectly in the middle of the tight landing that there wasn't room on either side for another landing. Despite the setback, Cass was stoked. He looked up at the cliff, his crater, and then back down to us. The day was getting late, and he rode down, stopping next to me.

"Great one," I said, leaving the analysis for later, perhaps. Cass smiled, and continued down toward the trailhead, outpacing us, taking his own path.

CHAPTER 12

The Mountains Are Changing

The planet is warming at an unprecedented rate. This warming creates extremes in both our climate and weather, which in turn results in extremes for mountain snowpacks. Predictability with regard to snowfall and temperatures has changed radically. Slopes are sliding in a manner and size we've not seen before. On average, thirty thousand global warm-weather records are being broken each year, and that number is rising. One way to combat climate change is to embrace other types of change: with more diversity in the mountains, we'll see more paths to stewardship—more interest in protecting these wild places.

I was nine when I stood on a snowboard for the first time, the same year scientists first testified before Congress and outlined the threat of human-caused climate change. NASA scientist James Hansen explained that climate change stemmed from pumping CO_2 and other gases into the atmosphere, from burning fossil fuels and thus warming the planet. CO_2 emissions had increased drastically since the Industrial Revolution, and, if they were not reduced, the scientists cautioned, the warming would continue, creating dramatic changes for the planet. Ice cores and tree rings showed that the climate changes over the very long term, hundreds of thousands of years, but this rapid increase of

Never have I heard scientists say: "Actually, the problem is not as bad as we thought."

CO_2 had amped up the rate of warming. Those warnings from decades ago are today's reality, and the pace of change has been faster than initially predicted.

The mountains are changing. This increased fluctuation in extreme temps, droughts, and storm events leads to less predictable snowpacks and avalanche forecasting. Rain for the first time during winter on high continental peaks and interior-like instability on traditionally wet coastal ranges illustrate some of these changes.

Dramatic Shifts, Everywhere

> "The mountains have changed more in our life span than in any similar period. Climate change is real. We're losing the mountains, we're losing the glaciers, and we're losing the equibalance of this planet."
> —Ruedi Beglinger

I've seen the most dramatic shifts in Alaska. Partly because it's been where I stuck my flag in the ground twenty-five years ago and said, "This is where I'm focusing on breaking new ground." And partly because scientists have explained that higher-latitude regions will feel the effects of climate warming first. And this change is playing out in many different ways. When the Prince Hotel opened in 1994 at the base of the north face of Alyeska, they built a tram, creating ski-in and ski-out lodging, as well as opening up some of the most impressive lift-service terrain in the world. Fast-forward to today, and it is now a struggle to get snow to ride on back down to the hotel. Just thirty years ago, this was never even considered a future threat. The change that has disrupted snowboarding the most, however, is severity of weather events. A stable snowpack forms when there are consistent temps and moderate snowfall over long periods of

Meadow Camp

Tripadvisor: 5-Star Review
"The location is tough to get to and very confusing, especially the last ten minutes. But the views are amazing, and I love the Creekside dining room. I highly recommend the star-gazing activity with the roofless bedroom option—very realistic. The menu is simple but good: best oatmeal and one of the finest cups of coffee I have ever had, and from the comforts of my bed. Recreation options are endless, but bring a book as there are no power outlets. The lodge has a carbon footprint of zero. Bonus: the sun seems to be on the same program."

Dusk to Dawn

PLEASANT MEADOW CAMP, SIERRA NEVADA, APRIL 2018

I am paralyzed by the view and the warmth of my sleeping bag. It's a different world down here. Trees, flowing creeks, and many birds are a sharp contrast to the last five days in the high alpine: lifeless there but dramatic, sharper edges, silent except for the wind.

I am grateful to be in this gentle meadow. A soft landing indeed. Soon we will return to the barren high country, our sights set on one of the tallest western peaks. First, we need to figure out how to get out of this granite-walled canyon. Maybe it is the wear and tear of the past days. Or the oxygen-rich land, flowing creek, or the sun's refusal to find the bottom of the canyon. But I am moving extra slow, pinned to my sleeping bag and waiting for the coffee to do its thing.

Our exit is at my back. It has me in a reflective state. A full day in the mountains used to be enough. The day would end with the closing of the lifts. Then, in Alaska, I fell in love with the evening hours. We would always push our day to the limit of light. Soon I stopped wanting to go in with the setting of the sun. I realized the transition between day and night is when Mother Nature paints her finest pictures. The dance between the sun, moon, and stars—each taking their turn to show their stuff. Sunsets and sunrises are special anywhere, but deep within the landscape is where nature puts on her greatest show.

I began with one or two days out. I made every mistake: pack too heavy, shitty food, cold nights. Things got figured out, peace of mind was found, realizing that cold, hard times would soon be followed by warm, happy highs.

We shifted to single camp, four-day missions. By day three we would be tickling the edges of the outer range and putting a few tracks in places that had probably never seen them. The method worked well, but just as we were getting in the groove, we'd turn our backs and head home. For years we did it this way. A mental barrier.

Finally, last season we busted down that door. A seven-day, point-to-point thirty-mile traverse. Nothing really changed to get to the seven-day mark. We packed as light as possible and started walking. The trip was a huge success. It showed me that we could travel deep into the mountains and still have the energy to ride the beautiful lines along the way. Seven turned to eight, eight to ten, and it's still not long enough. I would love to be picking up a gear stash and heading to the next chunk of terrain instead of heading home today. I am sun-cooked, exhausted. It takes so much to get to the back layers that once I reach them, I don't want to leave. I want to take every last step I can in this remote landscape. Reaching camp through a new valley last night, I passed by a beautiful couloir lined by granite. I was saddened that I will most likely never ride it, but I am happy it exists.

There are simply too many things to see, the map is too big, and the landscapes are too large to retrace steps. I will use what steps I have left on this planet to take me to new places and different zones. It is here that my heart beats the hardest, and my blood flows the fastest.

time. High winds, extreme snowstorms, arctic lows, and record heat waves or rain in the higher elevations make for a very unpredictable snowpack.

Haines, Alaska, hit 75 degrees F in mid-April 2021, effectively ending the winter at a time of year that normally marks the start of "trophy line" season. I was camped out deep in the Fairweather Range and watched as more than three hundred avalanches roared down the mountains on the first day of the record-shattering heat. The next day roughly two hundred more avalanches occurred. A season's worth of snow-covered peaks were stripped in forty-eight hours. The issue from a riding perspective is that the once flat and smooth outruns are now breaking up and becoming covered with open crevasses. I've camped next to one particular glacier because it had some of the biggest, most perfect spine walls above it with clean glacier outruns. It is now so broken up with severe crevasses that none of those dream lines will ever be ridden again.

Absolutely nowhere has escaped warming and erratic temps. The top station of the Aiguille du Midi in the French Alps is actually shifting, because the permafrost is warming. The word "permafrost" may need to be relegated to a historical concept. Chamonix mountain guide Pica Herry recently observed that climate change doesn't only affect winter in the Alps: "Guiding in summer was in many ways more relaxing, because we were not worried about avalanches. We have long been accustomed to avoiding slopes with consistent rockfall due to daily warm-ups, but now we're seeing huge chunks of solid granite start to come down in places that we always considered safe. There are no real safe zones anymore."

This statement coincides with the rate at which the famous Vallée Blanche glacier is melting. Working with French company Rossignol, I rode the famous glacier run many times, primarily because it was the safest run off the Aiguille du Midi. The locals have been marking the glacier's toe for more than 150 years with a dab of paint on the rock. Over the years, since the early 2000s, I've watched those dabs grow

"One life, live it. One planet, protect it."
—Ayla McConkey

farther and farther apart at an accelerated rate. Change at a "glacial pace" describes something that changes so slowly you cannot see it. Those days seem long gone, however, and the speed of the retreat continues to accelerate at a glacial warp speed around the world. Because people have been living in and around the mountains of Chamonix for hundreds of years we have a long historical record of conditions there, which helps bring clarity to just how much the mountains are changing. The concept of "last descents"—routes that would soon no longer exist—started being discussed a few years ago. It began with a handful of lines, but the list is growing rapidly.

We're also seeing record-setting storms due to the changes, which complicates things. I would rather see 10 feet of snow fall over two weeks than in just two days. In 2009, I met some guys in their thirties while hiking a closed ski area in northern British Columbia that was mostly grass instead of snow in February. They showed me

Connor Ryan: Sacred Stoke

Through his adventures and activism, skier Connor Ryan seeks to decolonize the outdoors, learn to better honor his mixed Hunkpapa Lakota and Irish heritage, and deepen his connections to the planet.

How would you describe your relationship with the mountains?
It's kind of multi-level, because I think about it as a filmmaker, an artist, a skier. But overall, I think it's familial, biological. These places are like my relatives. I feel lucky to come from a culture that understands and embraces that way of looking at places.

When or how did you first get into skiing?
My mom is Lakota and my dad is white. They were never married, and growing up I would see my dad on the weekends. Skiing was something he shared with me a handful of weekends a year until I was ten or eleven years old. After that, his financial situation changed and I didn't really have the opportunity to ski again until I was twenty-one. I was driving by Copper Mountain one day with a friend who'd never seen a ski area before, and we talked about him giving it a try. As soon as I was skiing, it just pulled me in. I had a lot of time but not a lot of money. I think that inspired me to improve quickly—I'd find people who had nicer gear than me and try to beat them down the mountain. I was my dad's ski partner when I was in elementary school, and I could ski anything back then. I just never had the opportunity to be in a race program or have regular access until this point in my life.

What has your progression been like?
The learning curve is the most exciting thing, really knowing how to step out there into the backcountry, to get yourself to the lines you want. For me, it's a way of learning to relate to the land. My body's made of the water that fell on the mountains above me that I ski on. That connection is like a liberation and re-Indigenization for me.

There aren't a lot of Indigenous people sliding on snow or at the resorts; how does that make you feel?
Well, I see it as a reflection of everyday society: resources are extracted from the land and become the wealth of people who aren't Native. In that way skiing can feel like an extractive industry. Even though I love skiing as much as I could possibly love anything, I still recognize how the industry exists by profiting off of stolen land. As an Indigenous person, I feel incredibly lucky to have a career where I get to be out on the land every day. But I also think, *Dang, if other Indigenous people could be a ski patroller or ski instructor or liftee or whatever, their mental health and well-being would be so much better.* Any job in the outdoor industry could be really impactful.

How do you stay positive then? How do we get more Indigenous people on snow?
I ski. And I try to focus on the good. It fills me up, finding ways to get more Native people out here, through seeing a film, or scholarships, or other ways. We have a shortage of access right now. Indigenous people should be more involved in the stewardship and decision-making around public lands. Ski resorts should be part of the process: hiring, creating programs, building community around something we all can love.

How would you like to see the outdoor community better acknowledge Indigenous lands?

It's a tricky thing, a process that's kind of unique to each individual. But it's like putting together an expedition crew: you fill all the different roles with talent—individuals who will step up and do the job. I think the same is true when it comes to Indigenous people and the outdoor community. Who is good at bringing people together or telling stories? We should be sure Indigenous voices can be heard. Environmental experts can learn from traditional ecological knowledge, for example. However you operate on the land or whatever role you play in the industry, there's a way to look at it through Native people who've had the same roles in our communities, who can inform. We have a set of guiding principles as Indigenous people based around the ecological facts of life. And that's tucked within all of our spiritual and cultural knowledge. So, I guess I would like to see people throughout the industry build those connections, really listen. And society is a lever for change. Ask the guide company you're hiring in the mountains if they have an Indigenous guide, and if they don't, ask why not. Ask the Forest Service where you live, "How do you work with Indigenous people?" And it's not just for Indigenous people. Look at the environmental, climate, and cultural mess that we find ourselves in right now. We've got to go back to square one, put the pieces back together. It's incredibly hard but we have to come together. Truth and reconciliation.

their favorite jumps and told me about the chocolate cookies they used to get at the warming hut. The ski area was no longer operational, because there were no longer enough reliable storms and snow. Hearing the stories was heartbreaking. I remember thinking, *At least I do not have that issue where I live.* But it made me wonder, *What am I going to see over the next thirty years?* When I returned home from that trip, I hopped on my favorite lift in the world, KT-22, and thought about the devastating impact to our local economies and saw vulnerability in the fact that the area base is only 6,200 feet above sea level—and our average annual temperatures keep rising. The opening and closing of KT used to mark the start and end of the season for the generation just ahead of me. If you did that today, your season would be very short.

Mountains for All

Another pressing issue is the lack of human diversity in the mountains. Black snowboarder Ryan Hudson literally grew up on the streets of San Diego. He now lives in Utah and has been a staple in the Snowbird tram line for more than a decade. Through a youth program and a solid mentor, Ryan discovered riding. During a discussion with

Coombs Outdoors is a foundation created by Doug Coombs's wife, Emily, in Jackson Hole, with a goal of empowering local youth by reducing barriers to outdoor recreation. As a result of its work, local Hispanic kids from Jackson are competing on the Junior Freeride Tour and proficient in the high peaks of the Tetons.

Nature Therapy

BELLINGHAM, WASHINGTON, 2018

Life evolves. It moves and flows and never stops. Get on the train or get left behind. Change is constant, adaptation essential. Stagnation and rigidity are the enemies of the mind, body, and soul.

A film tour is an example of change for me. Night after night I show my recent film, "Ode to Muir." Being on a movie tour is not new for me, but the subject matter of this film is. It is a climate film disguised as a backcountry snowboard film. A bit of a bait and switch, maybe, but it is working.

Questions have gone from "How do I manage risk?" to "Can I do more to save the planet?" Sluff-management tactics are replaced with voter-registration strategies among the youth. How I got here I do not know. It is both invigorating, because it is new, and heartbreaking, because the climate crisis is raging. However, my transition from being focused solely on shredding snow to protecting snow has been natural and steady. Some friends and fans have fallen away while others have joined me on a new path. My words come from my heart, and my intentions are pure and backed by science.

Nature fuels me, its spell becoming stronger and more important than ever before. Even with a stacked schedule of travel, daily media interviews, and shop visits, I find time for quick hits of forest bathing. Rushing to the showing of the film in Bellingham, this meant pulling over on the side of the highway, throwing the car's hazard lights on, and sprinting into the dense PNW rainforest for twenty minutes. The vibrant fall colors spiked the volume to 11, invigorating my lungs and clearing my head. I returned to the car sufficiently cleansed. Nature provides the essential clarity that gives me power and conviction to stay on my path.

him about why there is a lack of diversity, he brought up an interesting point: "These sports are passed down from generation to generation. If you're Black, you don't even consider skiing or snowboarding as something to do." On a recent trip to Alaska with Ryan, we talked more about this. "We need people of color to have role models to look up to, people they relate to," he told me. "It's really the first step. To show people that all skin colors are welcome in the mountains."

"It's best to always be a part of the conversation." —Elyse Saugstad

Ryan's path from the streets to elite-level snowboarding is a far greater climb than any I've seen before and tough to replicate. There are small signs of progress, of opening access and increasing diversity in these wild spaces. Ski areas, the backcountry, wild places are all escapes, for everyone. It is important that all of us have the opportunity to escape our daily worlds, to relax, to challenge ourselves, and to understand both ourselves and people from different backgrounds in these wild places. They should be welcoming spaces and available to everyone, no matter the economics. The first step involves realizing what is out there, sharing with others, and then welcoming, teaching, and progressing.

Sadly, we're still in what I would call the first phase of diversifying the mountains. It's easy to point a finger at the cost barriers; it's a real obstacle but we can

South American Revolutionaries

It hit me on a recent trip camping with Chilean mega-Shralpinist Sebastián Rojas Schmidt, during which we stayed in a rock cabin that he had built by hand, that all my South American friends who are really charging are in their twenties. Other than a few pioneers, this is the first real generation of snowboarders in South America. Rafael Pease is a great example of this. Now in his late twenties, he's been snowboarding for only seven years, and his mountaineering is at a world-class level, with dozens of serious descents in the Andes above 18,000 feet. The most exciting part is that his generation also happens to be the first large generation of Chileans also fighting hard to protect the environment. With the help of surf pioneer Ramón Navarro, the Chileans and Argentines designated the series of point breaks outside Pichilemu as a World Surfing Reserve. This would not have happened without the support of the thousands of new surfers in Chile.

Although the lift lines are longer and the surf spots more crowded, it is a prime example of what happens when people fall in love with nature—want to protect it. This younger generation has persuaded the Chilean and Argentinian governments to celebrate their natural resources and see them as a means of enhancing tourism, rather than relying on extraction to fund their economies.

Phil Henderson:
The Power of Representation

Phil is a climber, outdoor industry professional, and recipient of the Outdoor Afro Lifetime Achievement Award. In 2022, he organized the first all-Black expedition to Everest, on which seven Black climbers achieved the summit.

How did you fall in love with the mountains to the point where you shaped your life around them?
When I learned that you could work while being in the mountains, it changed my perspective. Once I started working in the industry and living in small towns, I really found the magic of the mountains.

Did you ever question your path? Did you ever feel unwelcome?
I never really questioned my path—however, others did, including friends and family members. "Being unwelcome" comes with the territory for me as a Black person in the outdoors. Not saying it is 100 percent of the time. However, there are times where someone or something will happen that brings a negative vibe that I recognize and others may not.

You are a husband and a father and well into your fifties (that is a guess). Not only do you not seem to be slowing down, but you are currently training for an Everest expedition. How do you stay fit? How do you still have an appetite for the sharp end?
Lifestyle! I do a lot of things that keep me moving, including yard work! LOL. I have three acres and it takes a lot of work. I have lots of trees at home. I need to climb in them to trim from time to time, but I also use it as training to keep sharp on

systems. Living in southwestern Colorado, I have access to mountain biking—something I have been doing for more years than climbing—it is one of my main activities. Backcountry skiing is probably the only thing that will get me up at 3 a.m. these days. My interest in snow science also keeps me out and about.

What was the inspiration for your Full Circle Everest Expedition?
It was knowing and meeting other Black people who like to get in the mountains, climb, and ski. I am inspired to create a connection between my culture and the Nepali and Sherpa culture as well. Wanting to provide an opportunity to build more friendships through climbing in the Himalaya.

The outdoor industry struggles with diversity and inclusion. How do you think we can inspire people of color to embrace these sports and feel more welcome?
People of color can be inspired to embrace these sports by opportunities to have positive, comfortable experiences in the outdoors. By seeing people that look like them and other POC involved in these sports, they are inspired to participate. They also need mentors to help them navigate the many different aspects of the industry.

How was it for you often being the only Black person at the crag, on the mountain, or on the trail? Has this evolved at all?

At times it felt very unwelcoming. There has been a tremendous evolution in the numbers of Black people participating in outdoor sports. However, they are still finding a lack of representation by people from their communities. This is still slowly evolving.

work harder to eliminate it. Discounted passes, increased public transit to resorts and trailheads, emphasis on ski swaps, access to used gear, and development of gear libraries are all ways to lower the financial barriers. Supporting nonprofit groups, like Outdoor Outreach, that work to get youth and/or traditionally marginalized communities into the mountains—and to make them feel like they belong there—is another way to bring more diversity to the slopes and to encourage their stewardship.

> There are no walls, there are no boundaries. Set your imagination free, dream big, and get moving.

Chilean snowboarder Rafael Pease was with Ryan and me on that trip to Alaska. Both Chile and Argentina hold a special place in my heart. The Andes probably has more unclimbed and unridden mountains than any other range in the world. My first real break to film for a snowboard movie company came when I was nineteen, when Steve Klassen and I filmed

Pica Herry: A Deeper Sense to the Journey

"I reckon being in the mountains is like a drug, it is addictive! I feel truly alive and happy up there and couldn't imagine spending the rest of my life down in the valley! More important, I wouldn't go with only a sportive and personal objective, but try to organize more altruistic missions with local communities as well. It gives a deeper sense to the journey and is as rewarding as riding a big mountain!"

for Adventure Scope. It was my first segment ever in a snowboard film, and I remember thinking that it was odd how empty the mountain resorts in Argentina were. I didn't understand then that these resorts had been set up and marketed exclusively toward Americans and Europeans, not Argentinian or Chilean riders themselves. In the early 2000s, however, I started seeing one or two locals on the mountains whom I would later befriend.

So when I started Jones in 2010, the mountains outside of Santiago, Chile, were a key spot for one last round of prototype testing before production. This is when I saw real change. An energized, significant-in-number generation of skiers, snowboarders, climbers, and surfers. Local brands and media companies had started up. This smoldering fire ignited and is today in full blaze. The once-dormant coastal town Pichilemu, which is home to multiple point breaks, now looks like Santa Cruz in the 1960s. Action sports athletes like Chilean surfer Ramón Navarro and snowboarder Manuel Diaz are international superstars.

The key to making the mountains, and all of the outdoors, for everyone is to work within an open atmosphere, where all voices can confidently speak, no matter the subject or question—engaging as equal team members and getting everyone's opinion on conditions and travel routes.

Protect Our Winters

These observations, along with more research and some generational thinking, led me to form the not-for-profit Protect Our Winters in 2007. POW started with what I knew best, the winter sports community and people who love snow as much as I do. People who could see the climate changing right before their eyes. Today it is so much more: a global organization with chapters in over a dozen countries working to create what we call the "Outdoor State." In the US alone, there are fifty million people who regularly recreate outdoors; a goal of POW is to unify them around climate action so they step up, speak out, and vote. Unified, we'd be one of the strongest voting blocs in America. Driven by our shared passion to sustain the places and lifestyles we love, we have the ability to protect everything that lives downstream from a healthy snowpack.

Hundreds of athletes worldwide, including some of my friends and heroes like Conrad Anker and Hilaree Nelson, have joined with POW to lead this effort. My goal was (and still is) to unite the outdoor community around climate action. To achieve this, I not only had to reach out to my friends, I also had to learn to get over my fears and talk to scientists and policy experts who could help me figure out the most effective ways that our community could slow global warming. It's not a surprise: we need to reduce large-scale CO_2 emissions, and it has to be done with large-scale, systemic changes to transportation and how energy is made. I learned that a clean energy future can only really happen through programs and policies at the state, national, and global levels. POW tries to inspire our outdoor community to influence decisions at these same levels.

And, hey, we have power! In the US alone, outdoor recreation creates 4.3 million jobs, significantly more than the fossil fuel industry at 1.7 million. Yet there are members of Congress who represent outdoor meccas, like my hometown, Truckee, California, and still fight against efforts to slow global warming. Of all the tactics the fossil fuel industry uses, the most effective has been politicizing climate change and its related advocacy. They've soaked our elected officials with billions of lobbying and campaign contribution dollars.

> My wife thinks I am obsessed, and she is probably right. Says I ride more than I used to. Tough for me to say, but as my world gets more hectic off the hill, the mountains become my spiritual power center. A haven to hide from the emails. A place to work out my many thoughts. A place to set my compass in business, climate, and life.

Getting Involved

What we lack in lobbying funds, we make up for in our numbers and our passion—but time is not on our side. A scientist recently explained it to me in this simple way: "If we continue on the current CO_2 emissions path, your grandkids will be the last generation of skiers and riders in the Tahoe Basin." As a community, we must come together and send a clear message to our lawmakers that if they're not serious about implementing policies that reduce CO_2 emissions, then we'll replace them with someone who is, regardless of political party.

In making climate change a political issue, the fossil fuel industry has managed to effectively divide people, including the Outdoor State, preventing them from taking coordinated action. And this stalemate is happening even though an overwhelming majority of people know that climate change is human-caused and want to do something about it. For example, nine ski resorts are located in my legislative district; along with summer sports activity and general tourism, outdoor recreation is

One World, One People, One Planet

Like it or not we are all connected: one world, one planet.
We all breath the same air, drink the same water, and weather the same storms.
My trash is your trash, your trash is my trash.
Your problems are my problems, my problems are your problems.
Hate a divisiveness is not the answer to those problems.
Solutions lie in empathy and understanding.
Science and knowledge need to be our compass.
Humanity is in an all-hands-on-deck scenario.
Find your lever, grab tight, and keep cranking it.

hands-down our largest industry and employer. How is it, then, that our congressman has voted more than 250 times against climate action?

Critics point to my own carbon footprint, which is fair, but also avoids looking at the big picture where change really happens. It doesn't help to vilify people driving big trucks, riding snowmobiles, or flying and say that's the primary reason the planet is warming. For sure, individual action plays a role, but it isn't the main reason we're experiencing such profound climate change. Corporations, marketers, lobbyists, politicians, and yes, we as consumers have created a society that incentivizes the burning of fossil fuels. I'm not saying that we shouldn't all be living an examined life. Doing so has inspired me to change my diet, sell my snowmobile, leave behind helicopters, and greatly reduce air travel, among other things. But the real change comes from advocacy and voting for climate champions. Since starting POW, I tell myself, "Get better every year."

A New Normal: Adapt or Die

The seriousness of global warming cannot be understated. This is the most pressing issue my generation and my children's generation will face. Life will go on, but the way we experience the world will be very different than before. It may sound trite, given the context, but "adapt or die" is the new mantra. These days, I now do 90 percent of my snowboarding in my home range. On drought years this might mean a hundred days on a 12- to 18-inch base—and I have the scars, both internal and external, to show for it. We're often forced into riding the upper 1,000 feet of the range to get above the rain. This requires more walking on dirt and embracing the art of bushwhacking.

As tough as it is seeing it rain on the top of mountains in January, I make a point of not complaining about it, especially in front of kids because this is their new reality. We now need to be more patient, more creative when seeking out our mountain experiences.

Technology and innovation are moving so quickly in the development of clean energy sources and electric transportation. These are, in most cases the cleaner, cheaper, and more efficient energy solution. So asking our leaders to move toward clean energy security and away from fossil fuels, is not only the right thing to do for endless reasons even bigger than snowboarding, it also just makes sense from an economic and jobs perspective.

We have the solutions and we have a community. But we are lacking the political will. It's time to demand more from ourselves and our lawmakers, to act with the urgency the earth requires.

Outro: Life Focus

I still remember my high-school graduation day. I could finally follow my own path. I thanked my parents, celebrated with my friends, threw everything I owned into my cousin Adam Hostetter's truck, and we drove west to Mount Hood in Oregon. The future was bright! Success came fast. By twenty-one, I was well on my way. I was renting a closet near Lake Tahoe. I met my lovely wife, Tiff. By twenty-three, I could afford to rent a much bigger closet and convinced Tiff to move into it with me. Every time I talked to my mother, she wondered aloud when I was going to college. But I took a different route and was happy living in the mountains, riding all the time, with great people, spending my days outside.

This is what I want to focus on: life is ultra-short, so chase your dreams. The size of your closet does not matter. Happiness is the goal! It's important to acknowledge that life is precious. We take up resources on this planet, and we should honor it by enjoying every day. I have some advice: work, seek, find joy, and define success for yourself.

WORK

Don't get out of shape. Keep moving. Keep going. When you get hurt (and you *will* get hurt), don't waste it. It's a time to reset and come back stronger. Someone always has it worse than you. Find mentors. Observe people older than you doing what you want to be doing at their age. Ask questions and work for free. The best jobs and experiences often come from volunteering. Your word is your strongest asset. Show up on time, and do what you say you are going to do. Better yet, overdeliver.

SEEK

A healthy mind is just as important as a healthy body. Work out the mind, seek knowledge, seek guidance, seek perspective, seek wisdom. Seek facts, trust empirical evidence, defend science. Right now, we're in an all-hands-on-deck situation in terms of the environment and our planet and humanity. We are on a dead-end path fueled by greed and selfishness. We need to roll up our sleeves and come together to move forward and progress.

> There was nothing left to give. No second-guessing, no hard feelings or missed opportunity. We put it all on the table day after day. No one complained, everyone contributed at every opportunity. We earned what we got and now I float down the trail with a feeling of contentment and gratitude for the mountains.

FIND JOY

Find what makes you happy, do it often, and the world will be a better place. One thing I'm very proud of about my path in the mountains, and in life in general, is that my ability to find joy and happiness is much simpler than it used to be. There's a saying: "Jobs fill your pocket; adventures fill your soul." If you can be happy without that many material things, you will always be content.

DEFINE SUCCESS

It's important to ask the question, *What does success look like for me?* Is it a house on the lake and a private jet? Is it helping those in need? Helping the planet? Is it a life of adventure? There's no wrong answer here. Asking the question is what's important. Discovering the answer is your job. Take it on and find what moves you.

Whatever your answer is, I've got some news for you. It's going to be hard, really hard. Nothing extraordinary happens without hard work. The more unorthodox your dreams, the more conviction and commitment and creativity you will need. The road is lined with critics, doubters, and naysayers telling you to get back in line or to try something else.

Follow your heart. Follow the passion. Go all in. Put your head down for ten years and see where it gets you; that is a good start. Outwork everyone. Put yourself where you want to be. Regardless of your skill level, by doing it more than anyone else in the world, you will be better than 90 percent of the people out there. If you do not know your destiny yet, relax. It's okay. Explore, seek knowledge, discover, have an open mind, learn, fail, evolve. Discovery is an awesome job! Stagnation is not an option.

In closing, I offer the main tenets of the Church of the Seven Day Recreationalists, as shared with me from one of my main mentors, Jim Zellers:

1. **Get outside every day.**
2. **Keep your house/life in order.**
3. **Don't let #2 get in the way of #1.**

Acknowledgments

My mountain playbook is a direct result of the people I have spent time with in the mountains. Early on it was local rippers, teammates, and competitors who shaped my technical foundation. As my focus shifted to backcountry freeriding, so too did the people I was in the mountains with. I get older, but the bond from being on the sharp end with them never fades. Snowboarding in serious mountains is a team effort. If something happens to you, it will be the people you are with who will be called on to save you. This trust creates a friendship that time does not diminish. The progression bar gets raised not by a single person but collectively. I have always tried to surround myself with the most talented, humble, and high-spirited souls who share my love-of-sport mentality.

This book could not have happened without the work of Chris Crossen and his willingness to dive headfirst into my words, journals, and memories. For years I had kicked around the idea of doing this book, but it was Chris who gave me the confidence to go for it. As neighbors and close friends, we've spent a ton of time together in the mountains and in the surf. He is that quiet charger who shares the same ethos and views when it comes to both the tactics and spirit of moving through the mountains. Besides being a writer and editor, Chris is a world-class artist and athlete—the perfect partner to organize and improve my writing. His calm and sturdy demeanor allowed me to put myself out there and share my approach to the mountains.

Special thanks to Kate Rogers, editor in chief of Mountaineers Books. Thank you for your persistent prodding to bring this book to life. Writing a book is one of the scariest things I have done, but your guidance and support of my writing and story gave me the confidence to spill my soul to the world. You are a master and I am grateful to learn from you. Thanks, too, to the rest of the Mountaineers Books team, especially senior editor Mary Metz and senior designer Jen Grable.

Deep gratitude to everyone listed below and beyond. You have all inspired, motivated, and educated me in one way or another:

Adam Hostetter, John Percy, Mark Fawcett, Jeff Greenwood, Mike Jacoby, Jason Ford, Bill Enos, Mike Kildevaeld, Jasey-Jay Anderson, Tara Eberhard, Julie Zell, Johnny Recchio, Jeff McKitterick, Steve Klassen, Tom Burt, Bonnie and Jim Zellers, John Griber, Andy Hetzel, Temple Cummings, Craig Kelly, Noah Salasnek, Kevin Jones, Megan Pischke, Dave Swanwick, Kent Kreitler, Jeremy Nobis, Victoria Jealouse, Brian Savard, Johan Olofsson, Alison Gannett, Brant Moles, Gordy Peifer, Axel Pauporté, Jonas Emery, Sage Cattabriga-Alosa, Ian McIntosh, Travis Rice, Bryan Iguchi, Xavier De Le Rue, Victor De Le Rue, Bibi Pekarek, Mitch Toelderer, Cody Townsend, Lucas Debari, Josh Dirksen, Ryland Bell, Jonaven Moore, Terje Haakonsen, Luca Pandolfi, Danny Davis, Nick Russell, Sammy Luebke, Julien "Pica" Herry, Matt Schaer, Thomas Delfino, Leo Taillefer, Harry Kearney, Elena Hight, Griffin Post, Forrest Shearer, Daron Rahlves, Nick Schneider, Ryan Hudson, Glen Poulsen, Jim and John Morrison, Hilaree Nelson, Michelle Parker, Mark Landvick, Nicolas Müller, Jonaven Moore, Ruedi Beglinger, Rafael Pease, Greg Hill, Jimmy Goodman, Iñaki Odriozola, Robin Van Gyn, Mark Carter, Lucas Merli, Sammy Carlson, Torah Bright, Connor Ryan, and Conrad Anker

Thank you to this book's early readers; your input was super-helpful: Lora Bodmer, Josh Nielsen, Kimberly Pinkson, and Mario Molina.

TO THE GUIDES

Thank you for keeping me out of trouble. You have helped keep me in check when the froth is maxing. You have carried the heavy pack so mine could be light. You have watched from the shoulder in order to get to the outrun faster. You have opened your playbook, let me in your snowpits, and answered all my questions:

Jim Conway, Zahan Billimoria, Ed Shanley, and Tom Burt.

TO THE CAMERA OPERATORS

Your trusted voice on the other end of the radio, whether it is helping to find a cornice entry or unconditional support when I decide to back off a line, or blow a line, is critical to my success as a snowboarder. You are the unsung heroes, thank you:

Beat Steiner, Mike and Dave Hatchett, Corey Gavitt, Dirk Collins, Tom Day, Matt Herriger, Tim Manning, Chris Figenshau, Steve and Todd Jones, Gary Pendygrasse (RIP), Chris Edmands, Curt Morgan, Ben Dann, Leslie Hittmeier, Nick "Ninja" Kalisz, Jeff Wright, Greg Weaver, Dan Gibeau, Scott Baxter, Aaron Sedway, Dan Milner, Adam Clarke, Eric Bergeri, Greg Von Doersten, Tony Harrington, Jeff Curley, Jeff Hawe, Ming Poon, and Andrew Miller

TO MY PAST AND PRESENT SPONSORS

You have believed in me and helped me achieve my dreams. I will be forever grateful for your support:

POC Sports, Karakoram, thirty*two*, Sierra Nevada Brewing Company, YETI, Palisades Tahoe, Etnies, American Pistachio Growers, Revelshine Wines, Bikes N Boards, Swag, Rossignol, O'Neill, Scott, Sony Action Cam, Swatch, and CLIF Bar.

To the people who have watched my movies, rocked my products Thank you. It is the ultimate honor. Without you I would not have a job!

TO MY FALLEN FRIENDS

We all die but we do not all live. Your lives ended too early but *you lived*. Your spirit continues to motivate and inspire me. I think about you when I am really out in it, hiking in the predawn hours to a serious line, standing on a mountaintop, and battling through long storms in my tent, or celebrating a sunset after a special day. You are gone but not forgotten:

Trevor Peterson, Tristan Picot, Craig Kelly, Mihai "M.C." Constantinescu, Doug Coombs, Shane McConkey, C.R. Johnson, Erik Roner, Joe Timlin, JP Auclair, Liz Daley, Noah Salasnek, David Lama, Tate MacDowell, and Luca Pandolfi.

TO MY FAMILY

To my mother. Thank you for the unconditional love and acceptance of my unconventional life path. I always knew that whatever happened there was always a hot meal waiting and a warm home waiting for me. To my dad. Your consistent but subtle life lessons opened my mind to the idea that anything is possible with grit and hard work. You taught me to not get caught up in the shackles of society and to prioritize family, fun, and dreaming big.

To my brothers. I owe so much of what is in this book to you guys. You let me draft off your tails my whole life. You taught me the fine art of dirtbagging and always had a spot for me in the car, tent, or behind the couch. I am so grateful that so many of the best days of life in the mountains were with you two. Our hearts and souls led the way!

My greatest gratitude goes to my wife, Tiffany. Although she has not read a single word of this book, nothing in it would be possible without her. The unwavering support she has provided me for the last twenty-five years is the backbone of all I have done in the mountains.

At thirty, when I walked away from making movies with helicopters and a career that was humming along to personally underwrite the start of my first foot-powered film, *Deeper*, as well as Jones Snowboards, she gave me the final nudge to cut the cord of security and embrace the path of the unknown.

Over and over, Tiff's unwavering support and her acceptance that me going snowboarding . . . *a lot* . . . was a good thing, is why this book exists. Knowing she will be there for me when I get out is critical. More importantly, the thought of not coming home at all due to a fatal mistake has made turning my back on dream lines so much easier. Instead of feeling dread, failure, and defeat, I have felt a warm wave of love overtake me because I know I will see my wife again.

Although the words "trust me, it's good to go" could be trigger points to go the other way, she has instead trusted and supported my outlandish dreams and ideas for almost thirty years.

Mia and Cass: You challenge, inspire, and motivate me in and out of the mountains. Leaving you and your mother behind while I go out into the wild has been the hardest thing about my mountain journey. It is for you that I work hard and always evolve my knowledge and training. You are always with me in the mountains. Watching you grow and evolve and sharing the life-of-glide with you has been the coolest part of my mountain journey. You are my favorite riding partners, and I can't wait for more to come! Keep learning, evolving, and following your heart, and you will be fine.

Resources

It is, in part, through reading, listening, and watching that I continue to evolve as a person. Below is a roundup of some of my favorite sources.

Required Reading

Articles

"Snow Fall: The Avalanche at Tunnel Creek," by John Branch, *New York Times* (December 13, 2012).

"Accident: Wilson Glade," www.utahavalanchecenter.org/avalanche/59084 (February 2021).

Books

All We Can Save, by Ayana Elizabeth Johnston and Katharine K. Wilkinson

The California Field Atlas, by Obi Kaufmann

The Chuting Gallery, by Andrew McLean

Classic Krakauer, by Jon Krakauer

The Daily Stoic, by Ryan Holiday

Endurance, by Alfred Lansing

Escape from Lucania, by David Roberts

Extreme Alpinism, by Mark Twight

Force of Nature, by Laird Hamilton

The Happiness Advantage, by Shawn Achor

Man's Search for Meaning, by Victor E. Frankl
The Mindful Athlete, by George Mumford
The Mountains of My Life, by Walter Bonatti
The Power of Now, by Eckhart Tolle
Rules for a Knight, by Ethan Hawke
See You Tomorrow, by Jeremy Evans
Select Peaks of Greater Yellowstone, by Tom Turiano
Speed and Scale, by John Doerr
Staying Alive in Avalanche Terrain, by Bruce Tremper
Stillness Is the Key, by Ryan Holiday
The TB12 Method, by Tom Brady
There and Back, by Jimmy Chin
Training for the Uphill Athlete, by Steve House, Scott Johnston, and Kilian Jornet
A Wild Idea, by Jonathan Franklin
Zen and the Art of Motorcycle Maintenance, by Robert M. Pirsig

Viewing and Listening Options

Movies

TB 6 Carpe Diem, Standard Films, 1997
The Continuum, Teton Gravity Research (TGR) 1996)
Deeper, TGR, 2010
Endless Winter, Warren Miller 1995
Exposed, Adventure Scope, 1995
Further, TGR, 2012
Harvest, TGR, 1997
Higher, TGR, 2014
Life of Glide, TGR, 2017
Lines, Quinta Films 2007
Mind the Addiction, TGR, 2001
Mountain Revelations, TGR, 2021
91 Words for Snow, Blank Paper Studios, 2005
Notice to Appear, Standard Films, 2002
Ode to Muir, TGR 2018
Paradox, Standard Films, 2005
Purple Mountains, TGR, 2020
Roadless, TGR, 2019
Saturation, Absinthe Films, 2003
Shelter, Almos Films, 2020

Podcasts

Drilled, by Amy Westervelt
How to Save a Planet., https://gimletmedia.com/shows/howtosaveaplanet
Rich Roll, by Rich Roll

About the Author

Photo: Ming Poon

An award-winning snowboarder, environmentalist, and entrepreneur, Jeremy Jones is widely regarded as one of the most accomplished action sports athletes of all time. Jeremy started his snowboarding career as a racer in New England but later switched his focus to freeriding, taking his technical riding skills to the steeps of Alaska and beyond. Later in his career Jeremy began to focus on foot-powered ascents in the most remote regions of the world, including Svalbard, the Himalaya, and Antarctica. He is largely thought of as the pioneer of splitboarding. Two decades of bold first descents and backcountry snowboarding expeditions around the world earned Jeremy eleven Big Mountain Rider of the Year awards from *Snowboarder Magazine* and a National Geographic Adventurer of the Year accolade. Adept at sharing his adventures on film, Jeremy has produced and starred in countless snowboard movies, including his signature Teton Gravity Research produced films, *Ode To Muir*, *Life Of Glide*, and the *Deeper, Further, Higher* trilogy.

A devout advocate for protecting our environment and addressing climate change issues, Jeremy founded *Protect Our Winters* in 2007, with the goal of uniting the outdoor industry to act on climate. He was named a Champion of Change by President Barack Obama for his work with the non-profit organization.

A lifelong passion for snowboard design led him to launch his own brand, Jones Snowboards, in 2008. Jones is committed to offering responsibly made, high-performance technical outerwear, snowboards, splitboards, and backcountry accessories.

In recent years, Jeremy has focused on exploring his home mountain range, California's Sierra Nevada, where he lives in the town of Truckee with his wife, Tiffany, and two children, Mia and Cass.

PROTECT OUR WINTERS

Where would we be without snow? No glaciers or icicles, no snow days or sledding, no skiing, skating, snowshoeing—or snowboarding. That's why Mountaineers Books is proud to donate 1% of all sales of this book to Protect Our Winters, helping their ongoing efforts to mitigate climate change, enhance mountain stewardship, and advocate for wild places:

Protect Our Winters (POW) helps passionate outdoor people protect the places we live and lifestyles we love from climate change. We are a community of athletes, scientists, creatives, and business leaders advancing non-partisan policies that protect our world today and for future generations.

POW was founded by Jeremy Jones in 2007 to address the gap between the impacts that climate change was already having on our mountain landscapes, and organized action to address it. With the help of other concerned pro athletes, individuals, resorts, brand partners, and passionate outdoor enthusiasts, it has since grown from a kernel of an idea into a worldwide network of more than 130,000 supporters. POW harnesses this group to give a national voice to the outdoor sports community and provide a unique perspective that de-politicizes climate discussion. Our key formula for engaging upwards of 57 million outdoor enthusiasts globally? Relevance and authenticity. For us, the outdoors aren't just a passion, but a way of life. That dirt on our shoes is authentic.

Right now, we have the luxury of worrying about how climate change might impact the outdoors. Right now, we get to help dictate the outcome rather than react to a foregone conclusion. But if we sit on our hands for the next two decades, we won't be worried about powder days, mountain access, or having fun. We'll be worried about the stability of our environment, our jobs, and our economy.

WE ALL NEED WINTER.

MOUNTAINEERS BOOKS

recreation · lifestyle · conservation

MOUNTAINEERS BOOKS is a leading publisher of mountaineering literature and guides—including our flagship title, *Mountaineering: The Freedom of the Hills*—adventure narratives, natural history, and general outdoor recreation. Through our two imprints, Skipstone and Braided River, we also publish titles on sustainability and conservation. We are committed to supporting the environmental and educational goals of our organization by providing expert information on human-powered adventure, sustainable practices at home and on the trail, and preservation of wilderness.

The Mountaineers, founded in 1906, is a 501(c)(3) nonprofit outdoor recreation and conservation organization whose mission is to enrich lives and communities by helping people "explore, conserve, learn about, and enjoy the lands and waters of the Pacific Northwest and beyond." One of the largest such organizations in the United States, it sponsors classes and year-round outdoor activities throughout the Pacific Northwest, including climbing, hiking, backcountry skiing, snowshoeing, camping, kayaking, sailing, and more. The Mountaineers also supports its mission through its publishing division, Mountaineers Books, and promotes environmental education and citizen engagement. For more information, visit The Mountaineers Program Center, 7700 Sand Point Way NE, Seattle, WA 98115-3996; phone 206-521-6001; www.mountaineers.org; or email info@mountaineers.org.

Our publications are made possible through the generosity of donors and through sales of 700 titles on outdoor recreation, sustainable lifestyle, and conservation. To donate, purchase books, or learn more, visit us online:

MOUNTAINEERS BOOKS

1001 SW Klickitat Way, Suite 201 • Seattle, WA 98134
800-553-4453 • mbooks@mountaineersbooks.org • mountaineersbooks.org

An independent nonprofit publisher since 1960

Mountaineers Books is proud to support the Leave No Trace Center for Outdoor Ethics, whose mission is to promote and inspire responsible outdoor recreation through education, research, and partnerships. The Leave No Trace program is focused specifically on human-powered (nonmotorized) recreation. For more information, visit www.lnt.org.

The Shralpinist

The Shralpinist is curious, open-minded, and present.

The Shralpinist is committed to a goal but nimble, flexible, and willing to change the goal as new knowledge is gained.

The Shralpinist has an intimate relationship with fear.

The Shralpinist respects nature.

The Shralpinist is sometimes bold but always humble.

The Shralpinist knows there is no shortcut to the top and remains patient and unflappable.

The Shralpinist takes what the mountains give and does the most with it.

The Shralpinist understands that less than optimal days . . . lead to optimal days.